The Hero in Scandinavian Literature

The Germanic Languages Symposia Series
*Sponsored by the Department of Germanic Languages
The University of Texas at Austin*

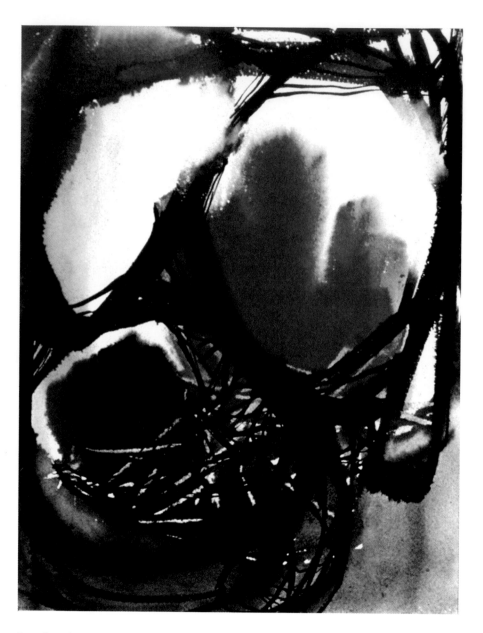

Interlaced Forms. Primitive forms laced together as with rawhide; sticks and mud comprise a sort of precious-stone setting; surprisingly attractive colors.

The Hero in Scandinavian Literature

FROM PEER GYNT TO THE PRESENT

Edited by

John M. Weinstock *and* Robert T. Rovinsky

UNIVERSITY OF TEXAS PRESS, AUSTIN AND LONDON

Library of Congress Cataloging in Publication Data
Main entry under title:

The Hero in Scandinavian literature.

Proceedings of a Scandinavian symposium, the 14th
annual symposium sponsored by the Dept. of Germanic Languages, and held in Austin, May 1972.
Includes bibliographical references.
1. Scandinavian literature—Addresses, essays, lectures. 2. Heroes in literature—Addresses, essays,
lectures. I. Weinstock, John M., 1936–   ed.
II. Rovinsky, Robert T., 1940–   ed.   III. Texas.
University at Austin. Dept. of Germanic Languages.
PT7067.H4   839'.5   74–26815
ISBN 0–292–73001–2

CONTENTS

ILLUSTRATIONS

ACKNOWLEDGMENTS

An undertaking of the magnitude of the Scandinavian symposium could not possibly have succeeded without the selfless participation and support of many individuals and organizations. We would like to take this opportunity to thank the Department of Germanic Languages of the University of Texas; the Royal Swedish Embassy, which in addition to financial aid also provided the Strindberg films; the American-Scandinavian Foundation, which arranged for Professor Ingwersen to participate; the College of Humanities of the University of Texas, particularly Dean Stanley Werbow, who followed the Symposium from its inception to successful conclusion and offered many valuable suggestions along the way; the European Studies Center of the University of Texas; and the Swedish Information Service, which provided the highly acclaimed Strindberg exhibit.

With the assistance of the above-mentioned persons, departments, and organizations, as well as that of the contributing speakers and discussants, and the numerous students and spouses who volunteered their time and energies, we were encompassed by a true *embarras des richesses*.

Introduction

by JOHN M. WEINSTOCK and
ROBERT T. ROVINSKY

University of Texas at Austin

On the morning of May 1, 1972, President Stephen H. Spurr of The University of Texas at Austin officially inaugurated the fourteenth annual symposium held under the aegis of the Department of Germanic Languages. The seven essays appearing in this volume were originally contributed to the symposium, which bore the rubric "Scandinavian Symposium 1972: The Hero in Scandinavian Literature from *Peer Gynt* to the Present," as lectures by the distinguished authors, among whom were counted two prominent literary historians from Scandinavian universities, a leading contemporary Swedish author, and four of this country's most respected professors of Scandinavian languages and literatures.

It was decided that continuity would best be preserved by setting aside, at the conclusion of the three days' activities, a separate section for discussion of the papers. On the second day, a special discussion group, led by the invited moderators, Professors Helmut Rehder and Oets Bouwsma (of the University of Texas), convened to consider the intellectual background of the symposium's theme, with Kierkegaard and Nietzsche as the philosophical *Sprungbrett*. An unscheduled "bonus" section was spontaneously formed immediately upon the conclusion of Professor Steene's provocative lecture, due to the great interest manifested by the enthusiastic, as well as sizable, audience. All three of these most stimulating discussions have been included in this book, as they played a significant role in the progress of, and conclusions drawn at, the symposium. Acting as catalysts for these fruitful discussions, it should be noted, were, besides the lecturers, four invited participants: Professors Erik Wahlgren, William Mishler, Søren Baggesen, and John Greenway.

Other events held in conjunction with the symposium included the showing of several films (Bergman's *Hour of the Wolf* and Strindberg's *The Father* and *Miss Julie*); a Strindberg exhibit, provided very generously by the Swedish Information Service; and an art show entitled "The Northlanders," including, as the title suggests, paintings with a Scandinavian motif by the noted San Diego artist Jim Kacirk, who, far from incidentally, contributed as a discussant as well.

While the theme of the symposium demanded exploration of an enormous literary corpus, considerations of practicality (alas!) forced constriction of our boundaries to allow inclusion of only the most significant authors and works, those very few seminal figures whose presence upon the literary scene helped shape succeeding generations of writers. Thus it is that the focus is directed toward Ibsen, Jacobsen, Hamsun, and Strindberg as central representatives of an earlier era (earlier *chronologically* only, it must be mentioned, as each of these authors, firmly rooted in the nineteenth century, has a very tangible relationship, be it primarily in content [Jacobsen] or form [Strindberg], with modern literature), while the movement toward nihilism shown by Ingmar Bergman, whose every succeeding work seems to take a new creative tack and who is seen by many as the most innovative artist of our time, is treated as exemplificative of this present, disaffected age. In addition to the individual attention afforded the foregoing figures, Professor Linnér provides an ambitious, comprehensive overview of the contemporary (post–World War II) Swedish fictional hero.

In seeking the archetypal Ibsen hero, one must, as Professor Arestad's lecture clearly indicates, wade through a pair of related preliminary questions, namely "What is a hero?" and "What is *the* Ibsen hero?" Compounding the difficulty of the search is the fact that three different types of hero appear in Ibsen's works: the literary, which traces its lineage to earlier writings; the modern, reflecting man's con-

The Conversants. A bleak, somewhat ominous area of Northland; a relatively pleasant time, but with all the signs of the harsh onslaughts of the elemental forces.

Red and Blue Shapes. A Northland still life; an arrangement of objects grouped in a lovely but primitive manner.

Viewers.   A pair of visitors to a dynamic area of thicket and underbrush; natural forces at work.

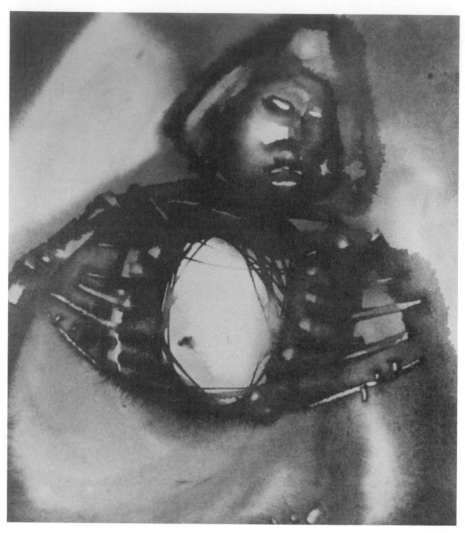

Nordic Man. A mythical figure of the Northland; coarse and earthy, and yet marvelously adapted to the severe, primitive life in which he exists.

Nordic Warrior. A staunch, aggressive, solitary figure, clad in strange garments, pondering meditatively over the world about him; a suggestion of the sea.

Ovoids. Composition in oval-shaped objects; primitive shapes, laced together into a setting; suggestion of a human form with white face in profile; lovely, tender harmony of tones as of strains of music.

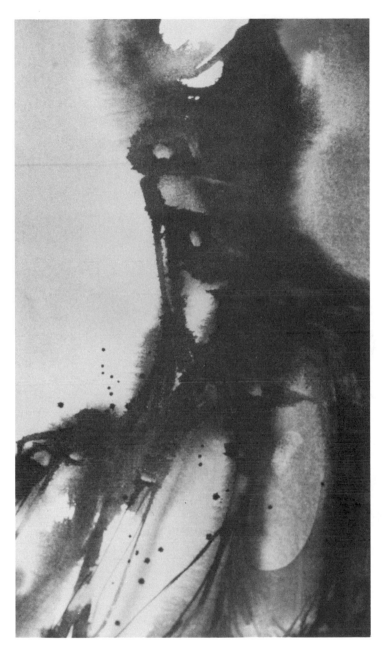

Northland Formation. Human figure created by the elements from the sheer, barren cliffs; perhaps overlooking the sea; warm tones suggesting latent energies.

Jagged Landscape. Dynamic landscape, fierce and potentially dangerous; elemental forces at work eroding, dislodging, and so on.

flict with a newly emerged naturalistic universe; and, finally, the particularly Ibsenian hero, who tackles the most significant of Ibsen's fundamental concerns, the individual's freedom of choice. With this central problem in mind, Professor Arestad traces the dramatist's early wrestling for some sort of solution, from *Lady Inger of Østråt* (1854) to *Brand* (1866)—whose protagonist he regards as one of four Ibsen heroes—in each case finding that, despite no small amount of heroic stature, the pivotal figures are not operating with full freedom: ultimately, their destiny is to "will under necessity." Interestingly enough, Peer Gynt, the second candidate for hero's status and, in Arestad's view, "the genesis of the antihero"—often treated as a human failure, an indecisive, self-centered individual with buffoonish qualities—is seen as possessing a goodly amount of sense by virtue of this very vacillatory nature, especially when compared with Brand, who is propelled toward his inexorable fate by unrelenting intransigence. Mrs. Alving, of *Ghosts*, a contemporary heroine, reflects Ibsen's concept of modern man's inherent tragedy: ". . . how meaningless existence becomes for an idealist who must seek to surmount the jungle of a mechanistic order." Representing an essentially incongruous *Weltanschauung*, she cannot do battle with the naturalistic windmill on equal terms.

If, as in each of the foregoing paradigms, other men do not possess freedom of choice, perhaps the exceptional man—in this case, the artist, Ibsen means—who is beyond such mundane considerations as the conventions, traditions, and morality of society, can achieve this personal freedom. Solness, the master builder, lives according to his own system of values and considers himself strong enough to challenge the might of God. He loses, of course, but his life, and the very loss of it, represents a consequent struggle on his part to evolve at least a modicum of individual freedom, and it is for this reason Professor Arestad considers Solness to be *the* Ibsen hero. The master builder's demise in the pursuit of his goal gives rise to a paradoxical situation, in that as an artist he has been instilled with the *need* to create. This would imply, it seems, the reemergence of Julian's predicament (*Emperor and Galilean*, 1873): the need to "will under necessity." Thus even the Ibsen hero who best exemplifies the playwright's most central concern is shadowed by a conundrum whose answer is pitifully wanting: "How free then can any man be? Perhaps he can only achieve a limited freedom."

For many scholars, the conclusions of Jacobsen's great novels, *Marie Grubbe* (1876) and *Niels Lyhne* (1880), have seemed curiously out of step with the Breakthrough climate in which they were created. On the one hand, there are proponents (as found in the journal *Kritik*) of the belief that a "new perception of existence" did surface in Jacobsen's language and that this signaled a modern breakthrough, whereas other researchers, most notably those involved with *poetik*, another literary journal, maintain that the author upholds "the dualism of the idealistic nineteenth century" in his works. Very briefly, the problem is one of lack of consequence, that is, the factor of sheer chance seems to play a decisive role in the fates of both central characters: Marie Grubbe, who had apparently given up hope after a long life of struggle, is suddenly united, happily, with Søren, whereas Niels Lyhne, who had acquired happiness, just as suddenly loses it completely as his family dies. While chance, too, is a function of modern life—and the Breakthrough recognized this—Professor Ingwersen finds it inadequate as a solution and, in seeking to provide a more elucidative approach to the problem, suggests instead an underlying, implicit mythical narrative structure to account for the *seemingly* inexplicable conclusions.

With the three phases of the *Bildungsroman* or, more precisely, of the Danish version, the *dannelsesroman*, as a starting point (i.e., the hero's journey from his state as a man of ideals—and the potential to achieve them—through a temporarily disastrous "fall" from innocence, and, finally, to the reacquisition of equilibrium based upon the lessons learned in his confrontation with the error of his ways), Ingwersen examines Hans Egede Schack's *Phantasterne* (1857), which had great significance for J. P. Jacobsen. Conrad, the hero of Schack's novel, follows this formula rather well, first losing himself in dreams of ever-increasing erotic fantasy, then going through a completely opposite stage, becoming antipoetic and inordinately critical of his earlier excesses, and ultimately emerging as the "harmonious man" under the influence of love. Significantly, Conrad reenters the dream plane, but now his fantasies are constructively directed toward reality. He has boldly confronted his demonic nature, and this requisite meeting transforms sexual fantasies into understanding of love.

The lesson of *Phantasterne*—one closely related to myth—"if man is consistent . . . in his endeavor to realize what his nature bids him, he will be rewarded and gain complete happiness," is directly applicable to *Marie Grubbe* and *Niels Lyhne* and supports Ingwersen's suggestion of an underlying mythical cohesiveness. Lyhne's dreams are wholly escapist, "without content," "derivative, borrowed from literature," for, despite his advocacy of new ideas, he refuses to recognize the existence of an erotic aspect in his nature. In short, he avoids the vital recognition of his erotic fantasies and thereby fails to achieve *Bildung*, for, just as reward is associated with gaining of insight into one's own inner makeup, punishment is the ineluctable consequence of deliberate rejection or unwitting ignorance of this confrontation. Niels Lyhne's fate is both Breakthrough, as his inability to manifest a positive dream is the result of determinative factors beyond his control, and myth, within which framework the punishment he suffers is highly appropriate and consistent. Marie Grubbe is a dreamer, also, but the fantasies to which she gives herself in searching for the right kind of man are unmistakably erotic and, in the mythical context, fulfilling. She, like Conrad, reaches *Bildung* through a confrontation with her inner faults and is rewarded by a viable relationship with a member of the opposite sex. Professor Ingwersen shows cogently that, whether by design or not, Jacobsen allowed his Breakthrough novels to exhibit, if only implicitly, the ethics of an age that was anathema to the spirit of his own time.

Can a general, all-inclusive formula for defining *the* Hamsun hero be extracted from the author's prose production, which stretches over some six decades, beginning with *The Enigmatic One* (1877) and concluding with *The Ring Is Closed* (1936). Although Professor Naess holds that such an equation is not very easily derived, he is able to illustrate convincingly the fact that the title of Hamsun's final book, while not necessarily a signal for "the hero's return to the point of departure," may be regarded as "a ramification of his road, with two major avenues parting and converging as the ring is closed." Within each of the three broader artistic phases of Hamsun's life, that is, the nineties, the first decade of this century, and the years during and subsequent to World War I, can be found central characters so similar to one another as to be readily assignable to the chronological periods of their "birth" by virtue of their behavioral patterns. And while there are certain common qualities shared by all of Hamsun's heroes, there is a definite shift—one bifurcation of the ring—from, as Naess states it, "the colorful Byronic hero of the nineties into the pitiful nonhero of the twentieth century."

Hamsun's controversial nature finds its first fictional literary manifestation in the novel of 1877, which, written during the height of Norwegian realism, is characterized by an undeniable romantic spirit in the person of its central figure, Rolf Andersen. Of interest for Hamsun's later writings, particularly the products of the nineties, is the nascence, in *The Enigmatic One*, of his romantic irony. During the nineties, his central characters all reflected Hamsun's ideal of the literary hero as one of extreme sensitivity, of complex psychological constitution, and of a convoluted, fascinating personality that he, the novelist, would explore. Each of them—"Tangen" (*Hunger*), Nagel (*Mysteries*), Glahn (*Pan*), and Johannes (*Victoria*)—is mysterious, artistic, strangely androgynous, sadomasochistic, and, as would befit Goethe's great romantic figure, Werther, "not made for happiness." Professor Naess discusses a most interesting aspect of Hamsun's "double consciousness," namely, the use of a Doppelgänger to reinforce his irony, as in the conflict between Nagel and the Midget: ". . . everything beautiful must call forth its counterpart." The character of Knut Pedersen, who is the cohesive element in the *Wanderers* trilogy (1912), best illustrates the author's change from what some regard as decadent concern for the "excessively nervous temperament" to concern for a figure more in tune with the tenor of the New Age. Pedersen shows certain similarities with the heroes of the nineties, to be sure, but he is much more representative of Hamsun's own problems of domestic maturity than is the introspective ransacking of the psyche illustrative of his earlier period. The author's great character portraits from this point on all exemplify his feeling that Society is destructive to the individual, and his growing disillusionment, exacerbated by the Great War and the general condition of humanity:

Lieutenant Holmsen (*Children of the Age*, 1913), "tenacity embodied," was the middle-aged author's answer to Ibsen's *Rosmersholm*, whose central character he found lacking in true aristocratic fortitude; Isak Selanraa (*Growth of the Soil*, 1917), the sole example of the "active man" as hero in Hamsun, despite moving treatment, lacks the dynamic personality of the earlier (nineties) figures; Oliver (*Women at the Pump*, 1920), Hamsun's first pure artist, is painted in a distressingly negative light to mirror the writer's pessimism after World War I; then there is August (of the *August* trilogy, 1927–1933), "Hamsun's Peer Gynt," so much like Oliver in his inability to find a niche in society or success in love; and, finally, Abel Brodersen (*The Ring Is Closed*), the reflective nature related to Nagel as well as Edevart (*August* trilogy), is Hamsun's last prose reiteration of his most persistent theme, the pernicious influence of society upon the individual's development.

Given the diversity of characters and sheer volume of Hamsun's literary production, Professor Naess's assessment of the futility of seeking a single definition for the Hamsun hero proves to be very valid indeed. (Hamsun's hero: a Scandinavian Yankee with Russian ancestry?) Perhaps, in the end, one might best define this theoretical construction, that is, *the* Hamsun hero, with the title of his initial novel, "the enigmatic one."

Continuing her sedulous investigation of Ingmar Bergman's works (see *Ingmar Bergman*, New York: Twayne, 1968), Professor Birgitta Steene charts the Swedish cinematist's philosophical shift to a nihilistic position in her perceptive analysis—centering about the "antiheroic stance"—of six of his films: *Secrets of Women, Brink of Life, The Seventh Seal*, and the Chamber Film trilogy (*Through a Glass Darkly, Winter Light, The Silence*). Of great interest—one would like to insert the word *relevance* somewhere in this context, but shudders at the thought—are Bergman's concern for and handling of women in the initial film, in which, rather than exhibiting qualities that would endear them to the modern Women's Liberation phalanx, they exist, as Steene notes, "within the traditional radius of womanhood." These characterizations, it is explained, are not the result of male chauvinism on Bergman's part; in fact, his use of women as main figures is pragmatic in a very positive sense: he feels that they can become more easily involved in "crucial situations," are a good deal more adaptable to life's hardships, and, in their ability to view existence emotionally, rather than on an intellectual plane—they seek answers "in their own experience, not in the rhetoric of the mind"—are more readily able to create interpersonal relationships, an ability that, in the Bergman idiom, is synonymous with an asseveration of life. One is reminded, in this last regard, of Ingwersen's remarks on the importance of sex in *Phantasterne* and the works of Jacobsen, in which women are far better able to seek harmony than men, who seem to need intellectualization of even sexual contact and, as he states, have difficulty "in reconciling the sinful flesh with the worthier soul."

Despite their greater ability to cope with life, however, Bergman's women still manage to evince the feeling of loneliness that is perhaps most characteristic of the modern age. With *Brink of Life*, Bergman abandons the portrayal of women as "victims of society"—which in itself represented a shift from the earlier Swedish cinema's view of woman as either siren or country lass—and takes his first significant stride toward nihilism. The lesson of Cecilia and Hjördis, that no lasting relationships between man and woman can be established, and that of Stina, who must suffer apparently senselessly, point up mankind's tragic existential plight and the anguish of the antiheroic soul. Antonius Block, of *The Seventh Seal*, is a perfect example of the male tendency to seek a solution to life's riddle by withdrawing to intellectual, static speculation, rather than by responding emotionally, dynamically, as do the women. He is, as Steene notes, "the modern, post–World War I antihero who has come to replace the tragic hero as the central figure in the most serious efforts by contemporary artists to explore the human dilemma." Block hungrily seeks answers as to the nature of existence, but his destiny is to be surfeited only with loneliness.

The Chamber Film trilogy, with its all-pervasive mood of self-abnegation, examines the ultimate nihilistic choice in the face of an existence devoid of meaning: death. One of Bergman's most consequential issues concerning human alienation is the role of language, which Professor Steene shows to be not merely empty, but simultaneously terribly destructive: Jonas Persson, of *Winter Light*, is annihilated by the priest's words (or, better stated: his *life* is destroyed, in contrast to the contemplated self-destruction of David, of *Through a Glass Darkly*, which is less a result of life's meaninglessness than of his *own* personal failure). Tomas, the priest, also uses words to conceal his inner bankruptcy, to *escape*, in keeping with the actions of so many Bergman men, whereas the woman, Märta, not unexpectedly, is strong enough to eschew such a façade. It is in the figure of a woman, too, that a Bergman character first comprehends the intrinsic impotence of language: Ester, of *The Silence*, witnessing the death of "hope, love, and faith," and the chilling advent of total loneliness, bravely follows the only course open to the nihilist—by dying. Thus the antiheroic stance is ultimately related to the inability of language to create meaningful, enduring human relationships, a condition that evokes the atmosphere of *tristesse* associated with these six Bergman films and the age in which they were conceived.

One wonders then—given the estranged, oppressive character of the time in which Bergman's figures function—whether a truly *positive* contemporary heroic personality can evolve and sustain himself or herself. There are several possible candidates for this appellation in the Swedish fiction of today (post–World War II), but, in most cases, Professor Linnér's close scrutiny reveals, either a negative aspect precludes elevation to the heroic level or, in several instances where clearly heroic action is evident, the figure is not in the true sense contemporary. Ingenjör Andrée, of Sundman's *Ingenjör Andrées luftfärd*, as an illustration of the first category, is only *apparently* heroic, a superficial hero, for while his journey is doubtlessly courageous—one of Linnér's prerequisites for heroic status—he is motivated by "sinister" impulses. In some instances, finding no suitable modern exemplars, authors have sought to re-create the hero of antiquity, as in Johnson's retelling of the *Odyssey* (*Strändernas svall*) and Moberg's emigration tetralogy, in which an apparently late nineteenth century man, Karl-Oskar, adheres to a misplaced classical ideal; in both cases, while they exhibit heroism in stature, these figures are part of an irrevocable past and unrecognizable from the modern point of view.

There are, however, at least two contemporary, recognizable hero figures in modern Swedish fiction, which thus provides an affirmative answer to Linnér's pointed queries: "Where are the heroes who crowd the subways with the rest of us or, at least, walk streets that we *might* have walked? Is a realistic depiction of heroism still possible?" In contrast to the ideal nihilistic Bergman hero (cf. Ester's final action), Linnér's heroic personality shows courage in continuing to live even in the face of life's devastating assault upon the individual. As in Bergman's films, on the other hand, it is the woman who shows great strength in the face of adversity; one is simply confronted here with two definitions, which, however different, still amount to courage: the negative and the positive, the strength to leave life and the capacity to endure. Professor Linnér's suggested heroines—Paulina, "that wonderful middle-aged woman who pronounces her fragrant Yes to life," of Ahlin's *Natt i marknadstältet*, and Linda, of Lidman's novels *Regnspiran* and *Bära mistel*—while noble characters in the classical mold, operate within the framework of the present, a setting far removed from antiquity, and they are readily recognizable to the modern mentality.

Besides courage, Linnér states, a simple clear-cut moral alternative is prerequisite for heroic stature. This precondition accounts in part for the absence of the political hero from the contemporary fictional scene, for the Byzantine machinations of modern politics are far too involved to allow for precise moral boundaries. (Once again, particularly in this year of disclosures, one would like to raise the cry of "relevance" but fears that the term, not unlike *Spöksonaten*'s kitchen bones, has lost its marrow.) Professor Linnér touches upon a number of possible causes for the nonappearance of a political hero in modern Swedish fiction (he discounts Forssell's Lenin as being romantically anachronistic), including Lukács's distressing assessment of Tolstoy's world, but his concluding statement amounts to an optimistic admonition to persist in the struggle for a viable, meaningful existence despite the absence of such heroism in today's literature.

The concluding articles in this volume, while not delivered together at the symposium, are considered here in the same breath, so to speak, as they both center on the relationship of August Strindberg to the modern literary scene. With the assistance of a research group at the

Lund (Sweden) Drama Institute, of which he is the leader, Professor Holm has meticulously studied the phenomenon of expressionistic drama, particularly as practiced by Strindberg, whom, as does Lars Gustafsson, he calls a forerunner of modernism. Delving into the post-*Inferno* works, Holm shows their essentially expressionistic character in typification, dream quality, naturalistic detail, violence, and the all-encompassing Strindberg ego (cf. Dahlström's *Ausstrahlungen des Ichs*), which comprised the central cohesive element of these later dramas. From the naturalistic "consistency of psychological realism" characterizing *Miss Julie*, Holm travels to the new view of humanity gained in Strindberg's neurotic Purgatory and expressed in such works as *A Dream Play* and *The Ghost Sonata* ("a glimpse into the soul"), noting that the dramatist anticipated Freud's concern for the dark Cimmerian corners of the subconscious and provided as well the impetus for "the most fertile of ideas for twentieth-century fiction." The illustrations that complement this essay, as well as Holm's treatment of Schuh's innovative production of *A Dream Play* in 1955, mirror the different approaches taken to Strindberg and (most forcefully in the contrast of plates 9 and 10) emphasize the fact that he was light years in advance of the theater of his time.

Using a Strindberg poem ("Mörk är backen" from "Gatubilder III") as his point of departure, Lars Gustafsson not only discusses Strindberg as a forerunner of Scandinavian modernism, but also summarizes the salient features of modernism in the process. He guides the reader on an extended artistic tour through such diverse minds as Lagerkvist, Huysmans, Stravinsky, Freud, Schönberg, Ungaretti, and Ekelöf, to give but a sampling. The problems of establishing the incidence of direct literary influence versus correspondence, the author recognizes, are legion, yet in his discussion of Strindberg's novel, revivifying use of the Swedish language, which manifested a characteristic refusal "to regard the exterior world as entirely exterior and the interior as entirely interior," Gustafsson holds persuasively that Strindberg answers a question far more interesting than "Who influenced whom?" namely, "What, of certain significance in the work, is it that made later achievements possible?" In obliterating the once-clear dividing line between exterior and interior, observation and emotion,

Strindberg, as in the introductory poem and post-*Inferno* dramas (*A Dream Play*: the dramatist's attempt to "say something about ordinary life in the grammar of dreams"), creates a new totality, in Gustafsson's words, "the totality of classical European modernism."

The Ibsen Hero

by SVERRE ARESTAD

University of Washington (Emeritus)

The subject of Ibsen's hero is so very nearly synonymous with the totality of his production that a consideration of all his protagonists would seem to be in order. Since this task obviously presents insurmountable obstacles, certain characters will have to be selected to represent the several kinds of heroes that Ibsen depicted. The selection cannot be arbitrary, for it is essential to choose the most representative one from each of three categories. When this has been accomplished, the discussion of Ibsen's hero can proceed. This matter is a bit complicated because two of the heroes to be discussed, Brand and Solness, are quite alike, and they therefore constitute one category, while Peer Gynt and Mrs. Alving represent two categories of the Ibsen hero.

Two matters need to be set forth as a preliminary to the whole complex problem of Ibsen's hero. First of all, I must state that I have worked with the Ibsen hero, directly and indirectly, for a number of years and have, from time to time, made public certain views concerning this topic. I now find myself drawing upon some of those views, and, consequently, I am consciously placing myself in a position that Peer Gynt, unknown to himself, was guilty of when he drew upon the whole repository of secular lore and of biblical tradition to prove a point and, finding these inadequate to his purposes, resorted to quoting himself.[1] In the second instance, I want to acknowledge a debt to numerous students, both undergraduate and graduate, who, over the years, have wrestled with me on the problem of the Ibsen hero, and I want to get that acknowledgment in before any of them begin to accuse me of plagiarism.

I believe it was Paul Valéry who once cited the mathematician Gauss's observation that one must put a problem in such a form that it can be solved. When a poet must cite a mathematician, there may be trouble for the lesser man who attempts to emulate the admonition. It is reassuring therefore to draw upon the more comforting formula of the philosopher. As Bertrand Russell stated in his essay "On Scientific Method in Philosophy," the discovery that a question is unanswerable is as complete an answer as can possibly be obtained. My task, therefore, will be to state the question and attempt an answer; Ibsen himself would hardly have demanded more.

If one asks the simple question, "What is a hero?" in the present context, the problem is immediately complicated, because forthwith one must pose the ancillary questions of "What is an Ibsen hero?" and "What is *the* Ibsen hero?" There are thus three aspects to the question, which is proper, because there are actually three different kinds of hero in Ibsen's plays: the literary hero, the modern hero, and *the* Ibsen hero. It is the final definition that will present the greatest difficulty, because a formulation of it involves a subjective, a value, judgment, but it is the hero image of central concern.

There can be no doubt that some of Ibsen's heroes reflect prototypes from earlier literature, from Shakespeare for instance, and some reflect features from sources other than drama or belles-lettres, like the Bible or Kierkegaard. These heroes I call literary heroes. Now these questions must be asked: Are, in fact, any of Ibsen's heroes commensurate in stature with the most notable of those in Greek drama? In Shakespearean drama? In the tragedies of Racine? I should answer all three questions in the affirmative, although I have ringing in my ears Butcher's admonition to all Ibsen admirers that he was limited and provincial and that, although he achieved intensity, he failed to achieve greatness as a writer of tragic drama and, consequently, as a creator of heroes of tragic stature. It is comforting to have on one's side in this debate several astute students of Ibsen who are also sensitive interpreters of tragedy.

I shall refrain from involving T. S. Eliot in my discussion of Ibsen's

hero, except to cite his view that the mirror of wholeness or complete-
ness had been shattered into a thousand pieces by the time of Shakespeare and that one would have to go back to Dante for a valid portrait
of the whole man—the Renaissance Man—and, consequently, for an
acceptable basis for the true tragic hero. It follows from the above that
I regard Ibsen's hero to be essentially tragic, and that I shall discuss his
hero from a more traditional point of view than that proposed by T. S.
Eliot.

The question now arises of the nature of an Ibsen hero. Is the Ibsen
hero a universal, timeless abstraction that can readily be equated with
the classical hero of earlier literature, or is it identifiably Ibsen's own?
Moreover, does Ibsen's concept of the hero shift with time and still
retain its validity? Finally, does Ibsen's idea of the hero evolve from an
earlier concept, then change, and finally revert to the original one?

My discussion will begin with Brand and will continue with Peer
Gynt, Mrs. Alving of *Ghosts*, and Solness of *The Master Builder*. I
must, however, make a few remarks concerning earlier Ibsen protagonists before proceeding to Brand.

The key to Ibsen's hero lies in his understanding of man's tragedy.
Ibsen's concept of tragedy centers on the question of whether or not
man is free to order his life as he chooses, a question that he tested
against both the conventions of the early nineteenth century and the
naturalism of the 1870's and 1880's. The three tragic heroes chosen to
be discussed are markedly different, although there is a much closer relationship between Brand and master builder Solness than there is between either of these two protagonists and Mrs. Alving. This is due to
the fact that Ibsen conceived of *Brand* as high tragedy, that he abandoned high tragedy in middle career, when he wrote *Ghosts*, and that
he restored high tragedy in his last period, when he wrote *The Master
Builder*. Peer Gynt is not mentioned here, but he will be considered in
due time.

The tragedies of Ibsen's first period—from *Lady Inger of Østråt*
(1854) to *Emperor and Galilean* (1873)—revolve around the broad
theme of *idealism*. *Brand*, written in the midst of this protracted speculation on the nature of individual freedom of choice and action, became
Ibsen's most profound tragedy.

It will be profitable to look briefly at the manner in which Ibsen evolved and extended the character of Brand. At the end of *Love's Comedy* (1862), the poet Falk assumes a position that can loosely be called idealistic. He has freed himself—so he thinks—from the "manacle of slavery" (tradition), and he can now carry on the war against the lie: social hypocrisy. But there is no assurance that he will succeed, because he relies on Svanhild's belief in his mission rather than on his own. The idealist Falk, who goes forth to do battle on borrowed goods, becomes the doubter and the procrastinator Skule of *The Pretenders*. Skule demonstrates that one cannot live for another's view; the best he can do is to die for it. Although Skule is one of Ibsen's finest tragic heroes, he falls far short of being *the* Ibsen hero. Another hero in *The Pretenders*, King Håkon, bears a curious relationship to Brand. Håkon had complete faith in God's support of his endeavors, but his faith was based on arrogant presumption. He is finally made to realize this after he has condemned Skule to death; Håkon says: "God, God—why have you stricken me so sorely, when I have not sinned?" (act 3).[2] Brand has the same view, perhaps as naïve as Håkon's, that his idea of his mission has God's sanction. But he is made to realize that it may be beyond man's ability to know absolutely what his fate or destiny is and therefore what his limitations as a mortal may be.

If this relationship is continued further into *Peer Gynt* and *Emperor and Galilean*, numerous facets of the character of Brand will emerge; Brand's character as hero will presently be considered in detail. *Brand* and *Peer Gynt* represent two aspects of the Kierkegaardian syndrome. Kierkegaard provided for three stages in man's moral, intellectual, and spiritual life: the aesthetic, the ethical, and the religious. These Kierkegaardian categories contain complete, complex analyses of three divergent views of life, but Ibsen has employed only one principle from two of them, the aesthetic and the ethical. Brand as an ethical character has assumed full responsibility for his decisions and resulting actions, while Peer as an aesthetic character has not committed himself to any such irrevocable responsibility. While an individual may rise or fall on Kierkegaard's scale, a character within the compass of a play cannot pass from one stage to another. The moment the hero did that, the play would have to end.

As an ethical character, Brand must constantly call upon all his powers to refuse compromise of any kind. He must adhere to the principle that to will a thing and fail is forgivable, but to refuse to will even the impossible and therefore not attempt it is not only unforgivable but also contemptible. Peer, as an aesthetic character, is the opposite of Brand. One's first impression of Peer might well be that he is an irresolute egoist, a fraud, a failure, a completely negative character, who never reaches a decision, never fulfills a promise, never attains a goal. But Peer cannot be dismissed so cavalierly, as a further comparison with Brand will show. Brand displays an inflexible adherence to principle, an inability to compromise, an absolute assurance of the correctness of his view of life, and a willful determination to achieve an ultimate goal. Peer, on the other hand, shows a seemingly casual disregard of principle, an unwillingness to commit himself fully when he cannot obtain absolute proof of the correctness of a tenet, and an inability to base his actions upon a view of life whose validity may not be questioned but must be accepted on faith. Brand bases his whole course of action upon the assumption that his particular view of life is infallible. Peer, however, tentatively tests the value of each principle of life, without finding any of them tenable. In a real sense, Peer's search for the meaning of existence and man's role in the world is much more sophisticated than Brand's.

Brand has assumed responsibility for his actions, but he at no time questions whether those actions result from his own decisions or whether the actions are dictated for him. Peer evades the problem. Julian, in *Emperor and Galilean*, however, comes to direct grips with the issue, and he rejects the condition, that is, "freedom under necessity," by which man is forced to assume responsibilities for actions that he does not himself choose. If Brand had questioned what he was asked to assume in the way of obligations, as Julian did, he never would have undertaken his mission. I conclude, therefore, that Julian also is a more sophisticated character than Brand.

I come now to a brief consideration of the nature of the hero Brand. Brand is an uncompromising idealist who has determined to fulfill his mission as an agent of God by bringing to the people the desire to live a Christ-like life and, by steeling their wills, the means to achieve that desire. He has married Agnes, a woman of as great a spirit as his own, compassionate, forgiving, considerate, aware of the weaknesses and limitations of man and willing to compromise with those weaknesses and limitations but forced to accede to Brand's inhuman demand for no compromise. He has assumed the family guilt, as a result of which he refuses to give his mother the last sacrament unless she will give up all her worldly possessions. When it is feared that his child will die unless he is removed from the damp climate of the cramped valley, Brand only for a moment wavers in his resolve to consider no obstacle too great if one but wills to overcome it. But when the doctor observes that it is strange that Brand should yield when his own son's life is in jeopardy, though he will not do so under any other considerations, Brand reverses his impulsive decision and declines to move away, and as a result his son dies.

Agnes must willingly give up all physical mementos of her son—a lock of hair, a cap—she must not look upon her son's grave; she must, in fact, divest her mind and soul of any remembrance of him whatever, and she must do this willingly and gladly, for such are the demands of God. Being inadequate to these demands, Agnes dies. Brand, without realizing it, has lost the one person who sustained him in his mission.

Alone at the end, Brand gives voice to his utter despair at the state of man.

God, I plunge into death's night,—
Shall they wholly miss thy Light
Who unto man's utmost might
Will'd—?   (act 5)

Brand's greatness lies in his unyielding and inflexible urge to attain the unattainable even after the impossibility of successful achievement has been inexorably demonstrated. Even in defeat, Brand leaves one with the optimistic, encouraging, and germinating idea that, although it has been demonstrated through him that he cannot attain the ideal, he will not admit that he cannot. In a very real sense, Brand's words, "But the path of yearning's left," are the most magnificent words that Ibsen ever penned.

The tragedy of *Brand*, then, is that of a man who, in attempting to live according to the ideal and demanding that others do likewise, realizes that his ideal is false because it is based on will and not on love, a realization that renders him incapable of fulfilling his mission.

Brand had voluntarily accepted responsibility for his actions, but he had not inquired whether his choice was free or whether it was predetermined. He failed to consider whether what he chose to do was what God had decreed that he should do. Ibsen clarified this aspect of Brand's character by presenting an opposite nature in the person of Julian in *Emperor and Galilean*.

Julian's task in *Emperor and Galilean* was to attain harmony of being by uniting in himself the forces of the flesh and of the spirit, whereupon he could proceed to effect a synthesis of the classical and the Christian traditions, that is, to institute harmony in his world. The Oracle had informed him that he was a chosen man under necessity, that is, the necessity of doing God's bidding, all the while assuming full responsibility for his actions. Julian refused to subordinate himself to a higher authority, for he would not accept any limitations on his freedom of choice and action. He rejected the formula "to will under necessity," and, in denying necessity and thereby a higher power, he discovered that what he struggled for he failed to achieve and what he struggled against he served to promote. The paradox is that, in refusing to will what he must, Julian willed what he wanted, only to discover, as Brand did, that that was what he was all along destined to do. These early Ibsen heroes are thus compulsive but, in actuality, not free individuals.

While Peer may well be Ibsen's most beloved character, and his search for the meaning of the self may perhaps be Ibsen's most sophisticated treatment of this central theme in all his works, Ibsen could not have condoned Peer's life style, although he tolerated it. Peer, therefore, falls short of Ibsen's ideal.

Peer Gynt is so great a drama that one feels apologetic about devoting only a few lines to it. In many ways it is as profound a work as has ever been written. One intriguing thing about *Peer Gynt* is its ability to arouse young people. They ask: How do I know what course to take? With every decision I make, I get into a mold. Do I know that I am proceeding in the right direction? What evidence do I have that what I am now doing is best for me? Where do my decisions lead? The basic element of *Peer Gynt*, as seen by the young, was well expressed by Kierkegaard, who said that life can only be understood backwards, but it must be lived forwards.

I have already commented on *Peer Gynt* in relation to *Brand*, and I need not repeat those observations. It only needs to be emphasized here that the negative aspects of Peer Gynt that were presented in the comparison are quite widely held, but they do not correspond to my view of *Peer Gynt* at all.

Although Peer may appear to be evasive and dilatory, he is so only because he acts according to a certain axiom: he will proceed only so far as empirical evidence of the validity of the tenets of life will carry him. The Button Molder's ultimate challenge to Peer, in act 5, is that, if he doesn't know God's purpose with him, he must divine it. Peer rejects this absurd demand, and rightly so. Two predecessors of Peer Gynt, the young King Håkon of *The Pretenders* and Brand, are relevant here. When Håkon's mother is performing the ordeal by fire on his behalf, an aide says to him, "Pray to the Lord, thy God." Håkon replies, "That is not necessary, I'm sure of him." Early in the play, Brand says, "I am on the mission of a great man. His name is God!" It is obvious how far off the mark these two characters were. Peer Gynt, in the opening scene, is asked by his mother to swear that what he is saying is true. Peer answers with a question: "Why swear?" That is, why commit yourself when you don't know what the score is? So, while Brand discovered that his protracted mission was based on a false assumption, which was his infallible belief that he had been chosen by God to play a specific role, Peer decided to find out something about this world we inhabit before he committed himself.

Peer's pilgrimage through life is known to everyone, so it does not have to be repeated here. Although he lived most of his life on the principle *"To thyself be—enough,"* he ultimately realized that this attitude toward life left one unfulfilled and that this view of life, moreover, deprived others of their share of life's rewards. While he was active, Peer drifted along on the currents of materialistic existence, but, when he had become sated with that life style, he paused to reflect. As Housman expressed it: "Some men think by fits and starts / and when they do, they fasten their hands upon their hearts." This is what Peer did. He succeeded ultimately in divesting himself of the Gyntian Self, but, as usual in an Ibsen play, there is a question of whether he realized his true self, that is, the recognition of what the self constitutes in the life of man. However one wishes to interpret the conclusion of *Peer Gynt*—whether he is saved or not; the skeptical will say no, the strong of faith will say yes—he nevertheless succeeded in demonstrating that man's knowledge of the world is insufficient to his needs. A faith of some kind is essential to survival, if not to triumph.

I want only to suggest here that critics, reading *Peer Gynt* in casual fashion, have found Peer to be the progenitor of Hjalmar Ekdal, in *The Wild Duck*, and Dr. Stockman, in *An Enemy of the People*. These suggestions, in a sense, are not invalid, but I doubt that Peer Gynt would ever have recognized Hjalmar Ekdal or, for that matter, Dr. Stockman. The matter of influence completely baffles me, but I should not think it unlikely that, fed by critical suggestions, subsequent authors may have seen in Peer Gynt the genesis of the antihero. If so, Ibsen would share with Dostoievski the distinction of introducing the antihero into literature, the latter's *Notes from the Underground* (1864) usually thought of as originating that concept.

Since Ibsen is the ideological forerunner of much of subsequent drama, one looks to him for the genesis of the modern tragic hero. Classical drama affords a wide range of protagonists, the few who are truly great and the many who are of lesser stature. The latter are called diminished protagonists. Ibsen has some of each of these, but he also has an entirely new hero—the modern hero—who, though of smaller stature, cannot be understood in terms of the diminished hero of classical tragedy. I shall give only one example, Mrs. Alving of *Ghosts*. In today's increasingly democratic orientation, Willy Loman, for example, has come to be accepted as a tragic figure, a protagonist who has his origin in Ibsen. It took Arthur Miller ten years, with fits and starts, to evolve a concept of modern tragedy that would include Willy Loman, the substance of which was that intent is primary and performance secondary. In other words, if a character in a modern play commits himself wholeheartedly to his goal, though because of almost total deficiencies he fails, he must nevertheless be considered a tragic figure. Ibsen would have agreed to this formulation of the modern tragic hero.

Ibsen's concept of the tragedy of modern man is nowhere more forcefully represented than in *Ghosts*. Mrs. Alving is a noble personality and a remarkable woman. She is thus, actually, a diminished protagonist in terms of the classical hero, but she inhabits a naturalistic world, and the tragedy therefore becomes a "mixed" tragedy, as I have called it elsewhere. Ibsen's intent in *Ghosts* is to demonstrate how meaningless existence becomes for an idealist who must seek to surmount the jungle of a mechanistic order.

Whether one reads or sees *Ghosts*, one leaves the reading or the performance with the feeling that this is one of the most powerful dramas that Ibsen has ever written. Mrs. Alving was conceived by Ibsen as a heroic personality, with diminished protagonist status, whose mission was to attain an idealistic goal: to create the basis for an environment that would make possible the achievement of the "joy of life." Far from being a cliché, the "joy of life" lies at the very center of Ibsen's concern in *Ghosts*. It is fundamental to an understanding of *Ghosts*, and to an appreciation of its tragedy, that Mrs. Alving be thought of as an unusual personality, a heroic or perhaps semiheroic character. But she is caught up in a nonidealistic situation, in which any choices she makes become meaningless because her choices are predicated on an idealistic view of life, while her environment is nonidealistic. Her efforts toward achievement are therefore totally ineffectual, and she becomes the victim of the circumstances she endeavored to overcome.

The feeling the spectator has in viewing *Ghosts* is that nowhere has he been elevated by a gigantic contest, because all efforts are doomed through negation rather than through meaningful struggle and conflict; and at the end one has a feeling of debility without any realization of compensation for the horrible fate that has befallen Mrs. Alving and her son. There is no rising to heights of emotion at the prospect of any notable achievement, and there is no possibility of accepting things as they are at the end, for they are too horrible even to contemplate. Leaving the theater after viewing *Ghosts*, one walks on shoes of lead.

Thus, if one looks for the elements of the classic formula of awe, catharsis, and the reestablishment of emotional equilibrium, one does not find them in *Ghosts*. They are absent because Ibsen substituted a naturalistic for a moral universe. *Ghosts*, despite all, is a remarkable play; the tragedy is undeniably powerful, but it must be considered on another basis than that of high tragedy, despite the presence of a protagonist of at least semiheroic proportions. And *Ghosts* is not a tragedy of character in the sense in which this term would apply to Ibsen's earlier tragedies, nor is it a tragedy of personal psychology, such as one finds in Strindberg's *Miss Julie*. It is the tragedy of situation or circumstances in which an individual of noble aspirations must contend, always ineffectually, against a hostile, nonidealistic environment.

A distinction must be made, finally, between a hero in an Ibsen play and *the* Ibsen hero. After three examples of the former, I can now formulate what to me, with perhaps some modifications, constitutes *the* Ibsen hero. I believe it to be Solness of *The Master Builder*. I do not make this commitment because I believe that *The Master Builder* is largely an autobiographical work. On the contrary, I hold that, despite certain resemblances to Ibsen's own life, *The Master Builder* is an objective consideration of the nature of the artist. After all, the stages in Solness's life parallel those of every individual. This play considers the demands he makes upon life; his choices, whose consequences are ultimately apparent to him; the question of guilt, or conscience; and, finally, what measure of freedom the artist has.

During his fifty years as a dramatist, Ibsen was concerned with only a few fundamental problems, namely, the will, love, man's calling, and the question of man's freedom of choice. All four of these are included to a greater or lesser extent in *The Master Builder*, but choice is predominant. This is by no means the first time Ibsen emphasized the problem of choice in his characters—in Brand, Emperor Julian, Consul Bernick, Mrs. Alving, among others—but in a real sense it is the most significant. This will become clear from a study of Ibsen's portrayal of the artist.

Ibsen portrays characters from many walks of life: churchmen, kings and emperors, politicians, doctors, lawyers, businessmen and entrepreneurs, and artists. Numerous callings and professions are thus represented in his gallery of portraits. He never consciously sought, however, to present a psychological delineation of a king or a churchman or a politician. In Ibsen's great historical drama, *The Pretenders*, there is no hint of the myth of kingship nor any attempt to understand a king as king. Ibsen's politicians in *The League of Youth* are at best stereotypes, and they bear little resemblance to the masterful portrait of the politician that Bjørnson created in *Paul Lange og Tora Parsberg*. Of Pastor Manders in *Ghosts* the best that can be said is that he is a flat character, but his is not a psychological portrait of a man of the cloth; at most, he is possibly emerging into the round. Referring to Brand, Ibsen dispels any notion that he ever attempted the portrait of a man of the church; he remarks: "I just happened to make Brand a minister: I could equally well have made him a member of any other calling." More important in this connection, however, is the fact that Ibsen did not and, indeed, could not have said the same thing about his entrepreneur- and artist-protagonists—Bernick, Solness, Borkman, and Rubek.

Though a weak character, Falk of *Love's Comedy* is portrayed as an artist per se. His is really the portrait of an early-nineteenth-century youth with some poetic pretensions, romanticized and idealized by others but cut to ribbons by Ibsen. While it is only a cameo portrait, Ibsen's portrayal of Jatgeir Skald in *The Pretenders* is one of his most brilliant achievements. Here is a true romantic poet, but somehow he does not seem to be Ibsen's ideal. Another artist in Ibsen's plays who displays the proper sense of independence is Oswald of *Ghosts*, but his destiny is determined by extraneous forces exclusively, so he cannot be considered. The self-declared artists in *The Lady from the Sea* and the unbalanced Eilert Løvborg in *Hedda Gabler* could hardly represent *the* Ibsen hero, even if he has to be sought among the artists.

All artists prior to Solness have been briefly considered and simultaneously rejected as possible candidates for *the* Ibsen hero. Why is Solness so special? The answer to that question lies in the exploration of two matters that become curiously interrelated for the first time in *The Master Builder*. The first is Ibsen's portrayal of an artist of stature, and the second is the question of freedom of choice.

I have already indicated who Ibsen's artists are. It remains only to reemphasize that Ibsen's preoccupation with the artist-protagonist intensified during his later years and to state that the artist and the entrepreneur (Solness and Rubek, Bernick and Borkman, respectively) are the only characters Ibsen drew who are to be understood in terms of their calling. In other words, these four characters are psychological portraits of the artist and the entrepreneur. While Ibsen could say of Brand that he just happened to make him a minister, but that he could equally well have made him a representative of any other calling, he could not have said that of the two artists and the two entrepreneurs whom I have mentioned. Moreover, Ibsen could not, except through complete and almost unrecognizable modification, have made Brand an artist. It has been suggested by a Norwegian critic that Emperor Julian, whose conflict arises by virtue of the "freedom under necessity" syndrome, could be equated with Ibsen's artists, namely with Solness and his *non serviam* view. This position is hardly defensible.

There is a very close affinity between Ibsen's two principal artist-protagonists—Solness and Rubek—and his two entrepreneurs—Bernick and Borkman. The latter I have called nonartistic creative personalities. Implicit in this designation are two important differences between the artist and the entrepreneur. The first lies in the different nature of their respective endeavors: the one creates poetry, music, sculpture; the other creates vast industrial empires. The urges, drives, compulsions of each are similar, and the goals (i.e., the achievement) are identical, but the end product is dissimilar. The artist, according to Ibsen, because of his special endowments, has an obligation to his fellowmen, but this obligation becomes effective only after the artist has performed according to his own satisfaction. The artist does not curry the favor of the public but does find a modicum of reward if his efforts are recognized. The entrepreneur, on the other hand, needs and curries public acclamation for his good works. It is sufficient here to note John Gabriel Borkman's procession down the street in top hat and a handsome carriage, drawn by a span of four splendid horses, acknowledging the acclaim of the public: King John. Ibsen's artist and Ibsen himself were above this sort of thing. This seems to me a strong argument in favor of Solness, rather than Bernick or Borkman, as *the* Ibsen hero.

Until *The Master Builder*, Ibsen had often considered the problem of man's freedom of choice. If other men are not free to choose, Ibsen said, perhaps the artist—who withdraws from repressive conventions and traditions, establishes his own set of values, and goes it alone—is free. In *The Master Builder* he set about to consider this matter. While Ibsen restored in this play the conditions for high tragedy—the artist's challenge to God to be permitted to do in his sphere what God did in his—his protagonist, Solness, obviously failed because he could not compete on equal terms, given his human limitations, against a universal force. But Ibsen's insistence that genius, at least, be free to choose goes by the board. *The Master Builder* represents a valiant attempt on the part of a select individual to gain complete freedom of action. Unfortunately, this freedom is not available to man, but the effort he makes to attain it in the character of Solness is Ibsen's supreme attempt to establish mortal man's demand of any and all forces that he be completely free to choose and do what he desires. There is, however, another aspect to this theme, because the artist has been endowed with certain gifts that drive him toward certain goals: he has creative urges over which he has no control. How free then can any man be? Perhaps he can achieve only a limited freedom.

Of course, this urge to be free—to be one's own man—is a universal quest for all except dolts. For Ibsen it became the most important of all human problems. And that is the reason I have chosen Solness as *the* Ibsen hero: he represents most clearly the force of this urge and displays the greatest effort toward noble achievement among all of Ibsen's heroes.

It has been suggested that Brand may have had a measure of the will to power, and that pride (hubris) may also have been a part of his nature. I doubt this. I should, moreover, like to make it abundantly clear that I do not agree with the usual interpretation of Bernick of *Pillars of Society* or, especially, with that of John Gabriel Borkman, who is supposedly a Napoleon, a man hungry for power, a "superman" who disdains ordinary man's morality. This is a popularized, though mistaken, Nietzschean concept. I hold that Ibsen does something with Borkman, a man of great talent and ability, who needs to find outlet for his talent and ability in order to realize his potential. Borkman is not seeking power for its own sake, but personal fulfillment through accomplishing what he can do and *must* do. Bernick, in effect, expresses this very well to Lona Hessel, saying that if he is restricted in his activities, he might as well be dead—as, in fact, Borkman is.

It should be emphasized that *the* Ibsen hero, Solness, is not motivated by a will to power. The source of his ultimate choice and resulting actions is not willed by him but dictated to him by the need to give expression to his creative talent. Will is, of course, operative and so is hubris, but I think Ibsen is subtly suggesting that an individual like an artist, a genius who tells society, tradition, or convention to go hang, is actually no more—and he may, in fact, be less—free than some more ordinary mortals who demand less from life.

My reason for choosing Solness as *the* Ibsen hero will become even clearer when I briefly refer to Rubek of *When We Dead Awaken*, an artist and another likely candidate for heroic stature. Although Rubek throws additional light on the artist as Ibsen ultimately came to see him, I think his apologetic tone is hardly commensurate with Ibsen's view of *the* hero. There is a note of resignation or reconciliation in the later or last works of other writers, Shakespeare or Racine, for example, as Tillyard has so succinctly pointed out with reference to Shakespeare. This same note in Ibsen permits the protagonist, Rubek in *When We Dead Awaken*, in this instance, to reduce his sights, acknowledge his limitations, and quit beating his head against a stone wall. Rubek speaks several times of the fact that his fate—because of his gifts as creative artist—is to go on creating one work after another until his dying day. This really is not freedom in the absolute sense that Ibsen conceived it, but it is a belated recognition, on Ibsen's part, of the human condition, at whatever level of human endeavor. The only consolation to be found here is that given by Niels Bohr after he had renounced any possibility of arriving at a complete understanding of the physical universe, namely, his *Komplementaritetsphilosophie*, which is the idea of complementarity. This simply means that by universal physical law, as at present understood, man is cast in a mold, but, aside from the predetermined restrictions, he has freedom of choice. I rather think that Ibsen recognized this principle in *When We Dead Awaken*, but that he would have looked back fondly and nostalgically to a man who had not yet accepted so sophisticated a view of the world that we inhabit, a view that, in a sense, makes us lesser men than we would like to think ourselves capable of being.

In a magnificent poem, "Timann skrid undan" [The hours flit by], Olav Nygaard reflects the ultimate in man's desire to be free from the constraining forces of universal law that curb his freedom of action or his desire for peace. Ibsen would have reveled in these sentiments. Nygaard, in effect, asks if there is nowhere in space a spot, hidden in dreams, beyond all man's fate, where he can sleep while galaxy after galaxy is extinguished, where he can rock and heal his searing wounds.

The Ibsen hero is an individual who demonstrates through action a professed belief in complete freedom of choice. But the triumph of the individual over circumstances or forces is not thereby assured, for his life appears to be predetermined. In spite of this, the Ibsen hero repeatedly refuses to accept the conditions that make him a subordinate individual, and, consequently, he openly opposes the forces, the circumstances, or the predetermined plan that prevents him from ordering his life as he chooses. In the resulting struggle values obtain, but there can be no absolute certainty; yet no Ibsen hero can find comforting assurance in a cynical rejection of the universal plan of which he is both product and victim. Ibsen's heroes reflect the noblest expression of the terror and the glory of life, and they make one sensitive to man's tragic fate. In spite of their imperfectibility, one comes to admire their struggle toward the achievement of complete freedom of choice and of action against the powers and the forces of a baffling and perplexing world.

Two matters remain to be explored briefly: Ibsen's supposed indebtedness to Nietzsche and the seemingly appalling seriousness of my discourse, which gives the impression that there is neither humor nor comedy in Ibsen.

Ibsen and Nietzsche were acquainted with one another's works and thought. Nietzsche went so far as to call Ibsen an "old maid." Why? Ibsen was soft on the woman question. This issue aside, there are numerous correspondences between the two. While Nietzsche may have reinforced Ibsen's concept of the artist-hero, there is no evidence that he led Ibsen to his view of him. Born in 1844, Nietzsche published his *The Birth of Tragedy* in 1872. This was just a year before Ibsen completed his first cycle of plays, ending with *Emperor and Galilean*, the first notations to which had been made eleven years earlier.

A few quotations from three Ibsen plays previous to Nietzsche's *The Genealogy of Morals* (1887) will be briefly considered. In *The Pretenders* (1864), Bishop Nicholas, having returned from the nether kingdom, encounters King Skule on his way to his death. He states:

While to their life-work Norsemen set out
Will-lessly wavering, daunted with doubt,
While hearts are shrunken, minds helplessly shivering,
Weak as a willow-wand wind-swept and quivering—
While about one thing alone they're united,
Namely, that greatness be stoned and despited,
When they seek honour in fleeing and falling
Under the banner of baseness unfurled—,
Then Bishop Nicholas 'tends to his calling,
The Bagler-Bishop's at work in the world!   (act 5)

At the conclusion of *The Wild Duck*, Dr. Relling says to Gregers Werle: "Oh, life would be quite tolerable, after all, if only we could be rid of the confounded duns that keep on pestering us, in our poverty, with the claim of the ideal" (act 5). Ulrik Brendel, returning to the house of Rosmer after his failure as a lecturer—he found himself bankrupt—speaks of Mortensgaard, who is in the ascendancy in the community, in undoubtedly the most discouraging passage in the idealist Ibsen's production:

Hush, hush, hush! Peter Mortensgaard is the lord and leader of the future. Never have I stood in a more august presence. Peter Mortensgaard has the secret of omnipotence. He can do whatever he wills. ("Oh, don't believe that," says Rosmer.) Yes, my boy! For Peter Mortensgaard never wills more than he can do. Peter Mortensgaard is capable of living his life without ideals. And that, do you see—that is just the mighty secret of action and of victory. It is the sum of the whole world's wisdom. Basta!   (act 4)

In his *Genealogy of Morals*, the following year, Nietzsche wrote:

Here I want to give vent to a sigh and last hope. Exactly what is it that I, especially, find intolerable; that I am unable to cope with; that asphyxiates me? A bad smell. The smell of failure, of a soul that has gone stale. God knows it is possible to endure all kinds of misery—vile weather, sickness, trouble, isolation, All this can be coped with, if one is born to a life of anonymity and battle. There will always be moments of re-emergence into the light, when one tastes the golden hour of victory and once again stands foursquare, unshakable, ready to face even harder things, like a bowstring drawn taut against new perils. But, you divine patronesses—if there are any such in the realm beyond good and evil—grant me now and again the sight of something perfect, wholly achieved, happy, magnificently triumphant, something still capable of inspiring fear! Of a man who will justify the existence of mankind, for whose sake one may continue to believe in mankind! . . . We no longer see anything these days that aspires to grow greater; instead, we have a suspicion that things will continue to go downhill, becoming ever thinner, more placid, smarter, cosier, more ordinary, more indifferent, more Chinese, more Christian—without doubt man is getting "better" all the time . . . This is Europe's true predicament: together with the fear of man we have also lost the love of man, reverence for man, confidence in man, indeed the *will of man*. Now the sight of man makes us despond. What is nihilism today if not that?[3]

These quotations need no comment, except that one would like to echo Kierkegaard: The times are not evil; they are contemptible, because they lack passion.

Having treated Ibsen in deadly serious fashion, how am I to relieve the tragic tension? Simply by indicating that comedy and tragedy are closely intertwined in Ibsen's entire production. *The Master Builder*, however, from which I have selected *the* Ibsen hero, is almost devoid of comedy—there are only two instances of it. However, as in all of Ibsen's plays, there is in *The Master Builder* an abundance of irony— a saving grace in all his work.

In his early plays, particularly in *The Pretenders*, Ibsen used Shakespearean comic relief. But in a later play, *Brand*, though the tragic tone is predominant, comedy is nevertheless ubiquitous. In *Peer Gynt* comedy pervades, but the tragic element rises up, on occasion, through the comic surface. I recall that Friedrich Dürrenmatt said, when asked why he wrote *The Physicists* as a comedy, that a subject so serious could not be treated as a tragedy. The paramount example of this concept in Ibsen is *The Wild Duck*. Here, as in *Peer Gynt*, the tragedy rises inexorably (as in *The Physicists*) through the comic overlayer. Ibsen's great achievement in *The Wild Duck* can be all the more appreciated when one considers how inferior this play would have been if it had not been conceived as a comedy on man's foibles. Perhaps Chekhov could have written a tragedy on the subject, but not Ibsen. So, while one thinks of Ibsen's hero in terms of tragedy, it should not be lost from view that this treatment of man by Ibsen would not have been endurable and it would not have been viable without the relief of a rich comic component.

Having dealt briefly with Ibsen's use of comedy, I should also indicate that, while I considered almost exclusively his unusual personalities, Ibsen did not neglect ordinary man, for his plays are peopled with individuals from all walks of life. A consideration of a single group of these, extending from *Brand* to *When We Dead Awaken*, will suggest the wealth of material that Ibsen included in his dramas to support the main action and, moreover, confirm the view that all mankind was his province. There is a peculiar fascination in a number of these minor characters, and in a real sense they serve to illuminate the nature of Ibsen's hero.

In almost every Ibsen play there is represented a male character, of middle age or older, who is either a remnant of former greatness and glory, like old Ekdal of *The Wild Duck*, or a complete bankrupt, like Ulrik Brendel of *Rosmersholm*, one of Ibsen's most tragic figures. Sometimes these human wrecks are saved from complete destruction by varying agencies. Thus Krogstad of *A Doll's House* is rehabilitated through the regenerative power of love, as is Ulfheim of *When We Dead Awaken*, while Engstrand of *Ghosts* keeps his miserable head above water through blackmail, a means of survival that Krogstad, to his everlasting glory, has abandoned. There are instances, too, in which men must accept compromise in order to survive, as does Aune of *Pillars of Society*. Life on the level represented by these characters can in turn be harsh, cruel, ugly, debasing, and degrading, but, as Dr. Rank of *A Doll's House* observed, they all regard the business of living to be excessively important, even for them.

In many respects old Foldal of *John Gabriel Borkman* most clearly illuminates these pathetic older men in Ibsen, and he most aptly illustrates their relationship with the chief protagonists. Like his counterparts in all the other Ibsen dramas, old Foldal serves a dual purpose. He is employed as a dramatic device to aid in the exploration of the character of Borkman, against whom he is pitted in the most unequal struggle conceivable, while he simultaneously serves as a commentary on that multitude who in one way or another fail of achievement or succumb to the adversities of fortune. Looking back over the road traveled, which is literally strewn with human wreckage, one discovers how well old Foldal symbolizes the destinies and summarizes the failures of those losers in the battle of life. Superficially, old Foldal's relationship to Borkman appears to be almost identical with old Ekdal's relationship to the elder Werle of *The Wild Duck*. However, as Borkman is a continuation of the study of Consul Bernick of *Pillars of Society*, so old Foldal has a closer psychological affinity with Aune, the shipbuilder of the same play, than he has with old Ekdal.

Ibsen's elder male characters, who play subordinate roles to the chief protagonists, are perhaps not very significant as individuals, but taken as a group they open up in vast perspective the author's brooding upon the human condition in general. Through these widely different secondary male characters, who dogged Ibsen for the greater part of his productive life, he reveals one aspect of the tragedy of man. Usually the hero is considered to be the sole tragic figure, and his destiny is set forth in what is called high tragedy. Ibsen was well aware that the noble protagonist was not present in naturalistic tragedy, but he also knew that there were tragic implications in the lives of any and all unfortunate human beings under any kind of order. Therefore, the most obscure person, for example, the man in *Brand* who has strangled his starving child and is now clutching it in his arms and calling on the devil for deliverance, may reveal elements of tragedy and of suffering of the same degree and of the same kind as do the lesser characters of the naturalistic plays. Rosmer of *Rosmersholm* may well be Ibsen's paramount example of the tragedy of the disintegration of personality, and, while he is a significant personage, several of the lesser characters share with him the same tragic fate. Through the minor characters one thus gains greater insight into Ibsen's unusual personalities.

NOTES

1 Some of my earlier articles I have drawn upon are "Ibsen and Shakespeare: A Study in Influence," *Scandinavian Studies* (August 1946); "Ibsen's Concept of Tragedy," *PMLA* (June 1959); "*Peer Gynt* and the Idea of Self," *Modern Drama* (September 1960); "Ibsen's Portrayal of the Artist," *Edda* (June 1963); and "Ibsen, Strindberg and Naturalistic Tragedy," *The Theatre Annual* (1968).

2 The quotations from Ibsen's plays are from *The Collected Works of Henrik Ibsen*, ed. William Archer (New York: Charles Scribner's Sons, 1906–1912).

3 Friedrich Nietzsche, *The Birth of Tragedy and The Genealogy of Morals*, trans. Francis Golffing (Garden City, N.Y.: Doubleday & Co., Anchor Books, 1936), pp. 177–178.

Problematic Protagonists

Marie Grubbe and Niels Lyhne

by NIELS INGWERSEN

University of Wisconsin at Madison

I shall readily admit that it was with some reluctance that I consented to discuss J. P. Jacobsen's *Marie Grubbe* and *Niels Lyhne*, for these two influential books and their protagonists have seemed problematic to literary critics for quite some time, and a wealth of analyses has been produced and must be taken into account. Let me state the problem specifically: how would it be possible to say anything even remotely new on *Marie Grubbe* and *Niels Lyhne*? I shall, however, just as readily admit that the topic for this symposium also requires that Jacobsen's works be considered: for years Jacobsen was a source of inspiration to young writers, and in the last two decades of the nineteenth century his writings were imitated and used as points of departure.

Let me briefly comment on recent Jacobsen research. The long-lasting and continuing, not to say increasing, fascination that these two novels have held is amply illustrated by two publications, one from 1970 and one about to appear; both belong to the newly established *vaerkserie*, each volume of which is devoted to a separate work of outstanding Danish literature. Each contains the author's own comments on his work, reviews contemporary with its debut, and many later analyses, which, in turn, mirror changing critical orientations. It should be added that, since the volume on *Niels Lyhne* appeared, significant new articles on this novel have been published.

One reason for this critical eagerness to reassess Jacobsen's achievement may be due, in part, to the Brandes centennial. This seems to be

true at least in the case of the journal *Kritik*, in which the circle around
the influential professor Aage Henriksen has taken upon itself the
task of redefining what—and how much—really happened at and
during the so-called Modern Breakthrough, a topic that for the last
decade has greatly concerned Danish scholars. If I may resort to a
grave simplification, I would say that the contributors to *Kritik* basically
assert that a new perception of existence was being expressed through
Jacobsen's language: a modern breakthrough did occur!

Another group of young critics, those whose main outlet is *poetik*,
a journal for *litteraturvidenskab*, *semiotik*, and *marxisme*, has also
made Jacobsen an object of study, and its findings may seem opposed
to those expressed by the circle around *Kritik*. In Jacobsen's works the
critics in *poetik* uncover ideological patterns that reveal that Jacobsen
is clearly adhering to the dualism of the idealistic nineteenth century,
that is, that beneath the surface of modernity he is reproducing a bourgeois ideology. Let me add that these critics have detected the same
phenomenon in most of the works of the authors of the Modern Breakthrough.

So much criticism has already been written that I, consequently, find
it difficult to present any significant new insights, and, even if I should
restrict myself to the useful task of presenting and analyzing the most
recent criticism, the subject would remain too large to treat in a paper
of this length. I shall, therefore, confine myself to some general comments that may be useful in the context of this symposium: I shall
speak briefly on the "hero" of the so-called *Bildungsroman* and, on
the way, present a mini-analysis of Hans Egede Schack's *Phantasterne*;
at the end, I shall attempt a comparison between *Marie Grubbe* and
Niels Lyhne that I hope will shed some new light on the forces that
are at work in Jacobsen's artistic universe and that determine the lives
of his protagonists. My analysis will definitely not be exhaustive; it
will only touch upon some aspects of the two novels, and it is intended
only as a sketch, a suggestion to an approach to Jacobsen and, perhaps,
to other works of the nineteenth century.

As a recognized member of a new orientation within literature, one
that had harshly broken with tradition, Jacobsen received much praise
from the members of the Modern Breakthrough, but it is nevertheless

obvious that their admiration diminished as the years went by. They did not let their friend down officially, but *Niels Lyhne*—a book that Jacobsen himself called *trist, men god*—was a disappointment to them. I can here refer to the dichotomy between the public statements and the private opinions voiced by the brothers Brandes. If one then moves up a few years in time, he will encounter what can nearly be called a writers' intoxication with Jacobsen. Those lyrical temperaments of the 1890's—a generation that to some extent, but not nearly so categorically as commonly assumed, reacted against the positivism of the 1880's—especially felt Jacobsen to be their harbinger and their aesthetic mentor. Here it should be noted that, while *Marie Grubbe* certainly was much admired, it was not embraced with the same exuberance as *Niels Lyhne*, a book that was apparently accepted as containing an experience of life with which the writers of the nineties could identify.

Before I turn to Jacobsen's novels I shall give the nearly canonized historical sketch of the Danish novel, one that characterizes its hero. The novel, which became a prominent genre during the nineteenth century, is predominantly the *Bildungsroman* or, more precisely, the variant called *dannelsesroman*. In this novel, for example, in the works of Andersen, Hauch, and Goldschmidt, as well as in those of Kierkegaard and Schack, a three-phased development of the hero occurs. The first stage normally presents the uninitiated child or young man who is evidently capable of realizing those values and goals that the age deemed to be worthwhile. The second phase, the bulky middle part of the narratives, depicts his journey from relative innocence to sophistication. In a sense one is witnessing the hero's fall, for, through temptations and seductions, one follows him as he strays away from the ideal path. He hardly ever arrives at total deterioration or corruption, however; this fate is reserved for secondary figures, such as Schack's Christian or, maybe, Kierkegaard's aesthetes. In fact, the hero, like the hero of the folktale, cannot really fail; in spite of his many mistakes, he manages to retain, albeit dormantly, a knowledge of his lofty, ideal goal. As a matter of fact, some of his erring steps may be seen as misguided attempts to realize these goals, and his errors may actually earn him the knowledge that will eventually enable him to continue on the right path. At some point—and this signals his progress toward the third phase—he understands that he has erred, and then, often enlightened and perhaps guided by a wise friend or an ideally cast woman, he can find his way toward his rightful destination. He emerges as the harmonious man, the ideal of the age; his education has been completed. *Wilhelm Meister* may have come to mind as I gave this rather flippant summary, but, since I have chosen to express myself so abstractly in my depiction of this typical process—the typical line of action—in the *Bildungsroman*, the description should also encompass the larger part of Danish novels written, say, between 1820 and 1870. There are, to be sure, many variations—and some exceptions—that I cannot discuss here; but no matter how the novel in question ends, with marriage, with asceticism, with the sacrifice of everything for an idea, or with death, the interpretation is always the same: the hero has realized his potential and is living or dying in accordance with the values to which the novel—and the cultural climate to which it belongs—subscribes. Jacobsen, in a letter to Georg Brandes, commented on this kind of novel and its hero, and he indicated that his Niels Lyhne belonged to a different breed: "At visse Folk troer at N.L. er Forfatterens 'Ideal' eller er opstillet som et Mønster til Efterfølgelse er jo blot en Vane erhvervet ved den aeldre, naive Litteratur hvor Forfatteren altid havde en Helt at ride om paa gjennem Tykt og Tyndt . . ." [The fact that some people believe that Niels Lyhne is the author's "ideal" or is set up as a model for emulation is merely a habit gained from older, naïve literature in which the authors always had a hero with whom they could ride through thick and thin . . .][1]

It is my intention at this point to keep the discussion on a rather high level of abstraction. Thus I can proceed quickly toward *my* goal and also take advantage of the thinking of the many theorists of the novel who use the *Bildungsroman* as the paradigm for the genre. This type of novel is a protagonist-oriented form, one that focuses on an individual's progress through time and space. This progress reveals what the laws of existence are and how man can and shall cope with these laws if he is to succeed. In a sense, one witnesses the protagonists' gradual and successful interpretations of existence. These interpretations may strike the reader—as they did the generations that followed

the age of romanticism—as interpretations producing, in Alan Friedman's terminology, "closed endings," endings that constrain or narrow
the human experience.[2]

I have paid some attention to the endings of these novels, because I
want to emphasize that there rests a rather solid interpretation of life
behind the *dannelsesroman*. Before 1870, interpretation was based on
variations of idealistic philosophy, which, at this point in history, had
not yet been damagingly questioned. This interpretation was, so to
speak, universally sanctioned, and not at all to be doubted; it allowed
man to reconcile himself with or overcome the dualistic universe in
which he lived.

I shall not elaborate much further but just stress that since provi-
dence, in a sense, ruled this world—for one must remember that the
hero will succeed—nothing in it was left to chance. If the world seemed
arbitrary, as it did to Kierkegaard's aesthetes, it was because man had
cut himself off from ideal thinking and had forgotten the goal for
which he had to strive. As soon as the hero found the right, ideal perspective again, he would realize that nothing had been left to chance,
that he, in fact, had been guided, tested, punished, and rewarded according to a plan. Chance, the grim accidental event that may leave
man suspended in a world beyond good and evil, in an indifferent
world, does not, if one commands the right knowledge, exist.

Such features as those mentioned have led Danish literary historians
to characterize Danish romanticism as uncommonly harmonious when
compared to that of other countries. Erik M. Christensen finds that the
period can be labeled "optimistic dualism," since the gap between the
heavenly and the earthly, between the immaterial and material,
always seems to be bridged.[3] Very briefly, I might add that I personally
find that some darker views of man's predicament seem to appear in
Danish romanticism, but I shall admit that it is the short story, rather
than the novel, that seems to project this less rosy outlook upon man's
successful quest.

Let me add, furthermore, that in some critics' opinion the genre
should rightly be seen as antiromance, a genre that plays Sancho Panza
to the heroic romance.[4] This may be true of many Danish novels of the
romantic period: they contain a criticism of society, as well as of many

of its members, and of the hero's too lofty dreams. One must, however, keep in mind that the hero's final phase of development is never seen in an ironic light. Actually, the hero inhabits—or comes to inhabit—a world that cannot be subjected to criticism. He emerges as a unique individual who, through his journey, has somehow separated himself from his group and his society, and his *Bildung* is of a higher value than that which other men may gain. He may often join society, work for social causes, marry, and so on, but his ideal *Bildung*, nevertheless, sets him apart from and above his fellowman. He becomes more than a protagonist; he becomes the hero. Like the protagonist in the closed-ended folktale, who is, by definition, the hero, this protagonist's successful quest results in his being rewarded with that which guarantees him a life of complete harmony. There is, however, a difference between the tales and the novels: in at least some of the latter, it seems that the protagonist is more severely tested than in the tales. In various ways, he must confront the severe dangers hidden within his own nature before he can rightly assume the title of hero and be granted happiness. To be precise, it seems the hero must learn that the blame for his many hardships shall not be sought in the world around him, but within himself.[5] The protagonist's journey is, thus, essentially an inward one, during which he wanders through the dark realms of the mind and battles all those forces that are destructive to the realization of his ideal nature. This battle is his *Bildung*, made up of the trials through which he must pass; thus, all stages of his development are of importance and cannot be shrugged off as mistakes. Through trial and error he gains the kind of knowledge that enables him to move forward and upward in perception.

In order to establish the approach that I shall be taking in my comparative discussion of Jacobsen's two novels, I must briefly refer to an earlier Danish novel—one that had impressed Jacobsen greatly—Schack's *Phantasterne* (1857). This novel joins hands with other works of the times insofar as it exposes how dangerous dreaming may be for man. Schack reveals how fantasies alienate man from life and may cause his destruction, but, as is the case in other romantic works, man's faculty for fantasy is also allotted positive values: the protagonist's *Bildung* reveals that if fantasy is rejected altogether, he cannot experience the fullness and beauty of life. Before the protagonist reaches this positive, third stage, he has gone through two stages, both of which limit him. In the first he becomes nearly totally lost in dreams, which gradually and simultaneously assume a more sexual and a more ominous character. After he has pulled himself out of this destructive realm, he enters into the second stage of his development, in which he reacts very strongly against his earlier excesses; he abhors anything poetic and appears to have become stolidly philistine. He is saved from this other extreme when he falls in love with a young girl who allows him to renew his contact with the world of fantasy, but to do so in such a way that fantasy enriches his experience of *this* world. Conrad emerges as a harmonious man, and the novel emerges as a good example of the *dannelsesroman*.[6]

All this is fairly obvious, but I should like to add a personal objection. It concerns the ending of this book, an ending that has disturbed some critics: the narrative seems to end in a fairy-tale universe, for Conrad falls in love with and wins the hand of a real princess. This ending seems to be a violation of the rules laid down by the work itself. Some readers have wistfully suggested that the ending is ironic, and some have seen it as an aesthetic flaw, pointing out that it is very close to a return to a world of romantic dreams; some years ago, however, Aage Henriksen, in a perceptive analysis, argued that the ending should be taken at face value.[7] But why, sigh our students, why a princess, why not an ordinary girl? Various answers can be given, but it seems to me that the most intriguing, if controversially simple, answer must be that Conrad deserves a princess. Overtones of the folktale surround the ending: he seems to regain his youth, and he is, indicates the narrator, much better off than his friend Thomas, who is merely allowed to marry someone who can be characterized most precisely as an ordinary girl.[8] Now, why and how has Conrad earned this elevated position, he who, in contrast to his friend, has wasted years on dreams and in philistine living? The answer might just be that his wasted years were not all that wasted, that during these years he has gained insights that make him superior to his fellowman. Let me explain: his early dreams, as well as those of his friend, were centered for the most part upon public honor; later he turned exclusively to sexual dreams in which he first reveled in being humiliated (imagining himself a woman) and then found pleasure in humiliating others as a mighty and pitiless ravisher. These two types of fantasies, those of honor and those of sex, may seem quite different, but their common denominator is power, power over other human beings. In Conrad's later dreams this power was most destructive, because its goal was the destruction of the sexual partner. The destructiveness of such dreams lay also in their effect of totally alienating the dreamer from the human world. What Conrad experiences through his fantasies is all that which destroys a relationship between human beings, a relationship that—asserts the book—allows man to live happily ever after in perfect harmony with the world.

How can such fantasies be considered in a positive light? They can be seen as positive, because Conrad, by an act of will, pulls himself out of their grip and *learns* from them. He becomes capable of choosing, and slowly he gains the ability to direct his own life toward eventual harmony. Sadism, as well as masochism, has totally disappeared from his sexual behavior when, years later, he meets Princess Blanca. He has also lost all lust for and awe of power, and, despite his few actual experiences, he has become a very capable man who copes with his environment with social poise, a sound critical sense, tolerance, and humor. As the book ends, it is made unmistakably clear that, during his years as a civil servant, he has been more than an unimaginative man married to his work, that, in fact, he has served his country very well.

My point is, then, that these two periods of his life—periods that he himself evaluates negatively at the novel's very happy end—are invaluable experiences that have taught him a wisdom gained by few other men. He dared, although not by a conscious choice, to descend into those dark realms of the mind where the forces that determine man's behavior are hidden. Through an extraordinary expansion of the mind, he faced all those forces that would make him dangerous to others and to himself. He focused on what this book considers to be the force most essential to man, the sexual, and through sexual fantasies he came to know himself. Few other men, hampered as they are by society, would dare to do the same, but Conrad managed this feat because he lived his sex life in the exclusive, but very "real," world of fantasies. He followed his desires to their ultimate consequences, but at the point where he seemed to take leave of the realm of humanity—he imagined himself to be the devil, Moloch, and even death itself—a warning bell rang. His nature reacted; he was beset by a very real headache, which prevented him (in contrast to his friend Christian) from becoming completely lost in fantasies. He woke up to a changed world: he found himself alienated not only from other people, but also from all absolutes, all those truths that create order in man's life. In the years that followed he seemed to be cut off from everything ideal and romantic, even from human emotion. He paid a high price for this experience, but one must remember that Conrad was finally allowed to pull himself out of this limbo.

My point is that, for a time, as unwittingly as the folktale hero, Conrad has managed something outstanding: by allowing his instincts free rein he has confronted all the destructive powers within himself and, thereby, rid himself of them. As mentioned, the results were dire, in that much else was simultaneously lost, but that loss was only temporary. The process had not been destructive, for during the following period he established contact with society by serving it well. Later, the positive forces within him were rejuvenated, whereas the negative forces were not. A transformation has occurred: from being a man with a destructive relationship to the other sex, he is transformed into a man who can respond to love in exactly the right way. It would hardly be correct to talk about a change of identity, but one can describe his transformation as the emergence of the ideal man. This ideal man, it seems, can emerge only if he has purged himself of the demonic sides of his nature. Such a man deserves a reward, for he has managed the nearly superhuman. He may, therefore, be seen as the archetypal hero, the prince who must be rewarded for his successful quest with the hand of the princess, with whom he will live happily ever after.

This pattern—a mythical one—most clearly shines through in the ending. It seems confusing, out of step with the book's psychological realism, until the relationship between the narrative function of the preceding parts and this puzzling ending becomes apparent. Conrad's daring descent into the darkness of his mind, his ability to pull himself out of that realm by an act of will, his demonstrated talent for serving his country, and his preserved ability to fall in love can all be seen as tests through which the hero has had to pass before he is allowed to gain everlasting happiness.

In its unconvincing brevity, this reading does not furnish much evidence for my interpretation, but I hope to present that evidence in another context at another time. To sum up, one might say that a pattern harkening back to myth would seem to emerge: if man is consistent, as Conrad was, in his endeavor to realize what his nature bids him, he will be rewarded and will gain complete happiness. It is this pattern, maybe a general one of the age, that in due course I shall attempt to apply to *Marie Grubbe* and *Niels Lyhne*, and I shall do so with the conviction that I am not superimposing it upon them.

In both these famous novels of the Modern Breakthrough a similar structural feature occurs, one reminiscent of *Phantasterne*. By a sudden twist of plot both endings abruptly take a new, startling departure: the no longer young Marie Grubbe, whose dream of finding the right kind of man has become dormant, suddenly falls in love with Søren and is allowed to live her life out in what she would call happiness; Niels Lyhne has finally found some kind of peace in his marriage, but then both his wife and child are suddenly torn away from him. As indicated when I discussed *Phantasterne*, realistically oriented readers have had trouble accepting such drastic changes, those suspiciously accidental turns of events that seem to leave verisimilitude behind. I have argued in favor of a reading of *Phantasterne* that shows how this book's ending functions within the narrative, and the question is now whether the same is possible in the case of Jacobsen's surprising conclusions.

The ending of *Phantasterne* is not accidental, but can Jacobsen's endings be ascribed to anything but the accidental? After all, he was writing in the midst of the Modern Breakthrough and its rejection of the romantic outlook. Space does not permit me to enumerate the many features of these two novels that make them representative of, and creative forces within, the Modern Breakthrough, but this should hardly be necessary, for others have done this in detail. Let me instead briefly point out one of the major effects of the rejection of the romantic philosophy: man was left without much guidance in a world of chance, forever exposed to the workings of the accidental. The cost of doing away with the romantic ideas, those that eliminated chance, was exorbitant, for even though new positivistic ideas, which explained much to man, were introduced—and hailed as liberating forces—these could not in the long run give man exhaustive, meaningful answers that could guarantee him order and harmony.[9] This knowledge is voiced in *Niels Lyhne*:

. . . men de fleste af dem var opfyldte af det, der den Gang var det Nye, drukne af det Nyes Theorier, vilde af det Nyes Kraft og blaendede af dets Morgenklarhed. Nye var de, forbitret nye, nye indtil Overdrivelse, og det maaske ikke mindst, fordi der inderst inde var en saelsom, instinkstaerk Laengsel, der skulle overdøves, en Laengsel, det Nye, ikke kunde stille, verdensstort som det nye var, Alt omfattende, Alting maegtigt, altoplysende. (P. 304)

[. . . most of them were full of ideas that were modern at the time, drunk with the theories of modernity, wild with its powers, dazzled by its clear morning light. They were modern, belligerently modern, modern to excess, and perhaps not the least because in their inmost hearts there was a strange, instinctive longing which had to be stifled, a longing which the new spirit could not satisfy—worldwide, all-embracing, all-powerful, and all-enlightening though it was. (P. 81)][10]

Man was proclaimed to be a healthy and free animal, but instead he became a hunted animal, and it seemed to be his dubious privilege to know that he was hunted and would be run down. The romantic hero had lived in a world that could be recognized as orderly and harmonious; the distance between subject and object could be bridged. The new ideas should ideally have eliminated all distance between subject and object by making man feel completely at home in this world and master of it, but, while the positivistic ideas beautifully managed to make romantic ideas look like fictions, they did not furnish exhaustive explanations of man's lot, and consequently they left him in a hostile world. The distance between subject and object widened, and one can rightly speak of alienation.[11]

Much of this can be found explicitly or implicitly in *Niels Lyhne*, which, among other things, is the story of the difficulty of being exposed to a philosophic reorientation, a story that portrays the taxing costs of this transition to the generation that experienced it. In *Niels Lyhne* the new truths figure dominantly: Niels Lyhne's development is explained in terms of heredity and environment; he is seen as a product of certain forces, which can be pinned down and analyzed quite exhaustively. The novel contains—and advocates—the new ideas that superseded idealistic philosophy, and, as mentioned, these new theories account for much that happens in *Niels Lyhne*. The ending, however, can be understood only as a cruel blow of chance. To sum up: if the book is considered as a product of the Modern Breakthrough, it contains not only a number of methods that man may employ in order to understand his life, but also the sad knowledge that these methods are not sufficient to explain everything. The new truths were partial ones; thus, they were scarcely all-important to the probing minds of this era. After all, the gaining of new truths could hardly outweigh the loss of the promise of harmony to an age that cherished above all the idea of the individual's right and duty to realize his potential, and this demand —as Julius Schovelin pointed out in 1889—was definitely not given up with the demise of romanticism.[12]

If chance then rules man's existence and at any time may wrestle from him the little control he has over life, man will naturally fear chance and begin to think of it in terms of a malignant fate. Such an interpretation, which looms in many naturalistic works, is in a sense unfair, for, theoretically speaking, chance may work in man's favor as well as against him. One may look at the ending of *Marie Grubbe* in this light and ascribe this book's harmonious outcome for the protagonist as an example of indifferent chance from which man benefited. In most works of this age—in those that in contrast to the *dannelsesroman* have been called the *udviklingsroman*—the protagonists, however, share the fate of Niels Lyhne and see their lives turn to ashes. Such endings, like that of *Phantasterne*, may strike one as a violation of verisimilitude: one asks why poor, hapless Niels Lyhne should be struck down so harshly. That question is exactly the right one to ask, and, in the same breath, one might ask why Marie succeeds.

The need to ask these questions indicates that the answer—that the cause is merely the workings of chance—is not sufficient, though, if one looks at the hard facts, it is the only answer that the Modern

Breakthrough officially can muster. One must go beyond the novels as mimesis, and this indicates, in turn, either that they contain elements foreign to the official aesthetics of the period within which they were written, or that not all currents within that period have been properly assessed. This point has already been brought home by some recent studies: Jørgen Ottosen and Jørgen Holmgaard have both pointed out that a romantic dualistic view of man dominates Jacobsen's works.[13] Ottosen, in his thorough analysis of "Mogens," uncovers mythic patterns and a folktale or mythic structure; furthermore, he maintains that such features also determine the organization of the two novels *Marie Grubbe* and *Niels Lyhne*.

One effect of the Modern Breakthrough seems, then, to be that certain features, mythical patterns, which in the romantic novel still could be detected rather easily, now were forced deeper into the narrative were, indeed, forced so far down that it has been considered ludicrous to maintain that they were there. In many cases, nevertheless, they can be uncovered, but they must be implicit, for, according to the positivistic outlook of their time, they are fictions that have been deprived of the universal sanction they enjoyed during romanticism.

The following comments presuppose that Jacobsen still saw the hero in the same light as did the authors earlier in the century, but I shall admit that it becomes increasingly more difficult to detect these mythical patterns in his writings. In "Mogens," as Ottosen has demonstrated, the protagonist has much in common with the hero of the folktale, but surely it is difficult to assert the same thing about *Niels Lyhne*. For the time being, however, it must be sufficient to suggest that the mythical features had become increasingly implicit in Jacobsen's works, but that he, nevertheless, exposed his protagonists to the same journey or quest as that found in *Phantasterne*.

It is necessary to determine how this quest shall be characterized, and as a model I shall apply the pattern that I found in *Phantasterne*: Conrad had to come to terms with that which is basically essential to all else, the relationship to the other sex; and, as several critics have pointed out, this is an issue very much at the heart of Jacobsen's work. Jacobsen's universe is peopled with men who fail miserably, if their lives are judged in terms of erotic success or failure—and their lives must be judged in these terms, for success or failure in this area determines whether they will or will not become harmonious men. The male characters, especially, seem destitute, while the women fare somewhat better, even though their chances of achieving harmony are often spoiled because of their sorry partners. It seems as if the men are suffering from an extreme case of platonic dualism and are having difficulty in reconciling the sinful flesh with the worthier soul; the women, on the other hand, seem to have a less awkward and a more earthy appreciation of the feasibility of a union between the sexes.[14]

Considering Niels Lyhne first, I can agree with Knud Wentzel that when Niels Lyhne interprets existence, he fails to include the erotic.[15] He, who, in a rebellion against the God who refused him happiness, has joined those in the ranks supporting the new ideas, thinks only in terms of ideas, and none of these refers to the erotic. To put it more precisely, the erotic certainly occupies his mind, but he refuses to cope with it and to make it an integral part of his interpretation of life. This psychological phenomenon is illustrated in different ways; it can be given the semblance of a positive reaction on the part of Niels Lyhne, but, no matter how indulgent the narrator is, the result is the same, for Niels Lyhne shies away from the erotic:

. . . der var saa megen Mandskraft i Niels Lyhnes Kjaerlighed, han ridderlig afholdt sig fra i sin Fantasi at tage, hvad Virkeligheden naegtede ham, og ogsaa der, i denne Sideverden, hvor Alting lystrede hans Bud, respekterede Fru Boye, som var hun virkelig til Stede. (P. 317)

[. . . Niels Lyhne's love possessed so much virility that he chivalrously held himself back from taking in imagination what the reality denied him, and even in that separate world where everything did his bidding he respected Mrs. Boye as if she was actually present. (Pp. 101–102)]

Han laengtes imod tusinde sitrende Drømme, mod Billeder af kølig Finhed:—lette Farver, flygtende Duft og fin Musik fra aengsteligt spaendte, bristefaerdigt spaendte Strømme af sølverne Strenge;—og saa Tavshed, ind i Tavshedens inderste Hjaerte, hvor Luftens Bølger aldrig bar et eneste Tonevrag hen, men hvor Alting hvilte sig til Døde i røde Farvers stille Gløden og ildfuld Vellugts ventende Varme.—Han laengtes ikke efter dette, men det gled frem, udaf det Andet og drukned det, til *han vendte sig fra det og hented sit Eget frem igjen.* [Italics mine.]

Han var traet af sig selv, af kolde Tanker og af Hjaernedrømme . . . Blot det vilde komme over ham—Livet, Kjaerlighed, Lidenskab . . .

Uvilkaarligt gjorde han en afvaergende Bevaegelse med sin Haand. Han var dog inderst inde bange for dette Maegtige, som kaldtes Lidenskab. Denne Stormvind, som hvirvled afsted med alt det Satte, alt det Avtoriserede, alt det Erhvervede hos Mennesket, som var det visne Blade! Han holdt ikke af det. Denne buldrende Flamme, der ødsled sig bort i sin egen Røg—nej—han vilde braende langsomt. (P. 307)

[He yearned for a thousand tremulous dreams, for cool and delicate images, transparent tints, fleeting scents, and exquisite music from streams of highly strung, tensely drawn silvery strings—and then silence, the innermost heart of silence, where the waves of air never bore a single stray tone, but where all was rest unto death, steeped in the calm glow of red colors and the languid warmth of fiery fragrance.—This was not what he longed for, but the images glided forth from his mood and submerged all else until he turned from them to follow his own train of thought again.

He was weary of himself, of cold ideas and brain dreams. . . . If he could only be overwhelmed by something—life, love, passion . . .

Involuntarily he made a gesture as if to ward it off with his hand. After all, he was afraid in his inmost heart of this mighty thing called passion. This stormwind sweeping away everything settled and authorized and acquired in humanity as if it were dead leaves. He did not like it! This roaring flame squandering itself in its own smoke—no, *he* wanted to burn slowly. (P. 88)]

This reaction on Niels Lyhne's part is in itself peculiar, for, like Marie Grubbe, he is beset by a desire to live life as fully as possible. Many passages in both novels are given to the formulation of exactly this dream:

. . . alle hans Sejl skulde flyve mod Raa for en Fart efter Livets den spanske Sø . . . Farvel til lykkelige, smaa Momenter; I leve vel, I matte Stemninger, der maatte pudses op i Poesi for at skinne, I lunkne Følelser, som maatte klaedes paa i varme Drømme, og dog frøs ihjel, I fare som I maa! Jeg staevner mod en Strand, hvor Stemninger slynge sig som frodige Ranker opad alle Hjaertets Fibre—en vildende Skov; for hver visnende Ranke er der tyve i Blomst, for hver blomstrende Ranke er der hundred i Skud. (Pp. 307–308)

[. . . his sails should fly to the yards for a merry run over the Spanish Main of life! . . . farewell to the pleasant little hours! Peace be with you, you dull moods that have to be furbished with poetry before you can shine, you lukewarm emotions that have to be clothed in warm dreams and yet freeze to death! May you go to your own place! I am headed for a coast where sentiments twine themselves like luxuriant vines around every fiber of the heart—a rank forest; for every vine that withers, twenty are in blossom; for each one that blossoms, a hundred in bud. (P. 89)]

Once more the erotic seems left out for the sake of vague generalities and flashy metaphors. The cause for this may be found in Niels Lyhne's early awakened fear, not of the erotic as such, but of the power of the erotic to crush all possibility of fulfillment in life. This fact of life had been disclosed to him at a very tender age when he inadvertently watched Edele reject Bigum (p. 283).

His "choice" to eliminate the erotic from his interpretation of life proves destructive to Niels Lyhne: he has repudiated the erotic; as a consequence, he can hardly cope with the women he meets, and all the women to whom he is drawn, without exception, repudiate him. Even his wife does so in her last hours, and she compounds her rejection by dying. At this point, my analysis, which has until now treated the novel as psychological realism, once more takes leave of the text as mimesis.

What I am suggesting is, bluntly, this: by not making Conrad's effort, by not confronting those inner forces of his mind that determine his relationship to women, Niels Lyhne forfeited his chance of ever gaining harmony. Niels Lyhne is surely a dreamer, but, while Conrad's dreams depend upon an expansion of the mind, Niels Lyhne's dreams can be characterized as a constriction, a narrowing of the mind: the latter's dreams are exclusive rather than inclusive. Conrad's dreams are directed toward reality; therefore, he truly develops through them. Niels Lyhne, through an unwitting choice that leaves him with dreams less directed toward reality, is not capable of developing; thus, he does not achieve the kind of *Bildung* that would enable him to cope with the erotic challenges life inevitably will fling at him. If one takes a close look at his dreams, one will discover—as Ottosen has pointed out—

that the erotic is present, but only vaguely, and it is, by and large, sup-
pressed; it does not present itself as containing the terrifying insistence
found in Conrad's fantasies. Those of Niels Lyhne's dreams that have
clearer contours are all centered about the cause of atheism: mankind
freed from lies and, therefore, happy. These are dreams that he never
manages to fulfill. It is quite typical and revealing of him that he per-
sists in "committing metaphor": in his mind the cause of atheism is
always referred to in military metaphors, as a battle to be won by the
brave warriors of truth. Niels Lyhne never wins such a battle; in the
end, when he actually dies at the front, he is merely escaping from life,
and his last ramblings disclose that his dreams have led him nowhere. It
may not be totally unfair to compare him to Christian in *Phantasterne*,
not only in the trivial sense that Christian, too, leaves out the erotic,
but also, more importantly, in the sense that both Christian's and Niels
Lyhne's dreams are without content. Although the former's fantasies
are dry and mechanical, and the latter's fuzzy and lyrical, both are mere
outlines of the future, forms lacking the content of real or imagined
experience. Conrad, on the contrary, definitely manages to fill his forms
with vivid and significant experience. Niels Lyhne dreams vaguely of
being a soldier in the spiritual army of atheism, of experiencing life
fully, of becoming a poet serving his cause, but his poetry reveals what
he himself realizes, that he is mired down in romantic dreams, dreams
that, like Christian's, are derivative, borrowed from literature, and do
not signify the individual's attempt to know and overcome those
destructive inner forces that, if not checked, will determine his future
existence.

The puzzling ending, when seen in this light, can be put into a correct relationship with the preceding parts: one witnesses here not only
the workings of chance, but also the punishment of the designated hero,
of the man who failed to pass the tests that would have entailed his
reward. Niels Lyhne neglected to follow the road that would have led
to the ideal *Bildung*. Here it is tempting to add that Niels Lyhne
should not be blamed too harshly, for he is shaped by factors beyond
his reach. In this deterministic view the novel is decidedly a product of
the Modern Breakthrough, but the removal of personal responsibility
rules out neither the presence of the described concept nor the profes-

sion of its validity implied by the work's author. The novel "knows" more than Niels Lyhne, and, although it may sympathize with him because of his place in time, it also judges him. At one point the novel's narrator offers this bit of wisdom: ". . . Den Tid, der er gaaet med Godt, kommer ikke tilbage med Ondt; og Intet i det Liv, der leves bagefter, kan visne en Dag, eller slette en Time i det Liv, der er levet" (p. 303). [". . . The time that has gone with happiness does not come back with grief, and nothing the future may bring can wither a day or wipe out an hour in the life that has been lived" (p. 81).] It is Niels Lyhne's tragedy that he never experiences such fulfilling moments, moments that remain meaningful and reconcile man to a difficult life. This, however, cannot be said of Marie Grubbe.

I suppose that my ensuing commentary on *Marie Grubbe* will not offer many surprises. My quite rigid view of the laws governing Jacobsen's fictional universe should already have made self-evident my reading of this novel. Marie Grubbe is a dreamer too. At first she is engulfed by erotic fantasies, but, although they may be derivative at this stage of her life, they certainly have content; the young dreamer adds so much detail to these takeoffs on the chapbooks that her dreams definitely emerge as experience. Although she is exposed to disappointing men, Marie Grubbe never gives up her dream of the right man. The erotic is given the highest priority in her personal world, and she does not hesitate to follow any avenue that seems to promise fulfillment, even if she must sacrifice much to do so. She, too, shares the dream of total fulfillment, but, in contrast to Niels Lyhne, she knows that the erotic constitutes fulfillment; thus, she achieves the right kind of *Bildung* and is finally—inevitably—rewarded.[16]

Jørgen Ottosen comments that men and women are essentially different in Jacobsen's works and maintains that Marie Grubbe should be seen as the harmonious woman who is looking for the harmonious man.[17] If this view is correct, Marie Grubbe has not had to face the same dangers as Conrad, but it is possible to argue that by the time she encounters Søren she has rid herself of the desire to humiliate and the even stronger desire to be humiliated, for neither of these traits—as Ottosen points out—is emphasized in her relationship with Søren.[18] It should, thus, be feasible to argue that she, like Conrad, has managed

to change in such a way that an ideal companionship with a member
of the opposite sex can be established. Such a change, the elimination
of those forces within the mind that spell alienation between two
lovers, seems to be the prerequisite for accomplishing the correct kind
of *Bildung*, which, in turn, grants the final reward.

I shall readily admit that Conrad's princess is a far cry from Marie's
Søren, but I am not trying to eliminate the Modern Breakthrough
altogether. It is, however, my contention that beneath the surface of
Jacobsen's works lies a mythical structure, a very simple one perhaps,
but one that, when its presence is observed, can satisfactorily account
for the endings of the two novels.

Perhaps this bare outline of an interpretation is somewhat tenuous,
and, if I have reduced the works to less than they are, or have made
them into something they are not, I deserve to be corrected. I realize
that my title for this article may have aroused expectations that I have
disappointed. "Problematic Protagonists" suggests Lukács and Gold-
mann and a more extraliterary approach than the one I have chosen. I
have, moreover, largely ignored the role of the narrator in *Marie
Grubbe* and *Niels Lyhne*, and I shall readily admit that, until the
tension between the narrators and their respective stories has been examined, my analysis must indeed remain partial. In a way Jacobsen
indicated this much in a letter to Vilhelm Møller:

. . . Paa Bogens første Side findes et Jeg, Bogens eneste; men det dukker
hele Vaerket igjennem frem som hvad man kunde kalde lyriske Udbrud af
en Livsanskuelse, der af Folk, som ikke kjende Pessimismen, benaevnes
pessimistisk, men som vi, naar vi blive gamle, maaske vil blive nødte til at
indrømme var optimistisk.

[. . . On the first page of the book there is an "I," the only one in the book;
but throughout the book this "I" appears in what one could call lyrical out-
pourings of a view of life. People who do not know pessimism call this view
pessimistic, but, when we grow old, we shall perhaps have to admit that it
was optimistic.][19]

A fuller, more carefully documented analysis is, of course, warranted,
and so is a further investigation into other novels of the period, which
may display a thematic similarity to Jacobsen's works.

I would like to make just one more comment: I noted earlier that *Niels Lyhne*, particularly during the 1890's, became a canon for subsequent young writers. This fact alone says a good deal about the development of the Danish novel and its hero. Many of the protagonists of the 1890's seem to be going through Niels Lyhne's motions as they vainly try to cope with existence; they, too, fail to gain a secure foothold on reality, and their *Bildung* seems arrested at the novels' conclusions. The spiritually paralyzed man becomes the dominant protagonist in the *udviklingsroman* of the 1890's, yet in one way these protagonists are different from Niels Lyhne: whereas he scarcely managed to understand the real nature of his crisis and, thus, could not resolve it, they are more knowledgeable; they yearn for erotic *forløsning*, but they tend to realize that this "solution" will not free them from their hopeless situation. The erotic solution as a saving force, as the one preserved "absolute," came to be questioned, and, although this topic requires further examination before anything even remotely conclusive may be said about it, it seems reasonable to suggest that the nearly mythical pattern found in Schack and Jacobsen was finally, if not unanimously, being discarded in the 1890's.

NOTES

[1] Niels Barfoed (ed.), *Omkring Niels Lyhne* (Copenhagen: Hans Reitzels Forlag, 1970), p. 103. (My translation.)

[2] Alan Friedman, *The Turn of the Novel: The Transition to Modern Fiction* (London: Oxford University Press, 1966). Friedman sees the transition of the novel as having taken place in the latter part of the nineteenth century. The older novel contained "closed endings," whereas the new novel is open-ended in the sense that it does not offer fixed and final interpretations of existence.

[3] Erik M. Christensen, "Guldalderen som idehistorisk periode: H. C. Ørsteds optimistiske dualisme," in *Guldalderstudier: Festskrift til Gustav Albeck* (Aarhus: Aarhus Universitets Förlag, 1966), pp. 11–45; Erik M. Christensen, *En fortolkning af "Høit fra Traeets grønne Top"—Verifikations—problemet ved litteraturvidenskabelig meningsanalyse belyst i praksis* (Copenhagen: Gyldendal, 1969), pp. 84–120.

[4] Maurice Z. Shroder, "The Novel as a Genre," *The Massachusetts Review* 4 (1963): 291–308.

5 Aage Henriksen suggests as much in his analysis of Ernesto Dalgas's *Lidelsens Vej*; see Aage Henriksen, *Gotisk tid* (Copenhagen: Gyldendal, 1971), p. 181.

6 Schack himself uses the term *helt Menneske*; see Hans Egede Schack, *Phantasterne* (Copenhagen: Hans Reitzels Forlag, 1969), p. 187.

7 Aage Henriksen, "Fantasiens vendekredse," *Kritik* 5 (1968): 5–17.

8 For the sake of precision it should be added that the narrator is Conrad, who by now has, presumably, married Blanca. The narrator's relationship to his material, his remembered life, is not examined here, but, as the novel's organization suggests, it requires analysis, since the older, humorous Conrad is quite far from the young man, whose diary straightforwardly describes his indulgence in sexual fantasies.

9 A number of recent studies have delineated this effect of the Modern Breakthrough very thoroughly: Knud Wentzel, *Fortolkning og Skaebne: Otte danske romaner fra romantismen og naturalismen* (Copenhagen: Fremad, 1970); Erik A. Nielsen, "En palmegrøn Ø: I anledning af et jubilaeum," *Kritik* 19 (1971): 5–25; Peer E. Sørensen, "Fascinationens overvindelse: Et essay omkring J. P. Jacobsen og det moderne gennembrud," *Kritik* 20 (1971): 20–56.

10 Page references given in the original text refer to J. P. Jacobsen, *Samlede skrifter* (Copenhagen: Gyldendal, 1948); quotations in English are taken from J. P. Jacobsen, *Niels Lyhne*, trans. Hanna Astrup Larsen (New York: Twayne Publishers and the American-Scandinavian Foundation, 1967).

11 Sørensen, "Fascinationens overvindelse," pp. 32–38.

12 Julius Schovelin, "Litteratur og Socialpolitik," *Tilskueren* 6 (1889): 321–335. Mainly through an analysis of Ibsen's *Et Dukkehjem*, Schovelin finds the demand of self-realization to be the shaping force behind the works of the 1870's and 1880's.

13 Jørgen Ottosen, *J. P. Jacobsens "Mogens"* (Copenhagen: Gyldendal, 1968); Jørgen Holmgaard, "Den 'forsvundne' produktivitet," *poetik* 4 (1971): 122–164.

14 According to Holmgaard ("Den 'forsvundne' produktivitet," p. 159), the women manage their lives better since they are purely "seksuelle praktikere" and not, like the men, caught up in "kunstnerisk eller religiøs praksisproblematik."

15 Wentzel, *Fortolkning og Skaebne*, pp. 85–99; see especially p. 90.

16 Sørensen, "Fascinationens overvindelse," pp. 34–36. Sørensen offers a view quite opposed to mine: *Marie Grubbe* is seen as another embodiment of the disillusionment and alienation that fill Jacobsen's chilling universe, in which all dreams of obtaining *Bildung* are illusions.

17 Ottosen, *J. P. Jacobsens "Mogens,"* p. 284.

18 Ibid., pp. 224–225.

19 Barfoed, *Omkring Niels Lyhne*, p. 17. (My translation.)

Who Was Hamsun's Hero?

by HARALD NAESS

University of Wisconsin at Madison

Knut Hamsun called his last novel *The Ring Is Closed*, and, though he is not known to have said in particular what he meant by the title, most readers will feel that it conveys some sense of finality, like a return to the original point of departure. But it is not easy to decide whether it applies only to the action of the novel in question, or to Hamsun's whole opus, symbolizing somehow the breaking of his magic wand. However that may be, I shall use the title metaphorically in an attempt to come up with a formula for the Hamsun hero. The ring will be taken to mean not the hero's return to the point of departure, but rather a ramification of his road, with two major avenues parting and converging as the ring is closed. Already Hamsun's first novelette, *The Enigmatic One*, which was referred to by its publisher as scribbled nonsense, has the beginnings of this dichotomy. The weft of Hamsun's rich texture—what Georg Brandes called "the infinitely small"—is almost totally lacking, but in return the warp—what Brandes referred to as "the infinitely great"—is almost entirely exposed, giving the book its special interest for students of literature. It is a very rudimentary tale of a poor country boy, Rolf Andersen, who wins the rich man's daughter—actually a variation of the myth of the disguised prince, since the boy, as it later turns out, is really Knut Sonnenfield, the son of a wealthy city merchant. Hamsun, however, is less interested in the dramatic effect when the enigmatic character finally throws off his guise, than he is in the way this character taxes the townspeople's curiosity. Hence Hamsun's first book is a romantic work, not only because of its fantastic course of events, but also because the author has chosen as protagonist an outsider who fools the whole parish.

The Enigmatic One appeared in the heyday of Norwegian realism, whose heroes, like Torbjørn Granlien (of Bjørnson's *Sunny Hill*), conquered themselves and then went on to become pillars of the community. This realism is not without sentimental moments, as when Torbjørn plants Solveig's flowers during the night, but it is still different from the kind of romanticism Hamsun displayed when he provided his budding businessman with the following burst of *Weltschmerz*:

Today—or rather this evening—Rolf had a different suit on. This time it was gray worsted. It consisted of: a coat, or jacket, pants, leather shoes with brass buckles, and a double-breasted vest, and finally a velvet cap with a visor, all of the latest cut. In these clothes, which suited him so well, Rolf looked like a gentleman, and he also walked on the road like one. When he had come to the top of the hill near Aabakken, he sat down on a place covered with red flowers and gathered some of the most beautiful into a bouquet. It was as nice a bouquet as anyone could wish for. Its center was a carnation. When the bouquet was done, he placed it in a rubber strap on the left side of his cap. It now suited him much better. He looked like a verituoso [*en Verituos*], on whose head a lady had placed a wreath. He then sat down supporting his head in his hand, looked straight ahead, and thought of the last time he was here and with whom. As he sat there, the bouquet fell from his hat. He looked at it. He said to himself: Dust. From dust we have come and unto dust we shall return. It will happen to us what has happened to these flowers, one moment flourish and bloom but then wither and fall into the grave. Oh "if we were only then prepared."[1]

The quote is meant to be as deadly serious as the rest of this curious first work, which Hamsun never wanted to see reprinted till after his ninetieth year. By that time he had created many practical country boys who tried to win princesses. And, if he temporarily repressed the "verituoso passage" like some dark shed where his hero first bared himself to innocent readers, after long years of failure in Europe and America, where he learned to laugh at himself, he turned that shed into a theatrical dressing room from which he fitted out a series of tragicomic protagonists in striking garments. Even if *The Enigmatic One* is scribbled nonsense, it contains the beginnings of the romantic irony that characterizes all Hamsun's art and that is already fully developed in his great novels of the nineties.

For all their differences—the humor of *Hunger*, the mystery of *Mysteries*, the poetry of *Pan*, the sweetness of *Victoria*—these novels do form some sort of unity, and in their roughest shape the protagonists have all come from the same mold. In them Hamsun has realized his own expressed ambition to arrive in a small town completely unannounced, live there incognito for some time, and then disappear as mysteriously as he came.[2] The protagonists are all visitors trying to make a living in a foreign milieu and, finding that the experiment does not work, in the end taking their leave. In *Hunger* a young writer from the country spends the fall season in Kristiania; in *Mysteries* another young man, presumably with some big-city background, spends a summer in a small coastal town; in *Pan* a lieutenant from Kristiania stays from spring to fall in a small fishing village up north. The case is somewhat different in *Victoria*, in that Johannes, a poet, is socially rather than geographically displaced; his temporary visit does not so much concern a different locality as a different class: he is the miller's son among the landed gentry.

Furthermore, the protagonists are androgynous in much the same manner as Strindberg in Hamsun's early description of him; Strindberg, he said, was partly coarse and tough as a butcher, partly delicate as a woman.[3] "Tangen" in *Hunger* is strong enough to push a streetcar, yet his poor eyesight makes him unfit for service in the fire brigade. Nagel is known for his broad shoulders, but he is of small stature and has the delicate mouth of a woman. Glahn is a commanding officer, yet in company with people he is not only unimposing, but also awkward and timid. Johannes again is somewhat different, actually quite a healthy farm boy, but he tortures Camilla by saying he has thrown away her gifts to him, and, on the other hand, the tone of his stories shows him as possessing the soft sensitivity of women. He, like the rest of these heroes, falls into a category usually referred to by psychologists as sadomasochist.

It is significant that all these protagonists are artists or at least artistically gifted. Johannes and "Tangen" are writers, Glahn is a very literary kind of diarist, and Nagel, the teller of fantastic stories, impresses the townspeople as being a rather unusual agronomist. The popular image of artists as unconventional people suits these characters; they are outsiders of a special kind looking for a lost paradise, even though their search has so far led them nowhere near the goal. Yet the fact that they are still at the scene, rather than dead by their own hands, shows that they wish to make one last attempt to find the lost paradise, even at the cost of having to adapt themselves painfully to the norms of modern society. This is their experiment, and its various stages are presented on many levels, realistic and symbolic, sometimes humorous, sometimes tragic or pathetic. More particularly the experiment is presented symbolically in the love story that each book contains. The protagonist finds that a woman is able to give new or different meaning to his existence. She appears at first like an exotic princess or a refreshing child of nature—Ylajali reclining on a bed of yellow roses, or Iselin, or simply Dagny; but this dream does not last. The original paradise gives way to its fake imitation: Ylajali is just an average Kristiania girl, Edvarda is an unkempt, ignorant child, and Dagny, whom the hero now refers to as Dangny, is nothing more than the perfect wife for her naval officer. Victoria is different, but, for all her admired aristocratic qualities, her allegiance is to society: she does the so-called right thing in order to save her family's reputation.

The attempt to approach society through a woman's love, then, is no more likely to bring success than is marriage to one of these women. These men are not made for happiness, and deep down they must know that their lovers are as fake as the society they represent. They are all romantic protagonists; their world is the dream world of Goethe's Werther.

At this point it might be useful to ask what Hamsun had hoped to achieve as a writer after his last return from America. In the articles entitled "Kristofer Janson" and "From the Unconscious Life of the Mind," and particularly in his three lectures on literature in 1890 and 1891, Hamsun had presented a fragmentary theory of a new fictional hero.[4] First and foremost, this hero would be more complex than the heroes of the Norwegian naturalist movement, who were made according to Taine's formula of the *faculté maîtresse*. In their stead Hamsun would place a personality that was split and multiplied, feverish, with bleeding nerves. The novelist's task was to investigate the roots of this hero's instincts, or, in his favorite anatomic terminology, the intestines of his soul. Hamsun, though he did not say anything about this hero's *Weltanschauung*, was very explicit about his own; he was against positivism, materialism, democracy, science, and Christianity, and his heroes naturally reflect these sentiments. Hamsun's novels, then, after a generation of realistic Norwegian *Bildungsromane* from *Sunny Hill* to *St. John's Festival*, reinstate the romantic protagonist. This protagonist shares the antisocial stand, if not the revolutionary spirit, of the early Byronic hero; he also shares the crippling ambivalence of the later romantic nonhero, as in the works of Stendhal and, particularly, the great Russians Lermontov and Dostoevsky. He is new mostly because of a self-consciously humorous approach to his own excessively nervous temperament, what Hamsun calls his neurasthenia, and what other people have called decadence.[5] The morbid disposition of Hamsun's hero, however, applies only to his mind; physically he is of extraordinary health, and for this reason alone the word *decadent* in its conventional sense may seem out of place. In the light of his later development, it would probably be correct to say that, under his neurasthenic surface, Hamsun's hero from the nineties possesses qualities that correspond to the following unusual definition. The decadent, says Anatole Baju, a literary critic of the period, "is a man of progress. He is clean, economic, hard working and regular in all his habits. A man of simple attitudes and correct in his morals, his ideal is to find the beautiful in the good and he strives to bring his act into harmony with his theories. He is a master of his mind, which he has learned to control, he has the quiet placidity of a sage, and the virtues of a stoic."[6]

This definition is a good starting point for a discussion of the concept of the double in Hamsun's novels, what Hamsun himself in one of his literary lectures referred to as double consciousness.[7] In *Hunger* there are several scenes in which the protagonist hears and sees himself as a strange person; parts of his body are alienated, then assume personality, becoming himself looking at himself. One further step is the

actual creation of a kind of double, in *Hunger* an old cripple who
waddles in front of the protagonist, stopping when he stops, walking
when he walks, and destroying his happy morning mood with his ugly
looks and gait. In Hamsun's next novel, *Mysteries*, the old cripple is
easily recognizable as the person called the Midget, with the difference
that in the latter novel he has a much more central position; he is an
important minor character and endowed with independent action: just
as Nagel observes and plots against the Midget, so the Midget observes
and plots against Nagel. More than any other single feature, the
presence of characters like the Midget in Hamsun's work shows him
as the new romantic writer. His mode is ironic; everything beautiful
must call forth its counterpart.

The master of romantic caricature in Norwegian literature is Henrik
Ibsen, but, with the exception of *Peer Gynt*, Hamsun had little understanding of the dramatist's work, as one would expect. The characters
Rosmer and Brendel are a romantic pair of the kind Hamsun used in
Mysteries, but with the important difference that Rosmer's aristocracy,
unlike Nagel's, is of a Christian kind: to be noble is to forgive. Hamsun, to whom aristocracy was synonymous with pride, strength, and an
inborn sense of security, had nothing but contempt for Ibsen's ideal.
"Rosmer is soft and tender," he writes; "he is so helplessly noble that
he is happy when Ulrik Brendel fools him again and again to get
money for drink."[8] Hamsun's romantic pair is differently arranged.
The Midget, as clown, provides a caricature of Nagel's exhibitionism,
but he is at the same time a carrier of Rosmer's Christian ideals, while
Nagel is a man of Nietzschean views. Since *Mysteries* is a detective
story, the difference between appearance and reality is particularly important. Nagel's task as private investigator is to search for immoral
motives behind the Midget's meek countenance of Christian love. In
later works the cripple from *Hunger* will undergo many changes; the
Christian elements will be fused with qualities found in the clown-
artist—such as inconstancy, drunkenness, impotence—but always they
will be defined by their opposite, which is a morality based on noblesse
oblige. Nagel, for all his clownishness, has a side to his personality
that refuses to be degraded by life; and the protagonist of *Hunger*, in
the midst of all his suffering, is always concerned about keeping up

his moral standards. A striking reversal of this dichotomy, whereby society is upheld against the outsider, is seen in one novel from the 1890's, *Shallow Soil*. Here the protagonist is a hard-working business-man surrounded by artistic parasites. His temperament is in most re-spects the opposite of Nagel's, but he shares with him a deep sense of moral propriety, which makes it impossible for him to go on living after his sweetheart's loss of innocence.

In addition to presenting protagonists who gradually fall more and more distinctly into categories that could be referred to as either moral-istic or artistic, Hamsun in the 1890's began to develop a technical differentiation that gradually assumed great importance. For all its advantages of immediacy, the first-person novel lacks the multiple perspectives of the third-person narrative, and authors have naturally looked for ways in which to expand its single-tracked viewpoint. In *Hunger* the protagonist is sometimes able to view himself from the outside; in *Mysteries*—a third-person novel with a single viewpoint—Nagel sees in the Midget a symbol of certain negative qualities in him-self, so that when Nagel and the Midget discuss a third person, for instance Dagny Kielland, one view serves as a corrective of the other. In *Pan* Hamsun provides two entirely different viewpoints: Glahn's diary is followed by an epilogue in which one of his hunting com-panions tells the story of Glahn's death in India. Hamsun, however, did not use this technique again. Rather than using two narrators, he construes the plot in such a way that the characters, regardless of temperament, serve mainly one of two functions, being either par-ticipants or observers. The observer is usually an artist-protagonist rather than a moralist-protagonist, and in most cases he is also per-sonally involved in the action. He is usually, but need not be, a central character.

Now, after these preliminary notes, I would like to approach some of the major protagonists in Hamsun's work in the twentieth century. In its first decade Hamsun wrote ten books that form an intermezzo in his production, pointing backward to the great individualistic works of the nineties as well as forward to the monumental epics of the World War I period. They are at once humorous, poetic, and polemic, and they illustrate not only his problems of marriage and age, but also a growing need to leave the fin de siècle camp and orient himself in the new century. Like his contemporary, the Norwegian painter Edvard Munch, who shifted his interest from the violent love and death scenes of the so-called *Life Frieze* over lyrical landscapes to the monumental Aula decorations, so Knut Hamsun moves from the city to the country, and, while he still worships the young, it is not now so much for their neurasthenia, as for their greater physical strength. Norway during these years gained independence from Sweden and emancipated itself economically, and Hamsun's attitude to such a show of energy can be seen in his praise of enterprise in the two great poems honoring Bjørnstjerne Bjørnson. However, his attitude is again one of ambivalence: he is of two minds about the industrialization of Norway, and he also recognizes that, at fifty, he cannot be part of the new order except as a spectator and commentator. This recognition colors the six novels he wrote between 1903 and 1912. They fall into two categories, one more humorous and purely entertaining—*Mothwise, Benoni*, and *Rosa*—and one more poetic and polemic—the trilogy about the wanderer.

The *Wanderers* novels do not possess the kind of unity one expects from a trilogy. The first two books, with their petty landed gentry, have a quasi-feudal atmosphere reminiscent of *Victoria*, while the third, with different characters and the setting of a modern mountain hotel, points forward to Hamsun's later social satires. What holds the works together, besides a general poetic tone, is the extraordinary protagonist Knut Pedersen.[9] He shares with Hamsun's older heroes a sudden and mysterious arrival on the scene, but his flight is less dramatic, as are his actions. His pains and pleasures derive from vicarious living; he is a masochist more than a sadist, less participant, more observer and voyeur. There is no mistaking his excitement as he watches the seduction of his beloved and much admired Lovise Falkenberg by a young, unsympathetic engineer; yet he identifies with her stoical husband and would do anything to help improve the relationship between this lord and his lady. In the last volume, Ingeborg Thorsen's adventures with a young actor strike him again with the painful pleasures of jealousy, but he is also instrumental in getting her married to healthy, uncomplicated Nikolai Palm. Just as these books, judged by their quality, could be referred to as an intermezzo in Hamsun's production, so the protagonist is caught, as it were, between the battles. Rather than concentrating on his own hopeless social experiment, he is helping others succeed with theirs: like Bjørnson's King Sverre (*Between the Battles*), Knut Pedersen is a disguised God. The author is actually describing his own problems of jealousy and age: Ingeborg Thorsen with her college degree and actor friends is easily recognizable as Hamsun's second wife, Marie Andersen, and this almost complete lack of distance has shaped the style of these books, which resemble nothing so much as Hamsun's autobiography (published in 1949). The exuberance of his earlier works is gone, and, though the humor of *Hunger* has been revived after several serious books, this humor is low-keyed; the irony, when it is turned against the protagonist himself, has a bitter quality not evident before. The protagonist of the *Wanderers* trilogy is closer than ever to Knut Hamsun, and, as narrator, he is closer than ever to the actual author. Indeed there are certain sections of volume three in which he addresses his readers directly; they read like letters to the editor or, rather, like reprimanding letters to his wife. This form, in which the distance between the implied and the actual author occasionally disappears altogether, was taken up with great force by younger Norwegian writers twenty years later, but in Hamsun's own production it marks a climax in the development of his narrator. Not only is the last part of the trilogy the last of his novels to be written in the first person, but also, in the half-dozen novels following, the implied author disappears steadily until, in *Vagabonds*, he is completely hidden within the work. The observer also disappears, giving way to new protagonists —artists, men of action, and, in one single case, the moral man.

After Hamsun had temporarily settled his own personal problems by taking up farming and producing children, he must have felt a need to create a fictional character whom readers could look to for inspiration. Life in the new Norway was characterized by enterprise and energy, but during this time new ways of thinking replaced time-honored values, and Hamsun, for all his modernism in form and style, was politically conservative. As a young man he had sympathized with the Haymarket anarchists[10] because they represented the rights of the young individualists against old oppressors, and, along the same line,

as a middle-aged man he had supported the liberals in their fight for
Norwegian independence from Sweden. But, being at heart a disciple
of Nietzsche, he had fought all along against Christian slave morality
and the demands of women and workers. He had attacked Rosmer's
humanism, and he, like his protagonists from the nineties, Nagel,
Høibro, and Kareno, had dreamed up the ideal leader, variously referred to as a Napoleon, a Byron, a man who strikes, a great terrorist.[11]
This person would have to be a man of high moral principles and great
personal fortitude, a man unbending in adversity. Hamsun conceived
such a character during his years in the United States, where he had
first come because Europe could not help a young farmer who wanted
to change his caste. After only a few years in America, however, Hamsun was cured of his belief in democracy as a means of avoiding social
conflict. He had never visited the South, but he now imagined that the
master-servant relationship there was on the whole a happy one, one
that could serve as a model for a harmoniously stratified society.[12] The
most striking example of Hamsun's curious preoccupation with aristocracy is probably the novel *Victoria*. Such names as "the castle" and
"the castle master" are particularly anomalous in a Norwegian situation and help give the novel some of its fairy-tale quality. However,
the "castle master," who ruins his estate because he cannot adapt to
modern industrial society and who then burns himself to death by
setting fire to the manor, is a type that then interested Hamsun considerably. In the first two *Wanderers* novels he returns as Captain
Falkenberg, this time a much more central character, with serious
marital problems, but it is not until *Children of the Age* that the
protagonist is fully developed as Lieutenant Holmsen. The ideological
content of the novel is not new—social satire is part of *Mysteries* and
the central issue already in *Shallow Soil*—but the style is different, as
can be seen in the novel's composition. The short lyrical chapters of the
Wanderers trilogy have given way to long descriptive chapters in which
more than thirty characters and much colorful detail serve as a broad
background for the Holmsen portrait. And this background is caricature of a new kind, not the crude exaggerated satire of *Shallow Soil*,
but more realistic, more subtly ironic. By placing his small town in his
own Nordland—as he had done before in *Mothwise, Rosa,* and *Benoni*

—Hamsun was able to give his little crooks an almost endearing touch of humanity. The least sympathetic characters are as always the arrogant civil servants from Kristiania; even the self-made Nordland magnate, Holmengraa, who brings industry and corruption to the place, is shown more respect. Above them all is Willatz Holmsen, a third-generation local landowner, who is defeated in his attempt to bend a woman to his will and ruined by coming industrialization, yet who remains upright till the end. Compared to Nagel, he is an uninteresting character, but Hamsun, because he admired him more than his other protagonists, has been able to give him stature. He is unique in Hamsun's production, unique also in his ridiculous pride and stubbornness, but the author has reserved for him some of his finest characterization; for example, he says of his lonely wandering in the night: ". . . he passes like a figure in a ghostly landscape—tall, upright—tenacity embodied." Lieutenant Holmsen must be mentioned in a consideration of Hamsun's hero, not only because he is the middle-aged Hamsun's answer to Ibsen's *Rosmersholm*, but also because certain character traits—which he represents in their purest form—are recurring features in the Hamsun hero. Still, it cannot be denied that many readers of this novel will take more interest in what Hamsun calls the landscape than in its lonely figure, probably because they find Hamsun's Holmsen about as abstract as Hamsun found Ibsen's Brand.[13]

Similarly abstract, despite his many human touches, is Isak Sellanraa in *Growth of the Soil*. While he has become Hamsun's best-known protagonist, this popularity is due to the fact that his attractive ideals are shared by city dwellers all over the world: Robinson Crusoe will always be more popular than Timon of Athens. *Growth of the Soil* has rightly been called the least typical of Hamsun's major works, but this does not mean that Isak is a stranger among Hamsun's people: even though *Growth of the Soil* is the only novel in which the active man is the central character, he has both precursors and successors in Hamsun's production, and, as is true of Holmsen, his personality is part of the Hamsun hero. In Hamsun's protagonists of the nineties, work in the sense of regular bodily activity does not exist. These people act only in extraordinary, usually heroic, circumstances, as when called upon to save people from drowning. *Shallow Soil*, with its hard-working businessmen, was therefore a surprising breach of the pattern when it appeared in 1893, though, as is evident now, it was also a sign of new things to come. Twelve years later, in the *Wanderers*, Knut Pedersen does not consider it beneath his dignity to cut lumber and dig ditches, and the farm hand Nils is a first step in the direction of Isak; finally, in the last *Wanderers* volume, Nikolai Palm is a direct forerunner of the great farmer-hero. Hamsun's negative attitude toward the farmer can be seen in all his writings from the nineties, for example, in the name of his chief villain from that time, Endre Bondesen, which means "son of a farmer." As late as 1908, when commenting upon Johannes V. Jensen's apotheosis of farmers, Hamsun still had no belief in them, and it was not until he married an actress whom he insisted on turning into a peasant girl that Hamsun changed his view and went on to create his giants in the earth, Isak and later Ezra.

Other novelists, such as Laxness, have felt a need to correct Hamsun's picture of the farm worker's social situation.[14] *Growth of the Soil* has also failed to interest most of the younger Hamsun scholars, and the reason is not difficult to see. It is not so much the novel's idyllic qualities, its clear message and happy ending, but rather the atypicality of the purely active man as Hamsun hero. One dimension is lacking here, the tension and ambivalence that are key criteria of the authentic Hamsun protagonist. For this reason, and in spite of the broad sweep of his biography, with its many humorous and moving details, this active-man protagonist is less intriguing as a character than is his guardian spirit, the bailiff Geissler. The bailiff, like Knut Pedersen, belongs to the observer category; he is a disguised God; and, from the evidence of one line in which he recalls his childhood at Garmo in Lom, he is clearly a self-portrait of the author: a somewhat shady character, quarreling with his family and, though a man of sound judgment and occasional enterprise, mostly lazy and given to dreams of grandeur. Not a very flattering picture, but, while it is a long way down from Nagel, it is also a long way up from Oliver in *Women at the Pump*, the novel with which, in 1920, Hamsun shocked all new admirers of the recent Nobel Prize winner. Oliver, the new nonhero, fits into none of the categories mentioned above; he is not a reflective observer, not a moral person; neither is he a man of action. He is not artistic in the sense that he creates works of art; therefore, a few words of clarification will be needed to explain why he should be called the artist-dreamer.

Hamsun's first fully developed artist, the protagonist of *Hunger*, combined strict moral standards with a lively imagination, which made him see his miserable existence reflected symbolically in the invalid beggar who always seemed to follow him. The situation is further developed in Nagel, a man of high principles and a teller of beautiful tales, who sees himself as a clownish entertainer in the character known as the Midget. Hamsun's apotheosis of the powers of nature is accompanied throughout his production by a corresponding downgrading of the artist. However, in his early work he did not present the artist-dreamer in pure form, or at least not as a main character. Either he was given added moral qualities—as in the early protagonists "Tangen," Nagel, and Johannes and the later observer types like Knut Pedersen, Baardsen, or Geissler—or he was presented as a minor character like the artist-scroungers in *Shallow Soil*, or the Midget, or Lars Manuelsen and Brede Olsen in the Segelfoss novels and *Growth of the Soil*. That Hamsun now introduces him in his ugliest form, and as a central character in a major novel, must have something to do with his deep disillusionment after World War I. Oliver is amoral, inactive, unreflective. He is misshapen and impotent, he has no dignity, even his jealousy is faked. He offers his creditors the sexual services of his wife and causes the death of his tormentor Olaus. Still, here as always, Hamsun reserves his worst sarcasm for the civil-servant class, the doctor representing science, and the lawyer and schoolmaster representing politics and useless learning. Oliver, however repulsive, is drawn without hatred and actually with some compassion. The reader is made to understand how, because of his misfortune, he has become an outcast, how he is forced to defend himself through lies and delusions.[15] The suicidal thoughts of early Hamsun protagonists never occur to Oliver. On the contrary, life has rewarded him considerably; miracles, when they happen, happen to him: not only does he salvage a whole ship singlehanded and find banknotes in the eiders' nests, but he, who can produce no offspring of his own, is a devoted father of his wife's children, who become a source of pride and joy to him as they grow up.

Oliver may well be the ugliest of Norwegian antiheroes—Hjalmar
Ekdal and Jakob Engstrand in one—yet he is very human and very
important for the development of a character known as August, the
greatest of Hamsun's protagonists in the new century.

German scholars have referred to Hamsun's hero as a Northeastern
hero, that is, a Scandinavian hero with Russian ancestry, and Hamsun's
neurasthenic temperament as well as his expressed admiration of the
great Russian masters of the novel would support such a label.[16] On
the other hand, the American qualities of the Hamsun hero have not
received much attention, even though it is common knowledge that
Hamsun spent his formative years in the United States and early developed a taste for the special humor of Mark Twain. Arne Garborg
felt that in his first literary attempts Hamsun had learned too much
from the Russians, but he later referred to him as a Yankee, as did
many other Norwegian critics after *Mysteries* had appeared, and
Johannes V. Jensen, in 1907, claimed that Hamsun's happy style was
a product of his years in America.[17] Furthermore, the emphasis on
physical health and activity that gradually emerges in Hamsun's writing is more typical of the West than of the East; particularly Western
is that spirit of restless enterprise that colors the trilogy about August,
Hamsun's most "American" protagonist, and his most elaborate
symbol of modern times, city life, business, and industry.

August differs from Oliver mainly in his greater activity and his
ability to tell tall tales. While Oliver's enterprise is limited to a little
fishing, August is busy in a hundred ways, draining a marsh, setting
up a bank and a shooting range, as well as a tobacco plantation and a
herring-meal factory. Like Oliver, August does not have much prestige
in his little society and needs to produce fantastic stories about himself.
August, however, tells them with special flair—there are art and humor
in his stories, and, not surprisingly, after his death he himself becomes
literature, when a street ballad about his colorful life begins circulating
among the common people. Like Oliver, too, August has little success
as a lover; not only does the novel describe his defeat in the wooing
of Cornelia, but also readers are made to understand that throughout
his long life he has mostly had to buy his love, and the girl with the
lion mane even left him with a "reminder," a "disease of two and a

half years' duration." August's disease is symbolic. "This single individual," says the author, "had it in his power to corrupt both town and countryside." However, as in the case of Oliver, that judgment is tempered with many positive traits—August is said to be unselfish, conscientious as an ant, innocent of malice. "Here he stands in his old age, and, in the language of Gordon's accountancy, his assets exceed his liabilities."[18]

Nagel had shaken his head and smiled at Ibsen's little verse about the poet sitting in judgment over his self,[19] but in the case of the August trilogy that seems to be exactly what the poet is doing, and with much the same result as in *Peer Gynt*: the final sentence is indefinitely suspended, but it is implied that, if the defendant were to be saved, it would have to be on the grounds of his artistic contributions. August is Hamsun's Peer Gynt, and, just as Norwegian folklore gave Ibsen's identity play its special texture, so in the August trilogy there is a youthful spirit, drawn, perhaps, from literary impressions of life on the seven seas and from Hamsun's reminiscences of his own vagabond days in North Dakota.[20] The tone is that of the popular ballad, not only in its mock heroism, but also in its anonymity: in no other work of Hamsun's does the story tell itself so spontaneously as here, where Hamsun takes one last good look, more distant, and more objective than ever before, at the artist-dreamer as good-humored clown.

In the novel August is defined through a variety of lesser characters, such as the farmers Ezra and Joachim, both firmly rooted in the microcosm of their home grounds, but particularly through Edevart, who becomes a victim of August's nomadic habits but differs from him in that he preserves a tragic sense of displacement. The pale cast of thought with which Hamsun tinted his early hero and the high ethical sense of Lieutenant Holmsen are recognizable in Edevart; he is a good late example of the moral-reflective type and a steppingstone to Hamsun's last great protagonist, Abel Brodersen, whose life style is oriental, though he lives in the West, more particularly in Green Ridge, Kentucky. At seventy Hamsun had taken up his old interest in the States, not now the bustling North, but the decadent South, which he knew from modern American fiction.[21]

Like the books of the August trilogy, *The Ring Is Closed* was probably meant to be a novel of good companionship, with Lawrence, who is only referred to, resembling August, at least in generosity and poetic imagination. As it is, there is only one protagonist, and, though he is more like Edevart than like August, he has in him some of both characters. In him that ring is closed which opened up in Nagel forty years earlier. He is called Abel, like the best of Oliver's stepchildren, and his name ought to be significant. It is confusing, however, that Abel's situation is that of Cain: he causes the death of his friend Lawrence and is uprooted from his home. He further resembles Cain's offspring in being technically and artistically gifted, and he uses these gifts for criminal ends: when Hamsun therefore calls him Abel, the reason may be not only Abel's extreme docility, but also a realization, later emphasized in Aksel Sandemose's work, that society is to be blamed for the character murder that finally kills all ambition in this protagonist. The son of an old, niggardly sea captain and his second, alcoholic wife, Abel was not socially acceptable to the novel's antiheroine, Olga. The early Hamsun hero could hope to win his princess only through his artistic powers, but Abel's weapon is a perverted art: Olga incites him to rob the church on two occasions; also on two occasions, the excitement of sleeping with a real murderer makes her spend the night in bed with him. The text says that, during the scene in which Abel mistakenly tells Olga how he shot Angèle and her child, he bared his teeth like an animal—a good starting point for critics who wish to place Abel at the definite low point in the development of the Hamsun protagonist.[22] It is true that, in addition to the ramification of the protagonist's road, there has been a steady downhill trend in his path, changing the colorful Byronic hero of the nineties into the pitiful nonhero of the twentieth century. This is a natural result of the author's growing age and general disillusionment, but it does not mean that he denies Abel stature. Indeed, a little listening to the novel's inner voice should convince the reader that Abel is intended to occupy a very prominent place in Hamsun's pantheon. The problem of Abel is an old and a difficult one: how to combine Rosmer and Brendel, or, as Hamsun says, gentleman and vagabond, in one character. Even Abel's vagabond years are not without style—his life among the Negroes in Green Ridge, Kentucky, and later in a shed in his home town, is not colorfully heroic, but it is based upon an Eastern philosophy that Abel is capable of defending with as much conviction and less rhetoric than Hamsun himself in his articles from Turkey.[23] As for his qualities as a gentleman, it is significant that, on leaving the scene after his "experiment in living," Abel, like only the great protagonists—"Tangen," Glahn, Nagel, Holmsen—takes great care to set his house in order.[24] It is also significant that Abel, so different from the many miserable cuckolds that people Hamsun's novels, will not tolerate his wife's adultery: his crime passionnel even appears to have the author's approval.

In *The Ring Is Closed,* as in all of Hamsun's work after *The Enigmatic One,* clothing is a very central symbol. But unlike Victoria's father, who even in death had the presence of mind to flick away a grain of dust on the sleeve of his evening dress, Abel sullies everything, both his uniform and his many new suits. In this way he is able to demonstrate a final and decisive unlearning of social ambition; dress has finally come to symbolize a perversion of art, as a means of achieving social disapproval. In Hamsun's early work, the protagonist, despite his romantic whims, wished to work his way back into society. Abel wants to get out of society. Also in this respect *The Ring Is Closed* resembles an end game, something like a blown-up denouement of an early Hamsun novel. In other ways, however, the ring is not closed: not only is the work incomplete, but also, like most of Hamsun's books, it is an open novel, a novel that leaves the reader asking at the end where the protagonist now stands, and also where he as reader stands in relationship to the kind of hero this protagonist typifies.

To sum up, I think it is important, if one attempts—as I have, perhaps unsuccessfully, attempted—to find a general formula for the Hamsun hero, not to concentrate only on the great works from the nineties. Holmsen and August are probably the most archetypal of Hamsun's protagonists and should not be left out of any full-size picture of his hero. It might also be useful to mention some of Hamsun's house gods, particularly the great ones, like Dostoevsky and Bjørnson, or even Strindberg and Mark Twain, but here it is important to draw a line between Hamsun's strictly creative writing and his political journalism. On hearing of Hitler's death in May of 1945, Hamsun published a curious eulogy of the *Führer*, which harmed his reputation and left the impression among readers all over the world that Hamsun approved of the authoritarian state.[25] Whatever views Hamsun expressed as a politically interested private person, his fictional hero can best be described as an anarchist in the sense of extreme individualist and social outsider. Such labeling is supported by his many conflicts with the central state authority, the police, who play an important part in *Hunger*, as they do sixty years later in the autobiography, when the old man is caught smuggling a letter out of the detention home. Otto Weininger's characterization of Hamsun as a *Verbrecher*—a criminal type—is interesting in this connection, as is Johannes V. Jensen's observation that Hamsun never learned to see the importance of governmental rules and regulations.[26]

Hamsun's question—how to avoid the corrupting influence of social institutions—is also Ibsen's, but Ibsen's answer—by changing the institutions—is not Hamsun's. Ibsen, with his persistent dreams of a third empire, could be called a romantic with regard to the future, just as in his earliest writings he was a romantic with regard to the past. Hamsun is a romantic only in his relationship to the present; his works are free from the trappings of history as well as from social programs of any kind. But Hamsun's hero exists in a social situation, and therefore he has to develop a set of simple rules to live by. Thus he is willing to sacrifice his life for his fellowmen; in most cases Hamsun has his hero save another person from drowning. Furthermore, the hero's generosity knows no bounds: the destitute protagonist of *Hunger* takes great pride in giving away his last pennies, and Abel insists on helping even when it means that he himself must do without. Finally, the hero keeps his promises. Not surprisingly, when asked in an *enquête* what human quality he held in highest esteem, Hamsun answered *redelighet* —honesty. In other respects Hamsun's hero is outside society, or rather he is a society all his own. Indeed, the word Hamsun uses repeatedly to sum up Abel's existence is *sovereignty*. One might interpret this word to mean "sufficient unto oneself" and see this as another contrast to Ibsen's ideal of being oneself in the sense of "becoming oneself." Hamsun is not concerned with improving the self ethically, but he is concerned with authentic living, and by his example his hero shows the reader how such authenticity can be achieved. Turning away from society, this hero communicates with nature in a manner not seen before in Norwegian literature. And it is not only Lieutenant Glahn, but also Isak and even Abel, seeing his soul reflected in the stunted cactus plants, who find fulfillment in such harmony with nature. Another, equally typical, way of transcending is through the experience of love, which Hamsun has described as no other Norwegian prose writer has, whether it be the delightful promiscuity of Ylajali, or Edvarda's more typical love-hate, or Eva's selfless passion, all terminating in tragedy. Another kind of love is everlasting and ideal love, often represented allegorically and summed up in the autobiography's story of Alvilde, whose memory Martin Enevoldsen hides deep in his humble heart. Finally, readers of Hamsun cannot fail to recognize the kind of transcendence offered by artistic experience, whether it be the passionate tales of Johannes, or Willatz Holmsen's opera, or the many technical inventions that color the more prosaic lives of the later Hamsun heroes, from Knut Pedersen's mechanical wood saw to Abel's lockless casket. Knut Hamsun, the greatest ecologist in Norwegian literature, had started out as an interpreter of what he called, somewhat mysteriously, "the whisper of the blood and the entreaty of the bone." What he meant was, more prosaically, the power of nature, love, and art to produce joy in our daily lives. Through Hamsun's protagonists these powers speak to the readers, sometimes in the tone of Don Quixote, sometimes in that of Sancho Panza, but in the final view of the Hamsun hero, those tones are harmoniously blended into one unique yet familiar voice. This is how Henry Miller describes it: "It was from your Knut Hamsun that I derived much of my love of life, love of nature, love of man. All I have done, or hope I have, in relating the distressing story of my life, is to increase that love of life, nature and all of God's creatures in those who read me. 'Praise God from whom all blessings flow!'"[27]

NOTES

[1] The original text of *Den Gaadefulde* (Tromsø, 1877) is available in Eli Krog (ed.), *Det første jeg fikk trykt* (Oslo: Aschehoug, 1950); the quoted passage occurs on pp. 102–121. (My translation.)

[2] Cf. the following lines from a letter to Bolette C. Pavels Larsen, dated October 10, 1890: "It has always been my ambition to be able to appear incognito, unexpected, with sudden effect, time and again, in each book with sudden effect, and then disappear again—till the next time." The original text is quoted in O. Øyslebø, *Hamsun gjennom stilen* (Oslo: Gyldendal, 1964), p. 122. (My translation.)

[3] Knut Hamsun, "August Strindberg," *America* (Chicago), December 20, 1888.

[4] "Kristofer Janson," *Ny Jord* 1 (1888): 371–386; "Fra det ubevidste Sjaeleliv," *Samtiden* 1 (1890): 325–334, reprinted in *Artikler* (Oslo: Gyldendal, 1939); the three literary lectures were reprinted by Tore Hamsun in *Paa Tourné* (Oslo: Gyldendal, 1960).

[5] Hamsun often used the word *neurasthenia*, as in the last lines of *Under the Autumn Star* (*Wanderers*, part 1). He may have adopted the term after reading—several times—the Danish translation of Otto Weininger's *Geschlecht und Character*. See David Abrahamsen, *The Mind and Death of a Genius* (New York: Columbia University Press, 1946), p. 213.

[6] Anatole Baju, *L'Anarchie littéraire* (Paris: Librairie Léon Vanier, 1904), pp. 7–8. (My translation.)

[7] Cf. the following lines from an undated (1892?) letter to G. Philipsen, now in the Royal Library Copenhagen: "Besides, in my book the Midget is always thought of as Nagel's *alter ego*, hence the mysterious confrontations, hence the dreams, hence the vision of the man who wishes to commit suicide, etc." (My translation.)

[8] Hamsun on *Rosmersholm*: *Paa Tourné*, pp. 34–35.

[9] Parelius, the narrator of *Rosa* (1908), provides a link between the narrator of Glahn's adventures in India and Knut Pedersen. Parelius is probably modeled after Blicher's Morten Vinge (*Journal of a Parish Clerk*).

[10] See my book *Knut Hamsun og Amerika* (Oslo: Gyldendal, 1969), pp. 86–87.

[11] See Hamsun's poems "Himmelbrev til Byron" (in *Det vilde Kor*) and "Verden Haelder." The text of the latter poem (originally published 1895 in the periodical *Juleaften* and not included in *Det vilde Kor*) is available in Sten Sparre Nilson, *En ørn i uvaer* (Oslo: Gyldendal, 1960), pp. 43–47.

[12] Hamsun on the American South: *The Cultural Life of Modern America* (Cambridge: Harvard University Press, 1969), chapter entitled "Etiquette."

[13] Hamsun on *Brand*: *Paa Tourné*, p. 37.

[14] Laxness on *Growth of the Soil*: see Peter Hallberg, *Skaldens hus* (Stockholm:

Rabén & Sjögren, 1956), pp. 249–253, and idem, *Halldor Laxness* (New York: Twayne, 1971), pp. 97–98.

15 "He had to rehabilitate himself by a fraud: in passing himself off as other men, as commensurate, the poor fellow was compelled to use his own standard and persuade himself to believe in it. Perhaps it gave him his own little share of happiness, at all events he had no other. Tricks all through, then? Tricks all through. But no bad trickery" (Knut Hamsun, *Women at the Pump* [New York: Knopf, 1928], p. 395). The original text has a word that might equally well be rendered as *art*: "Kunst altsammen altsa? Kunst altsammen. Men intet dårlig kunstverk" (*Samlede verker*, 6th ed. [Oslo: Gyldendal, 1963], VIII, 275).

16 Cf. Rudolf Kayser in *Wiener Allgemeine Zeitung*, July 30, 1929: "Knut Hamsun ist ein nordöstlicher Dichter . . . Aber in seinem Norden bricht auch der Osten ein: mit seinen tragischen Drohungen, seelischen Abgründen und dem frommen Willen zur Erlösung." The concept is further developed by Josef Graf Westphalen in "Der nordöstliche Typ," *Die Waldhütte* (Mölln in Lauenburg), no. 16 (1968), pp. 3–13.

17 Garborg and others on Hamsun as a Yankee: see my book *Knut Hamsun og Amerika*, p. 224.

18 Two quotes on August: *The Road Leads On* (New York: Coward-McCann, 1934), pp. 465 and 126 respectively.

19 Hamsun on Ibsen: *Mysteries* (New York: Farrar, Strauss & Giroux, 1971), chapter 4.

20 Hamsun and the seven seas: see his ballad "Gangspilvise," *Samlede verker*, 6th ed., XV, 233. Hamsun in North Dakota: see my book *Knut Hamsun og Amerika*, pp. 65–68.

21 Hamsun on American fiction: see article "Festina Lente," in *Artikler*, pp. 217–229.

22 See Alf Larsen's review "Hamsuns ånd," reprinted in *I kunstens tjeneste* (Oslo: Dreyer, 1964); and Aa. Brynildsen's article "Svermeren og hans demon," in *Spektrum*, 1952.

23 Hamsun on the Turkish farmer: see chapter 2 of *Under Halvmaanen*, in *Stridende Liv, Samlede verker*, 6th ed., IV, 271–272. Abel says: "Why must one strive to *be* something? All others do that, but they aren't happier, even so. They have had the struggle to come up, but they are compelled to look high and low for their reward. Their peace of mind is gone, their nerves are frayed: some take to drink in order to pull through and only find themselves even worse off. They insist upon high heeled shoes for all occasions, and I, who live in a shed—I pity them" (*The Ring Is Closed* [New York: Coward-McCann, 1937], p. 281).

24 Of Lieutenant Holmsen it was said: "Steadfast and firm of purpose to the end!" (*Children of the Age* [New York: Knopf, 1924], p. 286). The book about Abel ends with the following words: "He had ordered a child's velocipede sent to Lili's home

in the mill district, and had been to see photographer Smith and paid him" (*The Ring Is Closed*, p. 322).

25 "I am not worthy to speak in a loud voice about Adolf Hitler, nor do his life and works invite to sentimental thoughts. He was a warrior, a warrior for mankind and a preacher of the gospel of rights for all nations. He was a progressive personality of the highest order, and it was his historical destiny to be active in a period of exceptional brutality that finally felled him. In this light the average West European will view Adolf Hitler, and we, his close supporters, now bend our heads at the news of his death" (*Aftenposten* [Oslo], May 7, 1945. Reprinted in Nilson, *En ørn i uvaer*, p. 218; my translation).

26 Otto Weininger on Hamsun as *Verbrecher*: see *Über die letzten Dinge* (Vienna: W. Braumüller, 1907), pp. vii, 124, 126; Johannes V. Jensen on Hamsun: *Den ny Verden* (Copenhagen: Gyldendal, 1907), p. 179.

27 Letter to Trygve Hirsch, Oslo, printed in Thomas H. Moore (ed.), *Henry Miller on Writing* (New York: New Directions, 1964).

Bergman's Movement toward Nihilism

The Antiheroic Stance in Secrets of Women, Brink of Life, The Seventh Seal, *and the Chamber Film Trilogy*

by BIRGITTA STEENE

University of Washington

In Ingmar Bergman's film *The Silence*, there is a brief sequence in a hotel room in the strange city of Timoka that shows Johan, the film's young boy, lying on his bed reading a book. The camera dwells just long enough on the cover of the book to enable the viewer to read its title: it is Lermontov's novel *A Hero of Our Time*.

Bergman is fond of such casual allusions in his films. He likes, for instance, to tease the viewer with a set of Bergmanian family names that appear in film after film: Egerman, Winkelman, Vogler. He is also fond of using names with symbolic or Christian overtones: Ester, Alma, Anna From, Isak, Antonius, Jof and Mia, Tomas; names that have made some commentators, most notably theology professor Stig Wikander, turn into veritable Bergmaniacs approaching Bergman's films as though they were religious allegories or at least epistemological crossword puzzles.

Bergman himself, however, has stated a number of times that, apart from the playfulness of his name dropping, he uses it to elicit an *emotional* rather than analytical response from the viewer. A name or a book title serves no other purpose than to create a mood or trigger an association in the viewer's mind; it is not meant to be an intellectual key to the film.

Appearing in the context of Bergman's film, Lermontov's novel *A Hero of Our Time* becomes no more than an ironic name tag suggesting that in the decadent world of *The Silence* the real hero is an observant child. Johan is really too young to be reading Lermontov's novel with any great understanding. His reading habits are more likely to reflect an interest in the Monte Cristos and Robinson Crusoes of our early teens than around an alienated Byronic hero on Russian soil. Pechorin, Lermontov's hero, is surely too sophisticated and too much of a ladies' man to appeal to Johan, the child reader.

There is, however, by way of association a certain similarity between Pechorin's neurotic and callous way of life—his spleen, his inability to sustain love, his self-torture—and the world in which young Johan moves in Bergman's film. As in Pechorin's case, that world is spiritually adrift. Johan, however, is observer rather than perpetrator of a decadent life style. Caught up in it he suffers but can also withdraw from it, and there is even a suggestion at the end of the film that he might one day be able to challenge it: sitting in the train on his way home from Timoka, Johan begins to decipher a note that his dying aunt Ester has given him, a note containing such words as *kasi*, Timokan for "hand," a very central word in Bergman's vocabulary in that it suggests the most vital rapport he recognizes, rapport through touch.

Johan is the first child to emerge as a focal character in a Bergman film. In the 1940's, when Bergman started to make films, adolescent youngsters held much of his attention, beginning with the high school boy Jan-Erik in *Torment* (1944) and ending with the young couple, Tomas and Birgitta-Carolina, in *The Devil's Wanton* (Swedish title, "Prison," 1948). But in the early 1950's Bergman began to focus more and more on the mature woman and on an exploration of the female psyche. No doubt this change indicated a distancing and maturing process in Bergman, an attempt to transcend the world of adolescent *Weltschmerz* and egocentricity.

Bergman's approach to film making remains highly subjective, however. His use of women protagonists is, like Ibsen's, a camouflaged revolt, an attempt to hide his self in a female persona. But, like Ibsen, Bergman is also drawn to the world of women because he finds women less rigorously defined by social and professional bonds than their male counterparts. Women in Bergman's view—as in Ibsen's—can more easily be brought to crucial situations where, isolated in time and space, they are forced to face life as a phenomenon rather than a function.

Unlike the young people in Bergman's earliest films, who are unsuccessful rebels against society and against the patriarchal family life in which they live and who, if they survive at all, seem to do so by renouncing the world they have grown up in, the women in the films of the early fifties have a good deal of adaptability or, simply, resilience to life around them. This is not to say that their life is easy or happy; their psyches are often in a state of emotional turmoil before they achieve a certain peace of mind.

In Swedish films before 1950 two standard types of women appeared: the vamp and the country girl, the former inevitably dressed in black lingerie, the latter glowing with the health of a true child of nature. Eventually the vamp became a destructive neurotic and the folksy child of nature a Swedish Lolita aimed for export. But when Bergman first took over the two types in his films, he made the vamp a victimized slut rather than the self-destructive temptress of men (Birgitta-Carolina in *The Devil's Wanton*; Berta in *Torment*; Berit in *Port of Call*; Sally in *Ship to Indialand*; Monica in *Summer with Monica*), while the country girl became Bergman's innocent "girl of summer." The latter appears for the first time as young Mari in *Illicit Interlude* (Swedish title, "Summer play," 1951). She will remain a favorite with Bergman and returns in many later films—as Sara in *Wild Strawberries*, Mia in *The Seventh Seal*, Karin in *The Virgin Spring*, Annette Egerman in *Smiles of a Summer Night*, young Sanna in *The Magician*. Bergman's girl of summer displays some variations: carefree exuberance, coquettishness, timidity, and fragility; but she always has a pure and childlike view of life and refuses to accept the compromises of older women.

Bergman's film from 1952, *Secrets of Women* (Swedish title, "Waiting women"), is conceived as an object lesson for such a young girl. Following the popular cinematic structure of the early 1950's, *Secrets of Women* is composed of three separate episodes within a narrative frame. Like a twentieth-century Boccaccio gathering, a group of married women has left the city for a summer stay in the archipelago. While they wait for their husbands to join them for the weekend, each agrees to tell a revealing episode from her married life. The

teenage sister of one of the women is a passive listener; heedless of
the stories of disillusionment and jilted love, of the lonely moment of
childbirth and of marital neglect, the young girl elopes at the end of
the film with a young man. The elopement has all the touchingness
and awkwardness of young love and receives the blessing of the
worldly-wise parents and relatives. "Let them leave," says one of
them as the boat with the young lovers sets out to sea. "Let them leave.
They will know soon enough all the wounds of life, all this silly business of living."[1]

None of Bergman's mature women from the early 1950's would
please members of Women's Liberation, for Bergman's women exist
only within the traditional radius of womanhood. They become self-
contained only by playing the old-time maternal roles of women.
When husbands and lovers fail them, they take refuge in church and
motherhood; as one of them says in *Secrets of Women*, a woman's consolation lies in either "Jesus or the grandchildren."

To Bergman, marriage is not a social phenomenon or a religious
institution. It is based on a psychological necessity existing outside all
moral conventions. Women especially want to get married to alleviate
their loneliness; they show no great passion or interest in anything else
in life. It is true that Bergman's women of the 1950's are sometimes
professional people, such as the fashion manager Susanne and her
young model Doris in *Dreams* (1955), or Mari, the ballet dancer in
Illicit Interlude; but these women are strangely indifferent to their
work. Emotionally they are all absorbed in their erotic crises of the
present and the past. Professional independence becomes something
unimportant to them. They derive little joy from their work and it
cannot protect them from being more vulnerable, victimized, and disillusioned than the men they love. This indifference to their professions is one reason why they interest Bergman—no public role playing, no professional smoke screen can prevent these women from being
marked by an intolerable loneliness. They seem to demonstrate what
one of them says in *Secrets of Women*: "The most terrible thing is
not to be deceived but to be left alone." Their destiny, then, transcends
any moral tug of war between man and woman; their erotic disappoint-

ments simply catapult them into the modern world of the alienated human being.

In the world of the cinema only Antonioni has shown a comparable interest in the traditional female syndrome. Yet Antonioni's women seem strangely somnambulistic and passive and completely manipulated by the film maker's male ennui. By comparison, Bergman's women of the fifties—although they usually wax suicidal and bitter over men—emerge as rather dynamic characters. Bergman's women often have, in fact, a degree of dogged resistance lacking in the shiftless men that surround them, and a certain amount of tenacity in the midst of their misery. As Susanne says in *Dreams* after losing her lover: "One continues to live, hour after hour, day after day."

Bergman admits today that his image of female role playing in the films of the fifties is conventional. But in those days he would not have called it "role playing" but a genuine way of life, in which he could put a certain trust and with which he could partly identify. Thus Bergman's approach to his women characters in such films as *Secrets of Women, Dreams,* and *Illicit Interlude* is never contemptuous, and he lacks the male chauvinism that is a subtle presence in Antonioni's and Fellini's films and a blatant attitude in a great number of recent American films: Mike Nichols's *The Graduate* and *Carnal Knowledge* and Bob Raphaelson's *Five Easy Pieces.* All these films remain male observations of women; none of them presents a situation from the woman's point of view. Had Bergman looked upon *Secrets of Women* from a male perspective, the women's stories would almost inevitably have taken on a cute quality of kaffeeklatsch memoirs, whereas they now become, because of their subjective, confessional tone, the *active* reliving of the crucial moments that shaped the lives of these women for ever after.

Such is also the point of view of Bergman's most remarkable film about women from the 1950's: *Brink of Life. Brink of Life* (1958) is a film in the now, without any of the flashbacks used in *Secrets of Women.* Its less intricate cinematic pattern is in keeping with the psychological tenor of the film: this is a story far more naked and straightforward in its soul searching than *Secrets of Women.*

Brink of Life takes place in the maternity ward of a Swedish hospital. Three women, Cecilia, Stina, and Hjördis, share a room. Cecilia has had a miscarriage, Stina gives birth to a stillborn child, Hjördis is seeking an abortion. Hence, although the film deals with three women facing childbirth, no new human life is born. New attitudes emerge, however, from the intense experiences that rack the women. Cecilia says about expectant mothers that "they open not only their wombs but also their entire being." Bergman thus treats the prospect of childbirth as an existential phenomenon rather than a biological function; it is as inexplicable and lonely an experience as the moment of death.

Brink of Life opens as Cecilia arrives at the hospital after her miscarriage. She is filled with a sense of failure and gets no support from her husband. When the husband comes to see her, the viewer notices immediately his absence of love and becomes aware of what must surely be the imminence of a divorce. Cecilia's husband is a Bergman archvillain, the man of intellect, related to the self-absorbed knight Antonius Block in *The Seventh Seal* (1956) and to professor Isak Borg in *Wild Strawberries* (1958). When Cecilia needs affection, she gets it not from her husband but from Stina, an exuberant expectant mother, who seems to bubble over with love and energy.

A pattern of give-and-take begins to form among the three women in the ward. When Stina is taken to the delivery room, Hjördis, the young unmarried girl, comes over to Cecilia because she is upset and cannot sleep. Her talk with Cecilia is more important to Hjördis than all her other contacts in the hospital. It is because of Cecilia that Hjördis finally decides to accept the new life in her.

Stina, the strongest of the three women, is the hardest hit. After an agonizing delivery during which Stina cries out not for her husband but for her mother, her child is born dead. Bitterly Stina quotes the Bible: "Yea, a sword shall pierce thy Soul," and when she returns to the ward from the delivery room she is filled with hostility. As Hjördis moves to help her to a glass of water, Stina slaps her arm aside. She has come to know a world of meaningless suffering, and the viewer senses that, although she survives her ordeal, Stina will never again be the buxom wench she was in the beginning of the film.

With *Brink of Life* Bergman definitely leaves behind his earliest portraits of women as victims of society or as sentimentalized epitomes of the brave little girl who struggles alone in a world of male conceit.[2] Such a melodramatically heroic stance now gives way to an antiheroic attitude toward life, first noticeable in *Secrets of Women*. That is to say, Bergman's women now become relativists who recognize, like Cecilia and Hjördis in *Brink of Life*, that no passion will last and no bond between man and woman gives absolute comfort; or they learn, like Stina, that suffering is brought upon us by some capricious amoral force beyond our understanding, which leaves us drained of our self-confidence and shattered in our faith in a meaningful and joyful world. Like today's antiheroes, the three women in *Brink of Life* are constantly thrown back upon themselves. Bergman emphasizes their isolation by letting the camera register all the cold sterility of the hospital environment. It is an indifferent world where the pregnant women can expect nothing beyond a certain technical assistance. Like Estragon and Vladimir in *Waiting for Godot*, Stina, Cecilia, and Hjördis may at times form a community of spirit, a microcosm of life, so that they can say with Beckett's two tramps that they "represent all humanity"; but like Vladimir and Estragon they are surrounded by a wasteland, and the hospital becomes a metaphor for death. Young Hjördis, who leaves the ward at the end, tells a nurse: "It's so terrible in here; it's as if the whole world were dead."

Bergman's women respond to life on an elemental, emotional level. If they raise questions, they seek the answers in their own experience, not in the rhetoric of the mind. When Bergman attempts to express metaphysical angst through a male protagonist, as he does in *The Seventh Seal*, made in 1956, he ends up with a film that is much more intellectual and stylized in its pattern than *Brink of Life*. And, since he cannot camouflage his existential bitterness in a female syndrome, he removes his male counterpart from a contemporary milieu and places him in fourteenth-century Sweden.

The Seventh Seal is designed as a kind of cinematic station drama. Returning with his squire after ten futile years in the Holy Land, during which time God and the meaning of life have remained enigmas to him, Antonius Block finds his homeland ravaged by the bubonic plague. The finality of life is his only certainty, and it is fitting that his pilgrimage now turns into a chess game with the personified figure of Death. As its title suggests, the action of the film is to be considered as a prelude to that moment of transcendence described in the Book of Revelations as the breaking of the seventh seal, the last phase in the opening of God's Book of Secrets.

Antonius Block's self-absorbing religious quest is juxtaposed with the skeptical attitude of his constant companion, Jöns, the Squire. Jöns's behavior is a mockery of many of the old hero forms; he sings bawdy songs in the face of death and recites cynical witticisms while proposing to a girl he has just rescued from a rapist priest. Jöns in fact joins company with the comic or satiric forms of the antihero in Western literature: the *miles gloriosus* of Roman comedy, Falstaff, Candide, Sancho Panza.

Antonius Block, on the other hand, represents—for all his medieval trappings—the modern post–World War I antihero who has come to replace the tragic hero as the central figure in the most serious efforts by contemporary artists to explore the human dilemma. While Jöns exposes the incongruity of the heroic stance, Antonius Block displays the basic characteristics of today's antihero: his lack of affirmative pose, his inability to find a meaningful direction to his life, his futile search for a godhead. Like so many contemporary antiheroes, Antonius Block has to live and die faced with Nietzsche's dictum: God is dead. Like other twentieth-century antiheroes, from Hemingway's to Camus's, Bergman's Knight is at times heroic and noble in behavior, but his heroism seems quixotic and desperate. He rescues the young couple Jof and Mia from Death; yet his act and his total quest do not unite him with humanity. Except for a brief moment on a hillside when he shares strawberries and milk with Jof and Mia, the Knight's search alienates him from those closest to him, from his wife and his companions. In the end it seems that the only fruit he reaps from his quest is the one that Bergman's characters always get to taste: bitter loneliness.

Antonius Block searches for God and finds only a void that he recognizes as a reflection of his own self. When he prays in church the camera rests on his face rather than on the icons, traditional symbols of God's presence. The camera thus reinforces the Knight's verbal response to his attempt to speak to God: "The emptiness is a mirror turned toward my own face. I see myself in it and I am filled with fear and disgust." Except for its element of self-deprecation, this is a statement echoed by one of the minor characters in *Brink of Life*, Greta Ellius, who tells Cecilia: "True aloneness is a juggling act, and behind it lurks a constant fear."

Does that mean that *The Seventh Seal* and *Brink of Life* share a negative point of view? Not really. For, unlike Antonius Block, the women in the maternity ward know how to respond to the immediate reality around them. Their despair manifests itself in simple actions, their anger and frustration in spontaneous emotional outbursts, and in this very outlet of theirs lies a source of strength, the strength to commune. Antonius Block, on the other hand, withdraws into the artifice of his own mind. His isolation is obvious throughout the film, but his aloofness is also apparent. It is no coincidence that when the viewer tries to remember *The Seventh Seal* he visualizes the Knight facing the figure of Death, rather than Jöns, his traveling companion, or any other character in the film. And it is no coincidence that the film has been criticized by cinema purists for being too rhetorical. What the critics do not seem to realize, however, is that the rhetorical pattern is linked to Antonius Block's modus vivendi: he is a phrasemonger who escapes into verbalization. In one of the final sequences of *The Seventh Seal*, in which the Knight and his company face the arrival of Death in the castle, Bergman places Antonius Block behind the others in a last desperate prayer. It is in this kind of separation from his fellowmen that the Knight really parts company with the women in *Brink of Life*. Even Stina in that film, whose life seems shattered, will, one feels, somehow pull through and come out of her self-absorbing bitterness, for the sense of mutual support among the women in the maternity ward is so strong that it amounts to an affirmation of life.

To today's self-conscious antihero, of whom Bergman's medieval Knight is a tentative example, such affirmation seems absurd. In fact, one of the basic questions that the antihero asks himself, and then either rejects or evades, is this: Why should a man not embrace death; why should he go on living if his life is without meaning and if life itself is chaotic and without sense? It is a question that Bergman poses directly in his film *Winter Light* (Swedish title, "The communicants," 1963) through the character of Jonas Persson, a suicidal fisherman. But the question of self-annihilation haunts Bergman's characters in the entire so-called Chamber Film trilogy, of which *Winter Light* is the second work.

In the first film in the trilogy, *Through a Glass Darkly* (1961), one of the central characters, David, a widower and father of two children, has reached an impasse in life. Faced with his failure as a writer and as a parent, he has contemplated suicide. His self-destructive thoughts are prompted, however, by a sense of personal failure rather than a feeling that all of life is futile. In fact, David chooses to return to life because he claims he is convinced that there is a God and that this God is a *deus caritatis* who exists in the understanding and compassion we give each other. But David's positive stance has a curiously abstract and rhetorical ring to it, and it is much more difficult for the viewer to believe in David's humanity than in the bonds linking Cecilia, Hjördis, and Stina in *Brink of Life*. It is hardly surprising that David never reaches Karin, his mentally unstable daughter, with his "God of Love." Instead, Karin's search for God in a hideaway attic culminates in a hallucination in which she imagines God as an enormous spider coming out of a closet to crawl into her. In the end she is whisked off to a mental institution in a helicopter that descends outside the attic—a spiderlike *deus ex machina*. Karin chooses death, not physical death, but the spiritual death of the asylum.

In *Winter Light* Bergman moves outside the orbit of family life and attempts to set the question of suicide and rejection of life in relation to the malaise of the modern world. Tomas Ericsson, the film's Lutheran minister, has long been confronted with his own doubts, with the omnipresence of death and indifference, and the absence of love. Ever since the days when he was a seaman's chaplain in Lisbon and watched the Spanish Civil War at a distance, Tomas has questioned the loving nature of God.

Bergman provides Tomas with an irritating companion, an eczema-ridden, ugly schoolteacher by the name of Märta. The two live in a world of bleak winter; they meet in empty churches; they seem to share nothing but each other's despair; and they are either tortured or sickened by each other's presence. But in the end they choose to live on. Märta, the avowed agnostic, listens alone in church to the incantatory voice of Tomas as he intones, "Holy, holy, holy, all the earth is full of thy Glory." In the context of the film these are words of bitter irony, a desperate form of rhetoric that echoes David's reference, in *Through a Glass Darkly*, to the Christian cliché, "God is Love, Love is God."

Do Tomas and Märta pay lip service then to a God they no longer believe in? Yes and no. Märta knows that God is dead; she listens to the words spoken in the church out of a stubborn love for Tomas. Tomas, who could have canceled the service, insists on holding it, but less, the viewer feels, out of a sense of duty than out of a need to hide once more behind the words of the ritual. Märta is a woman whose psychic strength is such that she needs no such self-protection. Tomas, by comparison, is weak, an adult child who must reject the maternal offerings of Märta because they are humiliating to him, but who cannot live without illusions. Tomas's entire life has been a series of self-deceptions, some of which he sees through, but some of which he cannot face up to. The "security god" of his childhood and early priesthood has been replaced by a "spider god," from which he frees himself in the course of the film. Why then does he perform the service? Perhaps because he remains ignorant of the *complete* falsity of his life? He believes, for instance, that his earlier marriage was a perfect one, while in reality it was quite an ugly relationship, and he does not understand at all his great need for Märta. It is from that unpleasant truth, perhaps, that his ministerial role playing helps him take cover; the words of the ritual are a façade that conceals his naked face.

One is in fact tempted to say that ritualized language fulfills the same purpose for Tomas as artistic or pseudo-artistic language does for David in *Through a Glass Darkly*. In both cases words are used as a substitute for living and as an escape from personal responsibility. At one point David confesses to Karin: "When your mother got ill I went away and left you with Granny. After all, I had my novel to think about. When your mother died I had my big success, and it meant so much more to me than her death." Tomas is not so intellectualized a character as David and does not reach the latter's degree of verbalized self-consciousness, but his absorption in language and his escape into words are unmistakable.

Neither David nor Tomas uses words hypocritically or self-deceptively all the time, however. But beginning with Tomas in *Winter Light*, Bergman's skepticism toward language will become complete. Language can be used truthfully, yet only with a negative, destructive result. In an honest confrontation scene between Tomas and Märta in the schoolhouse, when Tomas pours out his disgust at Märta's physical ailments, he almost destroys her. When one of his parishioners, the fisherman Persson, comes to seek spiritual guidance from him, Tomas ends up revealing his own agony and skepticism, which only precipitates Persson's suicide.

Fisherman Persson is a big, awkward man who seems to have absorbed into his heavy, slow body a sense of absolute futility. He kills himself, not out of a sense of personal failure, but because he feels all life to be meaningless in our atomic age. Man is intent upon destroying the earth, and he, fisherman Persson, is unable to do anything about it.

Persson is married to one of Bergman's resilient earth women. She is pregnant, but it is as if her pregnancy merely throws her husband's despair into sharper focus: in a meaningless world, headed for annihilation, it seems meaningless to give birth to new life. In a way it is Bergman's rejection, as it were, of the last part of a statement made in the preface to the (unpublished) script of *Brink of Life*, in which his coauthor Ulla Isaksson wrote: "We may assail heaven and science with questions—all the answers are still only partial. But life goes on, crowning the living with torment and happiness."

The living in *Winter Light* seem to know only the torment of life. The film is the bleakest of all of Bergman's works for the screen. It seems shot in a grayish winter dusk, and the camera makes a special point of isolating each individual in close-ups and medium shots and of cutting abruptly from one face to another. When two people are in the same frame, they only rarely look at or speak directly to each other. The effect is a film where one senses, because of the closeness of the camera, the intimacy of the human struggle, but also an awkward and helpless lack of rapport between people. Unlike *The Seventh Seal*, in which the futility of the Knight was juxtaposed, at least in fleeting moments, with the idyllic and innocent love of Jof and Mia, *Winter Light* provides no glimpse of hope. The failure of Jonas Persson as a father and husband is an old Bergman motif, but the inability of his strong wife to save him is a new and poignant element in Bergman's movement toward nihilism.

It is hardly surprising that in his next film Bergman makes use of this disillusioned view of the role of women. In *The Silence* he projects his image of futility and decadence through the frustrated and hate-filled lives of two women, one of whom has separated from her husband, while the other is a masculine-oriented lesbian.

Most American critics discussing *The Silence* have concentrated on the film's lesbian conflict, an approach that says something about the sexual fixations of this country but ignores the fact that Ester's deviate sexual behavior is not the main issue but merely one of many symptoms that describe the collapse of a world where love, hope, and faith have died. Anna's heterosexual sensuality is as much a neurotic craving as is Ester's lesbian affection for her sister, a kind of angst expressed on the physical level. The sickness and decadence of the film also affect Johan, the young boy, although as mentioned earlier he seems to escape from these influences at the end. While in the hotel, however, he is wooed capriciously by his mother, only to find himself left alone as she goes to meet her lover. His negative experience of love is reflected in a puppet scene he performs for Ester. The puppets, who are husband and wife, attack each other furiously, probably a commentary on the hatred that Johan must have known in his own home, but also on the hatred that he senses between his aunt Ester, who plays a kind of father substitute to him, and his mother.

The abortive family of Ester, Anna, and Johan travels through a strange country whose language they do not understand. Because of Ester's illness, they have to get off the train in the city of Timoka. The main action of the film takes place in the old hotel where they have gone to rest. Outside the hotel a war is going on: tanks rattle by, officers mill around, air raid alarms go off in the night. Life inside the hotel has an eerie, ghostlike quality to it. No other guests are staying there except for a group of performing dwarfs. No hotel personnel are seen, except for a doddering old waiter who frightens Johan as though

he were some Dickensian bogeyman. In spite of the baroque décor of
the hotel, a tomblike atmosphere prevails. Anna, Ester, and Johan are
in fact as helpless in this voluptuously decorated world of Rubens
paintings and carpeted floors as were the three women in the frugally
furnished hospital ward of *Brink of Life*.

There are actually haunting similarities between *Brink of Life* and
The Silence. As Peter Cowie has pointed out, both films place the characters in very confined, stuffy rooms, which appear at the same time as
impersonal limbos, out of which the people can escape only into endless corridors leading nowhere in particular.[3] In both films people are
cut off from the world they normally inhabit; their new milieu, accentuated by its strangeness, makes tensions arise and emotions erupt that
might otherwise be kept under control.

The sense of threatening sterility and powerlessness, which in *Brink
of Life* was conveyed by having the camera register all the inanimate
hospital paraphernalia, is transmitted, in *The Silence*, by the use of a
prowling camera that creates the impression that the characters are followed by a stealthy, invisible spectator who comes crawling down the
corridors, observing every move the two sisters and the boy make. As a
result, the stopover quarters of the travelers are more reminiscent of
Kafka's mysterious castle than of any realistic facsimile of a European
hotel.

In keeping with the strange mood of *The Silence*, the viewer catches
only glimpses of the past of the two sisters and of Johan. In their background is Johan's father, alive but never confronted, whom Anna
never refers to as her husband. In the background hovers also the ubiquitous figure of Ester's and Anna's father, now dead but once an enormous ogre of a man who weighed over three hundred pounds. The absence of the men makes it difficult for Ester and Anna to challenge the
past; they can only sense it as a growing frustration, an emotional need
that can never be fulfilled. At the same time, by removing Anna and
Ester from any actual confrontation with the past, Bergman leaves
the psychological world of character conflict and moves into a metaphysical sphere of experience. This movement is underscored by the
rather schematic presentation of Ester and Anna as creatures embodying opposites: intellect versus sensuality, contempt of body versus con-

tempt of mind. In *Brink of Life* it is possible to imagine the three
women as having a psychological identity beyond the now of the film;
in *The Silence* it is difficult to visualize the women transcending their
symbolic roles as carriers of metaphysical dichotomies.

Anna, the sensuous but abstracted mother figure, survives her stopover in Timoka. But survival is small comfort if one lives one's life in
a limbo. Bergman stresses Anna's desperate situation by letting the
physical world bombard her with nauseating impressions: going to a
cabaret, Anna observes first the grotesque centipedelike movements of
the dwarfs linked together, then averts her eyes only to see the ludicrous lovemaking of a couple in the stalls; descending into the all-male
crowd outside the hotel, she is pushed or eases her way through the
throng of people mechanically; attracting a bartender to her hotel
room, she cannot enjoy lovemaking except as an act of revenge directed
at Ester.

The disappearance of the traditional father figure, with its protective
and Christian overtones, has left Ester as well as Anna in a desperate
state. As modern absurdist playwrights have demonstrated amply,
human beings living in a post-Christian, postpatriarchal universe tend
to become schizoid, fragmented. Bergman follows this assumption in
his dichotomous projection of the two sisters; they are two halves of a
human being, attracted and repelled by each other, each confused and
incomplete in herself. Anna, who complains that Ester treats her as a
half-wit and merely wants to dominate her, is struggling to set herself
free. Yet, whenever she falls back on her sensuality and sexual attrac-
tiveness (i.e., that which Ester lacks), she experiences life ad nauseam.

Ester is even more pathetic than Anna. She repels Anna with her
attempts at physical rapprochement, and she makes Johan withdraw
from her whenever she tries to touch him. As Ester is an intellectual,
language has always been her particular tool. Yet even with words she
seems powerless before Anna, for, unlike her sister, Ester cannot use
words as missiles that destroy. Anna, on the other hand, deals Ester her
deathblow by hurling at her the irrefutable charge of the antiheroic
age: "When father died, you said 'I want to be dead.' Why are you still
living then?"

Crushed by Anna's taunting words, Ester ceases to struggle against the disease that is killing her. The next morning she lies in bed, dying. Anna and Johan have left and Ester is alone, except for the old, skinny waiter who fusses around her like a tottering phantom. Although he must seem to Ester the very opposite of what her voluminous and auto- cratic father once was, she turns to the old waiter as to a father- confessor and sums up her life experience, Bergman's nihilistic credo: "We try them out, one attitude after another, and find them all mean- ingless. But they're too strong. I mean the forces that make us tremble. You must watch your step among ghosts and memories . . . All this talk. There is no need to discuss loneliness. It's useless."

Ester is an interpreter by profession. Through her dependence upon language Bergman links her to his earlier antiheroic brooders like An- tonius Block in *The Seventh Seal*, David in *Through a Glass Darkly*, and Tomas in *Winter Light*. At the same time he makes Ester ex- tremely sensitive to the destructiveness and emptiness of language. For an intellectual, Ester seems strangely powerless before Anna's verbal assaults. Perhaps she is helpless not only because Anna's accusations are true, but also because Ester realizes the futility of trying to explain anything through words. Ester has come to understand that, if people are to communicate meaningfully, a new language must be invented— either the language of music or an entirely new set of signs and sym- bols. She "speaks" with the old waiter via Bach's music on the radio. When nothing else works, she tries to reach Johan by providing him with a list of words in the unknown language of Timoka. But she re- jects the antihero's last holdout: conventional, petrified language. *The Silence* is the first film in which the evasiveness and lies and hostility of words—that is, language used as an evil magic to prevent real com- munication and love—are recognized not only by Bergman but also by one of the major characters in the film.

In his book *The Modern Century*, Northrop Frye has said, apropos of one of the earliest antiheros in modern literature, Dostoevsky's underground man, that the antihero may arrive at a position of abso- lute nihilism intellectually but survive because he has one crutch left, his possession of fossilized rhetoric, which he will use in a sadomaso- chistic fashion either to hurt someone else or to humiliate himself. The antihero, says Frye, is continuously possessed by rhetorical rages directed at himself or at some projection of himself. But this rhetoric is a device to keep himself from fully accepting the futility of his existence. Language is the antihero's way of planting "a series of anti-tank traps in the way of the rumbling and creaking invaders of his mind."[4]

Antonius Block, David, Tomas, and even the antiintellectual Anna succeed in planting such "anti-tank traps." All of them except Antonius Block survive and do so at least in part through the power of cliché-ridden, ritualized, or destructive language. Ester, on the other hand, sees through this trick of the antiheroic mind. That is why she does not engage, at the end, in a rhetorical outburst, like Antonius Block's final prayer in *The Seventh Seal*. Ester, choking to death, has the courage to admit: "All this talk. There is no need to discuss loneliness. It's useless."

NOTES

[1] All quotations, unless otherwise stated, are from the dialogue in the final Swedish screen version of the film cited.

[2] The melodramatic brave-little-girl portrait is exposed for what it really is—features drawn by male chauvinism—in an amusing encounter between consul Fredrik Egerman and his former mistress, Desirée Armfeldt, in *Smiles of a Summer Night* (1955):

Fredrik. What was that?
Desirée. That was Fredrik. [Their child]
Fredrik. Fredrik?
Desirée. Yes, Fredrik.
Fredrik. Fredrik?
Desirée. How strange you look.
Fredrik. Have . . . I . . . I mean have you . . . I mean . . . it isn't possible, or is it?
Desirée. [*laughs*] Look at Fredrik Egerman now. He's terribly shaken and as pale as a pickled herring. At the same time he's a little flattered, touched and terribly sentimental. "Desirée, my love, have you been struggling along by yourself all these years, sacrificing everything for our love's pawn?"

[3] Peter Cowie, *Sweden 2* (New York: A. S. Barnes & Co., 1970), p. 133.

[4] Northrop Frye, *The Modern Century* (New York: Oxford University Press, 1967), pp. 66–67.

The Hero in Swedish Fiction
after World War II

by SVEN LINNÉR

Åbo Akademi
(The Swedish University in Finland)

The central term of this article's title has two connotations: (1) main character or protagonist and (2) a person who is in some sense heroic. When I talk of heroes here I have the second meaning in mind. I am looking for the representation of heroism in modern Swedish fiction.[1]

The obvious starting point is Eyvind Johnson's *Strändernas svall* (1946). His Odysseus is the classical hero with modern man's sensitivity. Like Oreste in Sartre's *Les Mouches*, he is fully capable of action, even of violence if necessary, but he is tortured by a conscience of a very un-Homeric kind. Morally, he is in a more difficult position than Krilon, in Johnson's trilogy published during the war. In spite of his vacillations, Krilon's moral conviction remains steadfast. The writer's road from Krilon to Odysseus marks the shift from a spirit of resistance born out of the war to a realization of the price of that war and its aftermath in terms of human suffering. Nevertheless, Odysseus, whatever his disgust at the sight of his dirty hands, still has the power to form his destiny.

Some ten years later, Johnson published *Molnen över Metapontion* (1957), a novel that moves on different time levels: the past and the present. The principal character is Themistogenes, a close friend of Xenophon and partaker in the illustrious march described in the *Anab-*

asis. His story is reconstructed by a French archeologist, who is later killed in a Nazi concentration camp. The Frenchman has a younger Swedish friend, Klement, who follows his traces through Europe after the end of the war. In certain passages, the three men nearly merge into one. They share the experience of war and of organized cruelty, and also the quality of courage. The concluding words of the novel are written by Themistogenes, when he is aged and blind, but they speak not only for him: "Stundom vill jag kalla den Omega, det slutligas ö, eller det seende ögats ö, ja, jag ger den många namn. Ibland kallar jag den Uthållighetens ö" [Sometimes I want to call it Omega, the island of the Final, or the island of the Seeing Eye, yes, I give it many names. Sometimes I call it the island of Endurance].[2]

In his novel Eyvind Johnson forcefully demonstrates the dignity of man. Still, his story is fused with a tone of emptiness and loss: his view is directed toward an irrevocable past.

Odysseus appears again in Lars Gyllensten's *Lotus i Hades* (1966). Here there is no trace of heroism left. Odysseus—and other classical figures as well—is nothing but a shadow. Hades offers deliverance from suffering and striving, that is true, but is not morally structured in a way that makes it meaningful to speak of virtue. The very contours of individuality are blurred, identities exchanged: "Här är Kain kung, och Don Juan är kung, och Odysseus är kung, och jag är kung, och du är kung, och vi är alla kungar. Mitt rike är ditt rike, och ditt rike är mitt rike" [Here Cain is king, and Don Juan is king, and Odysseus is king, and I am king, and you are king, and we are all kings. My kingdom is your kingdom, and your kingdom is my kingdom].[3] In *Prästkappan*, of a few years earlier (1963), Sven Delblanc uses the Hercules myth, applying it to the central character of his novel. But Herman cannot be said to embody the greatness of the heroic ideal; rather, he embodies its absurdity: "a modern Hercules by necessity becomes a parody."[4] Herman is really an anti-Hercules.

The literary figures I have mentioned so far in rapid succession indicate that after the Second World War there is increasingly less room for heroes of a classical kind. This view would, I believe, be confirmed by a complete survey of the whole field. In addition, there is widespread suspicion of all power holders. The king of France, later the Emperor Charlemagne, His Grace in Johnson's *Hans nådes tid* (1960), is as terrible as the Easter storm with which the story opens. As the motto of the novel states: Man lives on an aspen leaf; there is no security to be found. But this is our world, *asplövsvärlden*. For most of us, life is a question of survival. Engineer Andrée, in Per Olof Sundman's *Ingenjör Andrées luftfärd* (1967), cares little about survival—his aims are set higher. He overcomes all obstacles, he carries the burden of responsibility alone, and he faces death without fear. So far he is designed according to the heroic pattern, but there is something sinister about him. The rationale of his enterprise is obscure, and his expedition to the North Pole was, in all probability, doomed from the outset. He is more or less forced into accepting an impossible role. Accused of expressing an authoritarian ideology in this novel, as well as in his *Expeditionen* (1962; about an African expedition reminiscent of the one made by Stanley), Sundman angrily replied that he had never had any intention whatsoever of setting up the "strong men" described in his novels as ideals. Rather, he had presented models of European pride and European stupidity.[5] In Artur Lundkvist's *Himlens vilja* (1970), the author's attitude is far more ambiguous than in Sundman's case. His book is about Genghis Khan, a man of absolute power and a dealer in large-scale death, destructive like a force of nature. Lundkvist passes no judgment on him. His lyrical imagination is caught by this man of fate. He is fascinated by him in a manner that his readers will hardly be able to call anything but problematic. This is a portrait on a grand scale, but I would hate to think that it depicts a hero of our time.

The heroes who are beloved by the readers are men with little power. Vilhelm Moberg's Karl-Oskar (in his series of novels about the emigrants from Småland; 1949–1959) is not dressed in classical robes but in the worn clothes of a nineteenth-century farmer. Still, he has those qualities that constitute heroism: strength, courage, tenacity, and, what is more, his actions have a clearly defined purpose. Like Aeneas, he builds for the future. But to us who have to live in that future, his world is romantic in a sense that the worlds described by Eyvind Johnson are not. The popularity of the emigrant novels stems from man's dream of a universe less problematic than the one he belongs to. In our world, the future is uncertain, and, more important still, all traditional moral values are questioned. The list of small men, insignificant from society's point of view but admirable or at least likable, could easily be prolonged (Bolle in Harry Martinson's *Vägen till Klockrike*, 1948; the father in Ivar Lo-Johansson's *Analfabeten*, 1951). But the point I just made about Karl-Oskar remains true. These men belong in another era than ours, socially and morally. The fundamental quality of their world is a simpleness that is no longer to be found.

To find a hero who is contemporary in a moral sense I will again turn to a historical novel, Lagerkvist's *Sibyllan* (1956). The sibyl has seen God. Everyone has learned that the human being who does so must die, but she does not. "May you be cursed and blessed" is her final judgment on God, and her strength is not broken. She has experienced everything that life can offer to men, extreme joy as well as extreme sorrow, and she carries the burden of her memories without shutting off her consciousness from them. Unlike Iokaste she does not abandon life when the pain it offers is unbearable. She remains upright, still seeing life with open eyes. In this respect, her spirit is akin to that of the prince of Emgión (in Gunnar Ekelöf's *Diwan*, 1965). Before he was captured and mutilated he was a hero, to speak in a technical sense. He was a gallant warrior, belonging in the epic tradition with Roland and Digenis Akritas. When the reader gets to know him, however, all this is past and he is a ruin of a man. But, blinded like Oedipus, he is still not blind. His mind remains open to the world:

Jag minns, och jag vet
Jag är därför inte blind
Jag är bara bländad
Jag har sett
och jag känner
flickans hand
. . . .
[I remember and I therefore know
That I am not blind
Only blinded
I used to see

And I can read the girl's mind

...]⁶

In spite of his tortures, his senses are open and his soul is alive, still receptive and expanding toward deeper experiences.

The heroism that I am speaking of here is not related to any kind of action. The fundamental quality (the quality that constitutes it) is courage, in particular the courage of a lonely man or woman. The hero stands apart from his fellowmen; this does not imply contempt for them or indifference—it is simply the basis of his existence. Characters like Lagerkvist's sibyl and Ekelöf's prince of Emgión are obviously very close to their creators: the poet and the fictional character have a profound experience in common. They both carry the burden of insight. It does take courage to go on living after one has seen the countenance of human existence, facing what Vilhelm Ekelund, more than half a century ago, called "allt det evigt oläkliga i tillvarons karaktär" [all that which is unbearable in the character of existence].⁷ Facing the truth of existence is perhaps the particular kind of heroism found in poets, and their most important business is to express that kind of courage and share it with us, more important than depicting heroes galloping into battle. Their place is what Johnson called *Uthållighetens ö*, the island of Endurance.

There is no denying that the experience expressed by Lagerkvist and by Ekelöf is a modern one: they speak for us. On the other hand, their works cited here are highly symbolic, and the question remains whether there are not any heroes to be found in a more immediately recognizable setting. Where are the heroes who crowd the subways with the rest of us or, at least, walk streets that we *might* have walked? Is a realistic depiction of heroism still possible?

I shall mention two such characters, both of them women. The world that they face is private only, and they do not speak for mankind the way the sibyl and the prince of Emgión can be said to do. Still, they have the quality of moral greatness that constitutes heroism. The first woman is Paulina in Lars Ahlin's *Natt i marknadstältet* (1957), that wonderful middle-aged woman who pronounces her fragrant Yes to life. In the end, she kills her husband because she cannot see him consistently debase himself (*förkasta sig*). The setting of her tragedy is as unclassical as can be, but the strength of her love and suffering makes her reminiscent of classical heroines. The same is true of Linda in Sara Lidman's twin novels (*Regnspiran*, 1958, and *Bära mistel*, 1960). Hers is an impossible love. She takes any humiliations and degradations upon herself to serve a man who does not love her. She is a sister of Hjalmar Bergman's "fru Ingeborg."

Lars Ahlin abandons Paulina when she mourns the husband whom she has loved and killed; it is difficult to visualize a future for her. But for her nephew Zacharias life is just beginning. He observes his aunt's tragedy and thereby acquires an understanding of suffering rare in mature people. He is the Alyosha Karamazov of Swedish literature. The novel ends before he has entered the world of the adult, but the reader has witnessed the initiation of the hero: as he appears at the end of the novel he is prepared for things unusual. The initiation of Axel Weber, in Sven Delblanc's *Nattresan* (1967), takes place at a later stage in his development. When the nightly journey is over, Axel is ready for more than married life only: he has faced the demons within him, but also the spirit of capitalism, represented by that grim de Sadean figure, Minski. "Socialize the lot" is Birgitta's motto, and her lover makes it his own. He stands on the threshold of political activity when the novel comes to its end.

Political involvement is strong among writers, particularly in the generation under forty. In a statement of 1960 (when a number of writers were asked to comment on their position), P. G. Jersild looked forward to a literature "which might perhaps affect our chances of survival."[8] It is not easy, however, to find in the fiction of these writers characters similarly involved; at least they are not portrayed in such a way that it is natural to call them heroes. Delblanc's Axel never enters the world of politics, as I just pointed out. Many writers give the better part of their effort to journalism and reportage rather than to fiction. This is true of Sara Lidman (that outstanding novelist), Jan Myrdal, Göran Palm, Sven Lindquist. Per Wästberg keeps on writing novels, and quite successfully, but in a spirit distinctly different from that of his journalism. Sundman's protagonists, with their immense will power, represent ideals clearly alien to the ones the writer is pursuing in his capacity as member of Parliament. The political novel most debated in recent years is Per Olov Enquist's *Legionärerna* (1968). There are several remarkable portraits in it, but hardly a hero. The central character of the novel is the writer himself—sensitive, trying in vain to understand, hampered by doubts.[9]

Where is the political hero to be found, then? There is one portrait on a grand scale, painted by that master of surprise, Lars Forssell. In his *Oktoberdikter* (1971), a group of poems is about Ulyanov, later known as Lenin. This man is truly capable of action; his faith in the future never wavers. But Forssell cannot be unaware of the distance between his poetic creation and the historical model. Lenin was a politician of utmost ruthlessness and of very rational calculation. Bertrand Russell observed in him "a distinct vein of impish cruelty."[10] It is almost as if Forssell has this in mind when, in one of his poems, he tries to encounter the moral objections raised against the dictator. Still, it seems quite obvious that the poet has idealized his Ulyanov. The revolutionary leader in *Oktoberdikter* is a hero in the romantic vein.

I should emphasize once more that heroism *is* found in modern Swedish fiction. Courage in facing the truth of human existence, ultimately the fact of death, may rise to heroic proportions and does; similarly, courage in carrying the burden of a passion that offers no reward, or in following the voice of one's innermost self, can be heroic. I insist on using the words *heroism* or *heroic* here. But what is lacking is heroic struggle or action in the sociopolitical field. Here is the reason why several Swedish friends, when I mentioned the topic of my talk to them, commented: "Well, of course, there aren't any heroes!"

How is one to explain the disparity between the strong political involvement among writers and the scarcity of political heroes in their fiction, and what conclusions should be drawn from it? Let me quote here, somewhat provocatively, a statement by Georg Lukács on the fictional world of Tolstoy: "Where in this world is there room for action? Tolstoy increasingly perceives and depicts a world that no longer offers to decent people a chance to act."[11] I believe Lukács's statement can be expanded thus: Action in the private sphere is not enough. Good men want to form the society in which they live. If, however, that society offers them no chance to act, there will be no such

action represented in fiction. And, on the other hand, if no moral action
is depicted in fiction (particularly not among outstanding writers),
one may conclude that the society in which these writers lived offered
no possibilities for good social action.

Lukács's theory is forceful and tempting precisely because of its simplicity. There are other factors, however, not contained in his formula,
that may provide at least part of an answer to the question. First, a
number of writers—some of them passionately involved in politics—
have turned their backs on fiction. The example was set by Sartre:
"Over against a dying child *La Nausée* cannot act as a counter-
weight."[12] In *Les Mots* he took his farewell of belles-lettres. In
Sweden, Jan Myrdal stated in his *Confessions of a Disloyal European*
(1968): "Storytelling is a danger and fictionalizing is a temptation to
be avoided. Art lies with form." European intellectuals are not, as they
would like to think, "the bearers of consciousness. We are the whores
of reason."[13] Although I do not have her own words for it, I assume
that Sara Lidman felt that, with her report on the Kiruna strike (*Gruva*,
1968), she had accomplished something far beyond the range of her
fiction. She has not published a novel since 1964.[14] Writers who regard
it as their foremost duty to strive for political effects may indeed have
reason to look upon their art with suspicion or regret. In their view,
political heroes belong in real life, not in novels.

A second factor in an answer to the question is that there are writers
who accept the limitation of their art without feeling inferior about it.
However strongly they may be concerned about politics, they are not
equipped for it: theirs is a different job. Thus Birgitta Trotzig points
out that art has little impact on political events:

. . . i en direkt politisk nödsituation är de specifikt konstnärliga medlen
trubbiga och ineffektiva. En konstnär som tror att han med konstens egna
medel kan *direkt* påverka en yttre situation måste alltid och med rätta känna
sig bekajad av mindervärdeskomplex, han åker i schäs bland tanks.

[. . . in the case of a directly political emergency the specialized tools of the
artist are blunt and ineffectual. The artist who believes that he, by art's
own means, can influence an external situation *directly* will always, and
justly, feel afflicted with an inferiority complex: he drives a brougham
among tanks.]

What art can do is something else: it can affect the basic attitudes of people, *livshållningen*, out of which norms and opinions will grow. I am convinced, she concludes, "att konsten på det viset—men bara på det viset, indirekt, som ett slags gödsel—har en vid och i egentlig mening opinionsskapande betydelse" [that art in this way—but only in this way, indirectly, as a kind of fertilizer—has a broad influence on the forming of public opinion].[15] Behind Birgitta Trotzig looms the mighty figure of Lars Ahlin; it is difficult to measure his influence on succeeding generations of writers. According to him, the writer's task is to change the language of his readers and through this their attitudes and their human and social relations. This process is a slow one, although it reaches far deeper than any political reform.

The writer does not simply choose to write according to his political convictions. (The same is true about religious convictions.) His creative sources are found on deeper levels and cannot easily be commanded. This is why there is in many authors such a marked difference between their political writings and their works of art. Let me quote Sven Delblanc as an instance. In his book about Persia (*Zahak*, 1971), he states once more his belief in political change, but he also speaks of his imagination, which is not willing to obey his reason:

Det finns ett möjligt system för omvandling av världen, och i detta system ser mitt förnuft vår enda möjlighet, vår enda räddning, det enda som är värt det höga namnet humanism. Detta inser och betygar mitt förnuft, medan min känsla och min fantasi hänger fast vid åldriga bilder och sköna, skuldbelastade idoler. Ja, jag är kluven, fördomsfull och krokigt växt, och med all min osäkerhet och vacklan dåligt ägnad att framträda som förkunnare och sanningsvittne.

[There is a possible system for changing the world, and in this system my reason sees our only chance, our only salvation, the only thing worthy of the lofty name of humanism. This is what my reason realizes and professes, while my feeling and my imagination are tied to ancient images and beautiful, guilt-laden idols. Yes, I am divided, prejudiced, and twisted, and, with all my uncertainty and wavering, I am poorly suited to go forth as a preacher and bear witness to the truth.]

Sven Delblanc demands the right to show in his books not only his

political vision of the world, but also the temperament through which
that vision is seen: "Och dessutom trodde jag, att bilden av min egen
kluvenhet, osäkerhet och vacklan kunde vara dem till hjälp, som
befann sig i samma belägenhet som jag" [And, besides, I believed that
the picture of my own dividedness, uncertainty, and wavering might be
of help to those who found themselves in the same predicament as I].[16]
The writer's mind is not simple enough for the job of political propa-
gandist.

Third, there are more factors to be considered here than just the
psychology of artistic creation. Political activities may not be apt for
heroic depiction, due to their complexity. I have described courage as
the moral quality that constitutes heroism. There is one more condition
to be fulfilled: the moral alternatives ought to be clear-cut and simple.
Heroism prefers dichotomies of the type Good versus Bad, God versus
Satan. If there is only *one* absolute norm the moral universe will be
structured by it, as by a magnet. In the personal area, being true to
one's love may serve as such a norm, or being true to one's deepest
conviction. The man or woman who pursues such a goal, whatever the
sacrifice, may be called a hero. In the political field, I would say that
Forssell's Ulyanov, in spite of all the subtleties of the poem, moves in
a world of fundamentally simple alternatives:

Det finns inga skäl för optimism
Det finns inga skäl för pessimism
Det finns skäl för revolution

[There are no reasons for optimism
There are no reasons for pessimism
There are reasons for revolution][17]

Minski, in Delblanc's novel, is unmistakably Satan, and resisting him
is Good. But this is where difficulties begin to appear. *Nattresan* tells
nothing of the ways capitalist and socialist economics function in the
actual world. Minski, the demon of capitalism, is defeated on a stage
that belongs in myth or in opera. There is no way of knowing what
Axel's future struggle might look like, whether it would be carried
out in his native Sweden or in the United States. Of course, he might
still be a hero, but then of a different kind from the one seen in the

novel. Saint George and the dragon are found only in the realm of imagination and myth. But, if the writer prefers to describe a world similar to the one we live in, the knight and the monster will both have to vanish.

Göran Palm's case is of interest here. His *En orättvis betraktelse* (1966), although not a work of fiction, has a quality of passionate anger that makes it a work of art. The writer's moral stance is that of an irate prophet. He sees Evil and Good standing against each other, and he makes no attempt to "understand" Evil. In his most recent book, *Varför har nätterna inga namn?* (1971), the attitude has changed. The writer reports his experiences as a factory worker. He brought with him to his job an arsenal of political concepts, but he soon learned that they did not cover the reality that he found.

När jag börjar på fabriken har jag händerna fulla med tungt vägande ord, alla i bestämd form.
Verkstadsgolvet / Det löpande bandet / Massorna / Proletariatet / Mono-polkapitalet / Klasskampen / Utsugningen / Fackföreningsbyråkratin / Ali-enationen
Dessa ord ska hjälpa mig att se.
Men var ligger verkstadsgolvet, och var går det löpande bandet? Jag ser bara en mängd vanliga golv på vilka en mängd individuellt skötta maskiner står uppställda, i regel utan förbindelse med varandra. Monteringsband saknas. Inte heller ser jag några massor eller något proletariat, bara en mängd människor som vad beträffar ålder, kön, klädedräkt, bakgrund, nationalitet, tänkesätt och allmänt uppträdande är mycket olika varandra; många ser inte ens ut som arbetare. Men hur ser arbetare ut?
Hur jag än spejar i korridorerna ser jag inte till några direktörer, ännu mindre några monopolkapitalister, bara en och annan verkmästare och på sin höjd en ingenjör som varken äger monopol eller kapital. Och klasskam-pen? Den tycks ha styckats upp i tusen och en smärre tvister . . .

[When I start at the factory I have my hands full of heavy, important words, all in capital letters.
　　THE ASSEMBLY LINE
　　THE MASSES
　　THE PROLETARIAT
　　CAPITAL
　　THE CLASS STRUGGLE

EXPLOITATION

UNION BUREAUCRACY

APATHY

These words are supposed to help me see.

But where is the assembly line? I see only a number of individually op-
erated machines, mostly unconnected to each other. There is no conveyer
belt. Nor can I see any masses or any proletariat, only a lot of people who
in age, sex, dress, background, nationality, attitudes, and general behavior
are very different from one another; many of them don't even look like
workers. But what do workers look like?

No matter how I keep my eyes open in the corridors I can't spot any
executives, much less any capitalists, only an occasional foreman and at the
very most an engineer, neither of whom have any capital. And the class
struggle? It seems to have been chopped up into a thousand and one lesser
quarrels . . .]

The concepts of militancy do not fit the facts observed. "Mycket
stämmer *nästan*; ingenting stämmer *riktigt*" ["A lot of things *almost
fit*; nothing really *fits*"].[18] There seems to be little room for a duel
between Saint George and the dragon on the floor of Göran Palm's
workshop.

The realization of the fact that in the realm of politics and economics
moral choices are rarely simple may lead to disillusionment. This is
hardly true of Göran Palm; he is prepared to carry on his political
work. There are others who detest even the dream of simple political
alternatives. Thus, Lars Gyllensten, in an angry rebuttal to an attack
from the revolutionary left, takes up Karl Popper's distinction between
piecemeal politics, on the one hand, and utopianism and perfectionism,
on the other. The attitudes of these ideologies toward social change are
radically different. To the utopian everything that happens in the
present is unimportant, secondary and ephemeral (*underordnat och
efemärt*), as compared to the great goal of a future society. "Stycke-
visa förändringar är lappverk, undanflykter och uppskjutanden av de
revolutionära omstöpningar som fordras" [Piecemeal changes are
nothing but patchwork, evasions and postponements of the revolutionary transformations that are required]. Gyllensten takes sides emphat-

ically with Popper's piecemeal politician. The perfectionist, in his opinion, tends to be inhumanly ruthless.[19]

My task is to discuss not the political implications of these two views, but the artistic ones. A utopian, or perfectionist, view is far more favorable to heroism on a grand scale: here the situation is stripped of its complexities. The piecemeal politician, on the other hand, cannot easily be a Saint George. His goals have to be limited; he looks for the compromises available at the moment and tries to do the best thing possible. The job he does hardly offers a subject to the novelist who looks for heroism, nor can it satisfy the critic who requires heroism.

This leads back to Lukács. In his essay on Tolstoy he sees the absence of positive heroes in fiction as a sign of the disease of the society that produced the fiction. He presupposes here a mirror relation, of a simplistic kind, between society and art. I have suggested several reasons, not taken into account by Lukács, why political heroes are not easily found in modern Swedish fiction. I want particularly to emphasize the fact that moral action of the piecemeal kind seems to have little or no place in Lukács's theory. He tends to see such action as a palliative for a disease for which there is but one cure: revolution.

For someone who does not accept Lukács's political and critical creed, there is no reason against hoping for and expecting meaningful moral action in society. One has to accept the fact that such action tends to be rather unheroic in the aesthetic sense; it may not be depicted in novels at all. It is important then to remember that the absence of political heroism in fiction warrants no conclusion to the effect that moral choice and meaningful action are not possible in today's world. The limitations of art must not determine one's political views and hopes.

NOTES

[1] My presentation is based on a personal selection that may be disputed. I am aware of several omissions, but restriction was necessary in order to make the main pattern

stand out clearly. On the other hand, I believe that most of the texts mentioned here would have to be included in *any* study, however differently conceived, of the hero in modern Swedish fiction.

[2] Eyvind Johnson, *Molnen över Metapontion* (Stockholm: Albert Bonniers Förlag, 1957), p. 404.

[3] Lars Gyllensten, *Lotus i Hades* (Stockholm: Albert Bonniers Förlag, 1966), p. 18.

[4] Lars Gustafsson, " 'Mer än sagor': Antikt mönster i tre moderna svenska diktverk," *Svensk litteraturtidskrift* 1 (1966): 23.

[5] Per Olof Sundman, "Om att övertolka," *Bonniers litterära magasin* 3 (1970): 414–418.

[6] Gunnar Ekelöf, *Diwan över fursten av Emgión* (Stockholm: Albert Bonniers Förlag, 1965), p. 86. English version from W. H. Auden and Leif Sjöberg, trans., *Selected Poems by Gunnar Ekelöf* (New York: Pantheon Books, 1972), p. 69.

[7] Vilhelm Ekelund, *Antikt ideal* (Stockholm: Albert Bonniers Förlag, 1909), p. 172.

[8] P. G. Jersild, in *Dagens nyheter*, September 9, 1960.

[9] See Sven Linnér, "Per Olov Enquists *Legionärerna*," in *Den moderne roman og romanforskning i Norden* (Oslo: Universitetsforlaget, 1971).

[10] Bertrand Russell, *Autobiography II* (London: Allen & Unwin, 1968), p. 110.

[11] Georg Lukács, "Wo ist in dieser Welt Raum zum Handeln? Tolstoi sieht und gestaltet immer mehr eine Welt, in der es für die anständigen Menschen keine Handlungsmöglichkeit mehr gibt" (*Der russische Realismus in der Weltliteratur* [Berlin: Aufbau-Verlag, 1953], p. 221). At the Texas conference, my copanelist Lars Gustafsson stated, with some emphasis, that my interpretation of Lukács was not fair. My answer was, and is, that a presentation of Lukács's theory of realism does not belong in my paper. It served my purpose to take out one strand of thought, found in that theory, and apply it to the Swedish situation.

[12] Jean-Paul Sartre, the famous interview in *Encounter*, June 1964, p. 62.

[13] Jan Myrdal, *Confessions of a Disloyal European* (New York: Pantheon Books, 1968), pp. 190 and 201.

[14] Sara Lidman's play *Märta Märta* (1970) is an allegorical, highly stylized (and of course partial) presentation of the history of the working class in Sweden. The title figure, Märta, is merely an outline of a political heroine. But if any writer, among those now visible on the literary stage, is ever to create a heroic character embodying the ideals of the radical left, it is Sara Lidman.

[15] Birgitta Trotzig, in *Dagens nyheter*, August 6, 1966.

[16] Sven Delblanc, *Zahak* (Stockholm: Albert Bonniers Förlag, 1971), p. 141.

17 Lars Forssell, *Oktoberdikter* (Stockholm: Albert Bonniers Förlag, 1971), p. 64.

18 Göran Palm, *Vaför har nätterna inga namn?* (Stockholm: Norstedts, 1971), p. 71. English translation from *The Swedish Dialogue* (Stockholm: Swedish Institute, 1972).

19 Lars Gyllensten, in *Dagens nyheter*, June 30, 1966. Compare Olof Lagercrantz in his reply to an article by Peter Weiss on Che Guevara: "Vi måste fortsätta empirikernas, revisionisternas, de ständigt upprepade experimentens, upplysningens och resonemangets väg. Ansluter vi oss till Peter Weiss' schematiseringar och 'optimism,' ger vi i själva verket spelet förlorat" [We must continue along the road of the empiricists, the revisionists, of the repeated experiments, the road of enlightenment and reasoning. If we accept the schematizations and the "optimism" of Peter Weiss, we will in fact give up the game] (*Dagens nyheter*, September 14, 1967).

Strindberg as a Forerunner of Scandinavian Modernism

by LARS GUSTAFSSON

University of Texas at Austin

M örk är backen, mörkt är huset—
mörkast dock dess källarvåning—
underjordisk, inga gluggar—
källarhalsen är båd' dörr och fönster—
och därnere längst i mörkret
syns en dynamo som surrar,
så det gnistrar omkring hjulen;
svart och hemsk, i det fördolda
mal han ljus åt hela trakten.

[Dark is that slope, darker is that house—
darkest still its cellar—
subterranean, windowless
the staircase serves as door and window—
and down there deepest in that darkness
is a purring dynamo,
with sparks around its wheels;
black and horrifying, hidden,
it grinds light for the entire neighborhood.][1]

This poem, the third of a cycle called "Gatubilder" [Street scenes] that forms the opening of August Strindberg's *Ordalek och småkonst* [Word play and minor art], from 1902, is a marvelous work. I do not know how many of the different ambiguities once mapped by William Empson can be discerned in it. Certainly Empson's "second-type ambiguity" is there: two or more alternative meanings are fully resolved into one. Also present is the fourth type, in which, according to Empson, "alternative meanings combine to make clear a complicated state of mind in the author." And it might be discussed whether the poem does not also contain an ambiguity of Empson's seventh type: "that of full contradiction, marking a division in the author's mind."[2]

The poem's dark house at the end of a sloping street has been seen before. It might have been in one of those strange paintings by Åke Göransson in Gothenburg at the end of the twenties, where half-unreal streets seem to vibrate in a strange green mist balancing on the very border of the unreal, of surrealism. Or it might have been in the stage design of an early expressionist drama by Pär Lagerkvist. At the end of the sloping street is a dark house; in the cellar of the house—hidden, black, and terrifying—is an electric dynamo with its humming sound, grinding light for the whole area.

The "grinding of light" (*mal ljus*) reminds one slightly of another, much more famous line in Swedish poetry, that strange and ominous "blommorna lutar sig mot natten och lampan spinner ljus," which opens, with a sort of somnambulistic perfection, the first major book of Swedish surrealism, Gunnar Ekelöf's *Sent på jorden*, in 1932.[3] There is, however, a considerable time-lag between Ekelöf's lamp spinning its light in 1932 and that dynamo grinding its light in the dark subterranean room.

It is a well-known fact that Sigmund Freud paid tribute in his *Psychopathologie des Alltagslebens* to August Strindberg for the latter's remarkable anticipation of Freud's concept of subconscious psychic activities.[4] This, as an isolated fact, is not very sensational, for it might be said with greater or lesser conviction about a number of authors that they had observed those facts about internal life to which Freud first gave a name. If it were not known that this poem appeared in 1902, and Freud's "Drei Abhandlungen zur Sexualtheorie" in 1905, it might indeed be a temptation to regard the poem as an almost perfect metaphor of Freud's concept of the libido. This coincidence, however, must be ascribed to the same type of accidental prefiguration that occurs when a Gothic gargoyle happens to be a perfect portrait of a Swedish minister of commerce.

"Gatubilder III" must be judged in its own right. Even then it remains an extraordinary argument for the much too often overlooked facts that poetic modernism was not born out of nothing, and that there is very little of real value in twentieth-century Swedish literature that does not, in one way or another, owe a debt to Strindberg. In the title of my article I have called him "a forerunner of Scandinavian modernism." In order to defend this rather strong expression, I think I must, if not define—a very difficult task—at least explain what I mean by such words as *forerunner* and *modernism*.

The first word leads immediately into that difficult area of literary criticism where one must discuss those vague relationships that obviously hold between different texts, even when it is not possible to speak of an immediate influence. Perhaps it would be better to speak of Strindberg as an "anticipator" rather than as a "forerunner," for saying that somebody "anticipates" something simply means that at a certain moment somebody says or does something, which at a later moment is said or done by somebody else in a manner that has enough similarity to the first occurrence to make it possible to speak about the same thing.

"Anticipator" does not have that very strong taste of causality that one connects with "forerunner." On the other hand, to describe as purely accidental the striking structural and atmospherical similarities between the quoted poem and other poems that would appear thirty years later, in the poetry and dramas of the genuine representatives of Scandinavian modernism, does not do justice to the situation. The main inspirations, for example, for Gunnar Ekelöf's *Sent på jorden* came from French surrealism (from Stravinsky's *Sacre du printemps* and from Mallarmé), from Persian sufic poetry, and from contemporary painting. Swedish modernism in poetry started within a small group of writers in Finland, the most prominent of whom was Edith Södergran (1892–1923). Like most of the writers in the Swedish language in Finland of the period, she took much of her inspiration from the members of the advanced literary circles of Saint Petersburg, who in turn were well informed of what was going on in Paris. So it might be maintained that some of the original impetus to Swedish lyrical modernism took the long detour over the East. German expressionism was important to the expressionistic drama of Pär Lagerkvist, and to his poetry. German expressionism, in its turn, owes a lot to the symbolist drama of August Strindberg, which, in Max Reinhardt's productions, developed its partly hidden properties and proved that a few things not considered possible before actually *were* feasible.

On the level of plain, outright, direct literary influence, if one goes from theory to the complicated realities of literary history, one very often gets the feeling of being lost in a labyrinth of echoes. Inferior authors strongly influence superior ones; young authors influence older and more famous ones (as was the case with Tomas Tranströmer and Hjalmar Gullberg). For example, the dramatic language of Pär Lagerkvist, transformed and conveyed through the workshops of German expressionism, is an echo of Strindberg's language.

Rather often the question of direct influence ultimately proves to be somewhat futile, as, in many cases, the streams of ideas and innovations that form a period in the major flow of literature seem to take on a stochastic, rather than individual, form of causality. The really interesting question is not so much "Who influenced whom?" but rather "What, of certain significance in the work, is it that made later achievements possible?" In this formulation of the question Strindberg is a forerunner of Scandinavian modernism: he made many later achievements possible.

He did this by creating a Swedish that nobody after him could ignore, a rich, nervous, explosive idiom, popular and, at the same time, sophisticated. Still more important, perhaps, this idiom is far removed from the official language of his own period. The language of the Swedish Academy and the language of contemporary criticism were, in different respects, the dialects of that centralistic, hypocritical power machinery which had successfully occupied Swedish literature as early as the eighteenth century and had turned the use of literary expression into one of those activities that the state could approve or disapprove of and control, as Bo Bennich-Björkman has proved in his well-documented study *Författaren i ämbetet*.[5]

Strindberg's appearance on the Swedish literary scene, from *Röda rummet* (1879) to the very end, marks a decisive turn in the long history of official dominance over Swedish literature. Like Ola Hansson from Sweden, Henrik Ibsen from Norway, and Georg Brandes from Denmark, Strindberg spent part of his life in exile, and in one sense his language could be described as one of exile, of opposition. It has the clarity and directness that results from one's refusal to commit oneself to the standards or the values of official Oscarian society, and in its very exile from Oscarian values it returns to the sources, to the popular, to the vulgar—in the best possible sense of the word—values of spoken Swedish. The power source is in its antirhetoric.

Strindberg's Swedish is a language freed from German idealism and the soft hypocrisy of early nineteenth century pietism, and he created it by introducing into Swedish literature a property that has very often since then been called his "reckless subjectivity" but in reality is much more complicated. Using himself as an instrument of experience and wielding that instrument far beyond the limits anybody before him in Scandinavian literature had dared to imagine, he made possible an expression of experience that had earlier not existed in that literature, refusing, characteristically, to regard the exterior world as entirely exterior and the interior as entirely interior. With this observation *anticipation* has become *modernism*.

Literary modernism is, in my view, much too often described as a syntactic phenomenon. Certainly there does exist a modernist syntax, even a modernist vocabulary that can actually be measured by investigations of word frequencies. Still, the syntactic aspect of modernism remains—perhaps for pedagogical reasons—a very exaggerated one, and, more important, it tends to blur the most essential fact about modernism: that it has a mentality. Modernism is not only, not even primarily, a formal movement; it is also a change in the mind. Maurice Maeterlinck and August Strindberg, in the nineties, are both considered to be symbolists. But what a huge difference one finds between them as soon as one passes from purely stylistic aspects to intrinsic ones!

It is time to return to the poem quoted at the beginning. Some properties are evident, such as the almost desperate contrast of deep darkness and sharp light, and the subjectivity that seems to make the external world part of a bigger context, perhaps even the occult. Or, if the scheme is inverted, there is described something seemingly belonging to the external world that essentially is a description of something else, something threatening and dark that produces light out of its very darkness.

Nothing is done to lessen this ambiguity; no reasons are presented to assist one in the confrontation with this obvious conflict. In this poem the world is described as ambiguous. The poem lacks any attempt to interpret what is seen: the world *is* ambiguous. Observation and emotion form a totality in the poem, the totality of classical European modernism.

The traditional approach to Strindberg has been psychological. There are different reasons for this, one being simply that his literary judges, for quite a long time, were people so completely different from himself. Those judges include not only such massive rocks of misunderstanding as C. D. af Wirsén and Fredrik Böök, but also gentler spirits like Martin Lamm.

The first critical portraits of Strindberg were drawn by people who were either openly hostile, like Böök and Wirsén, or those, like Lamm, who were in principle much more understanding, yet comparatively restricted to conventional views as to what was possible and advisable within human experience.

It remains a highly disputable question whether the right approach to *Inferno*, for example, is a psychopathological one. I think, in any case, it can be stated that no such analysis is needed in order to make that novel understandable. Strindberg's *Inferno* does not need psychiatry to any greater extent than does Dante's. Very much of what, in Strindberg's own time, was understood as psychological "crisis" and left that stamp on his official image for a considerable period can be explained in terms of literary form, rather than psychological peculiarity, and becomes, in the light of modernism, syntax rather than neurosis. This, of course, excludes neither the possibility of psychoneurotic or even psychopathological peculiarities in Strindberg's internal make-up, nor the possibility that investigations in this area might shed light upon certain points in his work.

Through use of Occam's principle, which is, perhaps, too rarely applied in literary research, it ought first to be asked what can be made understandable from literary facts alone, without resort to psychological analysis. This principle holds for a number of Strindberg's works.

In every verbal relationship some things must come into clear focus, while others must be described in a vaguer manner; every epic has a center of interest and a periphery. Proust, in his *Recherche*, for example, cannot describe all his characters with the same intensity and detailed attention. Some persons occupy the center of attention—quite a few—and the rest remain on the periphery. This position in the center of attention, of course, can be inhabited by various people as a long novel goes on, and, while the focus of the novel can be moved from one thing to another, it still remains a focus. To a much higher degree this holds true for such parts of the relationship as room interiors, landscapes, and various other elements.

This fact—that is, that the novel has a focus that can be occupied by different persons and things and that can change more or less as the story goes on—has, of course, a close connection with the linear character of verbal works of art: verbal relationships cannot, like maps or pictures, say everything at the same time.

The center of attention can be treated, changed, and manipulated in various ways: for example, something can be moved into focus that at the outset did not seem to belong there. Some detail that—conventionally—ought to belong to the marginal aspects of the action is moved into the focus of interest, becomes, so to speak, contaminated by the general flow and atmosphere of the action, and affects the entire reading. Too, the introduction of unexpected, seemingly extraneous material into the focus can have different effects: the reader can perceive the new element as a part of the action—as when unexpected details prove to have significance in a detective story. Or the reader may come to the conclusion that the action has a much larger range than expected. He may get the impression that the intrigue that has already been described is merely a part of a much vaster one, a plot that proves, in the final analysis, to be part of a metaphysical context.

This device plays a very important role in Strindberg's later works.

There may be a psychological explanation, but much more obvious is the fact that it marks a change in his composition.

The Chamber Plays provide many examples of this device. An example is the following passage in *Svarta handsken*, in which exterior details suddenly are drawn into the focus of attention, seem to become alive, and seem to imply a much broader intrigue than has been described from the outset of the drama:

Ellen.	Man skulle verkligen kunna tro på tomten, för ibland hittar man inte en sak där man lagt den: ibland går en dörr i baklås, ibland kommer det varmt vatten ur kallvattensröret—
Portvakten	[lystrar]. Är det någon härinne? Jag tyckte det skramla i nyckeltavlan—
Tomten	[gömmer sig].
Portvakten	[letar i nycklarne]. Jag tror att fan har blandat om nycklarna. —Här sitter 25: an på 13! och 17 på 81! Och grosshandlarns brevkort sitter på häradshövdingens! Och alltid talas det i trapporna: De grälar och gråter men när jag kommer ut, så finns där ingen.—
[*Ellen.*	One could really start believing in elves, for sometimes you do not find a thing where you have put it: sometimes a door gets jammed, sometimes hot water comes out of the cold water pipe . . .
The Porter	(listening). Is anybody there? I thought I heard some sound from the key-cupboard—
The Brownie	(hides).
The Porter	(searching among the keys). I think the Devil himself has mixed the keys. Here twenty-five is on thirteen! and seventeen on eighty-one! And the wholesale dealer's postcard in the judge's box: They quarrel and cry, but when I come out, nobody is there.][6]

This is, on the level of narrative structure, the imprint of that dominating idea of Strindberg's later years, which he summarizes under the heading *Makterna* [The powers]. In *Inferno* one can study this consequent manipulation of focus in detail.

It is remarkable how much *Inferno* has in common with the poetry of the early Ekelöf and the early Lundkvist, but it is possible to see the similarity only if one ceases to regard modernism as an idiom and turns to it, instead, as a structural property of literature. In a very special sense, the world view of lyrical modernism has a totalistic trend. Ungaretti's one-line poem, "M'illumino d'immenso," is more than a poem: it is the shortest aesthetic program ever written. Modernism's poetry seems very often to work toward a totality, a horizonless unity of interior and exterior, of time past and time present.

The three articles published in *Le Figaro* in the late autumn of 1894 under the heading "Sensations détraquées" are remarkable, well-known documents, later published by Strindberg in Swedish translation as "Förvirrade sinnesintryck" [Confused perceptions] in *Tryckt och otryckt IV* [Printed and unprinted IV] (1897). Hans Lindström, in his fine study *Hjärnornas kamp* [The duel of the brains],[7] has drawn attention to this piece of prose, which forms a sort of very free account of reflections and perceptions during several days spent in Paris and Versailles. Lindström stresses the connection between the interest in fragments of perceived, subjective reality in this essay and similar interests in contemporary French literature, such as those found, for example, in the work of Paul Bourget.

This interest in a fragmentized perceptual reality is, however, not the only interesting thing about "Förvirrade sinnesintryck." Still more fascinating is the way of dealing with subjectivity as such in this piece of prose. It contains, for example, a passage in which Strindberg describes the strange acoustic properties of the castle of Versailles, where it seems as if crowds of people can be heard although the place is almost empty. Suddenly Strindberg poses the question whether it is not, after all, himself he hears:

Som jag står och lutar mig mot muren, varseblir jag, att marmorgården bildar hörselgången till ett stort öra, vars mussla bildas av byggnadens flyglar. Medryckt av denna nya fantasi och glad att ha kommit på denna bisarra föreställning, att jag befinner mig som en loppa i örat på en jätte, lyssnar jag tätt intill väggen . . . Vilken överraskning! . . . Jag hör! Jag hör ett mullrande hav, folkhopar som kvida, övergivna hjärtan, vilkas slag pumpa upp ett utmattat blod, nerver som brista med en liten klanglös knall, snyftningar, skratt och suckar! . . .

Jag frågar mig om detta icke är subjektiva sinnesintryck, om det icke är mig själv jag hör.

[As I stand, leaning against the wall, I find that the marble court is the auditory duct of a huge ear, and that the wings of the building are the cochlea of that ear. Inspired by this new image and glad to have come to this bizarre idea that I am situated as a louse in the ear of a giant, I start listening, close to the wall . . . What a surprise! . . . I hear! I hear the thunder of oceans, crowds of crying people, deserted hearts, pumping an exhausted blood, nerves that burst with a little flat thrust, sobs, laughs, and sighs! . . .

I ask myself if these are not subjective impressions, if it is not myself I hear.][8]

This passage might be compared with Ekelöf's lines in *Färjesång*:

Det brusar i ådrorna, det skälver i nerverna men du är tyst.
Du rätar omärkligt på dig.
Du höjer dig sakta på tå.
Du lyfter dig upp till hans ögon.
Du ser hur syn och landskap plånar ut varann:
Den eviga fixeringsbilden.

[There is a surge in the blood vessels,
there is a reverberation in the nerves,
but you remain silent.
Imperceptibly you draw yourself up,
slowly you rise on your toes.
You elevate yourself up to his eyes.
You see how sight and landscape obliterate each other:
The eternal puzzle-picture.][9]

It is known from Arnold Schönberg's correspondence that one of the decisive impulses sending him into the realm of atonality and, especially, an impetus to his Drei Stücke für Orchester, was his reading of the German version of Strindberg's *Jakob brottas*.[10] This may seem strange if it is not remembered that what is often perceived as "subjectivity" in Strindberg's works from *Inferno* onward is more than a personal peculiarity: it is also a compositional principle. What from a "psychological" point of view might appear to be a perspective of the individual involved in an internal drama—a fight with invisible powers—becomes, on a formal level, something different. It becomes a major change in the arrangement of narrative perspectives, a new sort of use of realistic observation, by which that which is observed is not transformed into metaphor but is *born* as metaphor, because the world itself is not a passive *materia* but an intense agent in the drama of the mind.

Strindberg's development from *I havsbandet* to *Inferno* is a continuous one, his naturalism a necessary condition of his symbolism, for his symbolism is also, in a rather strict sense, based on observation. The method of *Inferno* might thus be described as the naturalism of Zola, applied to an internal world.

The very paradigm of anticipation of modernism, and especially surrealism, is, of course, *Ett drömspel* [*A Dream Play*] (1902).[11] The parallels are so many and appear already on such a trivial level that they do not really seem to be worth much hunting. There is that strange figure, Indra's daughter, forerunner of a new type of female personality that will play such an important role in the surrealistic writing after Apollinaire, culminating, perhaps, in André Breton's Nadja and Mikhail Bulgakov's Margarita. And there is the dream technique, finding its most appropriate expression, perhaps, in that famous trefoil hole in the door, which remains the same whether the door belongs to a house, a church, or a cabinet in the lawyer's office.

Gösta Bergman, in his excellent work on the breakthrough of modern theater, *Den moderna teaterns genombrott, 1890–1925,* makes the observation that the first performance of *A Dream Play* in Stockholm might have changed the entire course of modern Swedish theater history if the exterior means of the performance had been adequate to the text.[12] Of course, it *did* change the history of Swedish theater nonetheless, although the road had to be a longer one. The deepest influence of *A Dream Play* in Swedish literature was indirectly conveyed through the general modernist movement in Europe. This indirect influence is symptomatic of Strindberg's double role in Scandinavian literature from modernism onward. He exists as an obvious fact. His influence on all Swedish drama after him is obvious. His influence on literary language and especially on the language of Swedish prose, too, is obvious. But he exists as a hidden influence, as well as a part of that slow, enormous movement in art which, after the Second World War, in successive steps turns into modernism.

In order to be able to evaluate this fact, one must somehow approach the general problems of literary modernism, which, of course, in one way or another include some sort of modern evaluation. Very much has been said about this topic, and yet very much remains obscure. With all the necessary caveats due to such a difficult subject, modernism must, after all, be regarded as a unique major movement in the arts, with enough peculiar properties to sort it out from any other period. Between the clowns of Picasso's blue period and the frivolous trumpet in Stravinsky's *Petrushka*, between the poetry of Apollinaire and Eliot's *Waste Land*, or Erik Lindegren's "broken" sonnets in *mannen utan väg*, there is a subtle kinship.

What is it, except the nearness in time and the very name of modernism, that makes one recall these very different works of art as if they were parts of one and the same context? Of course there cannot be one single property that unites them, but rather something like the similarities among different members of a big family, in which, in spite of all differences, the similarities and continuities from one member to another are close enough to form a chain. Heresy, whether in a religious, political, or aesthetic sense, is very often found in the chain of modernism. An inclination toward the idea of the work of art as a *total* expression of man's place in the world and of his conditions of life is another link in the chain.

In the work of Strindberg—I think especially of *Inferno*, *Ett drömspel* [*A Dream Play*], and *En blå bok* [*A Blue Book*]—all these links of the chain are already present but ordered, as it were, in a different pattern, a pattern still dictated by major nineteenth-century forms. An experiment in thought that might throw some light upon this would be simply to ask what a drama like *A Dream Play* would look like, deprived of its title and all the explicit references to dream reality. As a matter of fact it would not be very much changed, for the dream atmosphere of the drama is an intrinsic quality, more or less concealed behind the external purpose of creating something like a series of dreams. The final ambition of *A Dream Play* is not to say something about dreams but to say something about ordinary life in the grammar of dreams.

In this respect *A Blue Book*[13] becomes very interesting. It has always been poorly understood and still is to quite an extent, a main difficulty being its classification according to genre. Seen as science, it is obviously mad. And at the same time it seems much too scientific to be able to pass as poetry in prose. From the point of view of the history of ideas, it seems rather clear that *A Blue Book* belongs to that same large wave of doubt about rational science, concern for mysticism, and renewed interest in Swedenborg that produced in Paris at that period such very different and still kindred products as Joris-Karl Huysmans's *Là-Bas* in 1891, or Gérard Encausse's *Traité méthodique de magie pratique*. The period did have an inclination to occultism so striking that it cannot be explained simply as an accidental expression of fin de siècle. The historical roots remain partly obscure, but it remains a fact that Strindberg not only took part in the ideas of this strange movement with fascinated interest, but even paid visits to the house of Encausse, who must be considered an extremist in the movement.

A Blue Book must be regarded not so much as a series of books in science, but as a series of books about science, expressing a refusal to accept the rational system of science as a whole. They differ very much from the works of Huysmans and Encausse and all the other contemporary French irrationalists in one very important respect: Zola, having read *Là-Bas*, described the book as a deathblow against naturalism, whereas Strindberg's reflections in *A Blue Book*—they may attempt to explain the synthesis of gold or to disprove the existence of the corn crake—always remain naturalistic.

As in *Inferno*, the change from naturalistic claims of objectivity to "symbolist" "subjectivity" never affects Strindberg's insistence upon observation as the fundamental method. Strindberg is not a naturalist writer who turns symbolist at the end of the eighties, but the naturalist of symbolism.

Somewhere here lies the key to Strindberg's ultimate role in Scandinavian modernism. Gunnar Ekelöf always protested zealously if anyone tried to describe *Sent på jorden* as surrealist poetry. The question whether it is surrealistic or not remains, perhaps, open for discussion. But Ekelöf certainly had an important point in insisting upon his independence from continental surrealism, and that is a point closely connected to the role of exterior observation in Strindberg's *A Blue Book.*

The mainstream of Scandinavian modernism, especially in its effects on Swedish poetry, always remained very close to this combination of the absurd and detailed observation. One can see this very clearly in the late poetry of Birger Sjöberg. Even Lindegren, with his strange combination of a big cantabile and a fragmentized form, retains this matter-of-fact attitude.

In Pär Lagerkvist's *Det eviga leendet,* there is a remarkable passage that through the years has retained its original freshness, its striking dramatic effect, and that might serve as a sort of emblem to the whole of Scandinavian modernism. It is that marvelous scene at the end of the story, where the dead, after such a long march in the dark, after so much suffering in their dark, anguished, fragmentized reality, at last get to see God. What they find is a very small, rather trivial, friendly old man, busily occupied, hewing his firewood for the winter.[14]

If August Strindberg had been able to see that scene he would have smiled—a smile of recognition.

NOTES

[1] [All references to Strindberg's work are to his *Samlade skrifter* (*SS*), ed. John Landquist (Stockholm: Albert Bonniers Förlag, 1912–1921). The year of the original edition is given within parentheses.] August Strindberg, "Gatubilder III," from *Ordalek och småkonst* (1902), *SS*, vol. 37, p. 233. (English versions are my translations.)

[2] See William Empson, *Seven Types of Ambiguity: A Study of Its Effects in English Verse* (Norfolk: New Directions, 1953), p. vi.

[3] Gunnar Ekelöf, *Sent på jorden: Dikter 1927–31* (Stockholm: Albert Bonniers Förlag, 1932), p. 2.

[4] Sigmund Freud, *Gesammelte Schriften*, vol. 4, *Zur Psychopathologie des Alltagslebens* (Vienna: Internationaler Psychoanalytischer Verlag, 1924), p. 236: "Von all den Dichtern, die sich gelegentlich über die kleinen Symptomhandlungen und Fehlleist-

ungen geäussert oder sich ihrer bedient haben, hat keiner deren geheime Natur mit solcher Klarheit erkannt und dem Sachverhalt eine so unheimliche Belebung gegeben wie Strindberg, dessen Genie bei solcher Erkenntnis allerdings durch tiefgehende psychische Abnormität unterstützt wurde" [Of all the authors who have occasionally expressed themselves concerning, or made use of, smaller symptomatic behavior or mental slips, none has recognized their secret nature with such clarity and given such great liveliness to the state of affairs as Strindberg, whose genius in such recognition was indeed supported by profound psychic abnormality].

[5] Bo Bennich-Björkman, *Författaren i ämbetet* (Uppsala: Svenska Bokförlaget, 1970).

[6] Strindberg, *Svarta handsken* (1909), SS, vol. 45, p. 304.

[7] Hans Lindström, *Hjärnornas kamp: Psykologiska idéer och motiv i Strindbergs åttiotalsdiktning* (Stockholm: Almgvist and Wiksell, 1952).

[8] Strindberg, SS, vol. 27, pp. 604–605.

[9] Gunnar Ekelöf, "Demon och ängel," in *Dikter* (Stockholm: Albert Bonniers Förlag, 1965), p. 134.

[10] Professor H. H. Stuckenschmidt, Berlin, in letters to the author January 20, 1972, and January 28, 1972.

[11] Strindberg, *Ett drömspel* (1902), SS, vol. 36.

[12] Gösta Bergman, *Den moderna teaterns genombrott, 1890–1925* (Stockholm: Svenska Bokförlaget, 1966), p. 275.

[13] Strindberg, *En blå bok*, vols. 1–4 (1907, 1908, 1912), SS, vols. 46–48.

[14] Pär Lagerkvist, *Det eviga leendet* (Stockholm: Albert Bonniers Förlag, 1962), p. 113.

Strindberg and the Theater

by INGVAR HOLM

University of Lund (Sweden)

I will confine my theme to an investigation of style done at my theater department in Lund. The work was originally directed toward those concepts in the history of literary style commonly known as *naturalism, symbolism, expressionism,* and *absurdism,* and the dramas usually labeled by these terms.

We in the department decided to work with these four styles by turning to the manifestoes and journals that publicized the style in question during any respective period. From the manifestoes we took names of plays said in these articles to be representative of one of the respective styles. When we had obtained enough references to plays, we chose thirty of the most frequently mentioned dramas for each style and made a rigorous, systematic, and quantitative analysis of their texts. (This method is known as content analysis in communications research.)

I will address myself to the results of an analysis of this kind made on various expressionist texts and a number of Strindberg plays. We set the hypothetical period for expressionism in the theater as the fifteen years between 1910 and 1925.

The manifestoes that we used for selecting the thirty expressionist plays consisted partly of program explanations, partly of reviews, essays, and yearbooks dedicated to expressionism, and partly of handbooks and dissertations from the years 1910 to 1925. This last group came from within the context of the history of literature and discussed expressionism under pronounced positive biases.

The same type of analysis was carried out with Strindberg's dramas. Resemblances and differences between Strindberg's methods and the four styles were analyzed from an ideological, social, and historical point of view.

I will not discuss our method of research in this matter—above all not the numbers in the content analysis; I will mention only some notes to that part of the total research associated with the question of Strindberg and expressionism. It is our experience that a certain similarity exists between Strindberg's plays and those of the expressionists. The expressionist playwrights also made special mention of the name of Strindberg. He, more than others, was pointed out as the forerunner of expressionism.

True to form, the Strindberg in whom the expressionists believed they had discovered a young revolutionary and nihilist was wildly irregular in his artistic work. Rudolf Kayser speaks of him in *Das Junge Deutsche Drama* as a background figure to the youth who "had built barricades against naturalism"; they had "experienced Strindberg and his undelivered suffering, a male iconoclast and impudent titan."[1]

The members of the youth movement created Strindberg in their own image. He was an iconoclast and a revolutionary, and his milieu a breeding ground for naked despair. Support for this view was sought in Adolf Paul's influential biography of Strindberg, written as early as the nineties, and in other early literature on the playwright. The surest signs of expressionist affiliation, however, were to be found in his own dramas.[2]

To Damascus, with the parts The Stranger, The Lady, The Beggar, The Mother Superior, and The Confessor, and the various collectively appearing "forms and shadows," begins on a street corner. A funeral procession approaches and recedes again into the distance. On the corner The Stranger and The Lady meet. Funeral attendants appear but they seem unreal. Something is wrong and out of place. In the dress of the funeral processioners the black of mourning has been exchanged for brown. The Lady draws down her veil of mourning to hide her face and hastily kisses The Stranger on the mouth. "From inside the church is heard a chorus, almost a wailing, of female voices. The illumined rose window quickly darkens, the tree over the bench trembles," and so on.[3]

The rest of the later Strindberg plays deal with the same type of material. People chase each other in the closed tower room in *The Dance of Death* or in the drawing room of *The Ghost Sonata*. Images of ghosts appear in full clearness in *The Bridal Crown*; in *Advent*, there is a patch of light that dances on a mausoleum wall long past sunset. A procession of shades glides by: Death with his scythe and hourglass, the beheaded sailor with his head in his hands. "Are they shadows, or ghosts, or our own bad dreams?" asks a terrified character.[4] Nightmares and realities blend into a terrifying chaos. Trivialities crop up. The evil mother in *The Pelican* drinks the bouillon while her family eats the overcooked meat. In *A Dream Play* one character is constantly attacking another with domestic terror. It would be easy to continue citing examples.

In the plays of the expressionists, Strindberg's vignettes are accented with violence: death by electrocution, or hanging on the stage, or a leap through the window; murder resulting from a fight over food; wildly ecstatic religious fervor. These vignettes, as well as the stereotyped nameless roles, chorus lines, and visions of ghosts, are usual in the plays of the expressionists.

Some critical observations should be made here. The similarities between Strindberg and the expressionists, both those that caused the expressionists to choose Strindberg as their idol and those studied later by literary historians, are almost always on a clearly visible but superficial level. It is just as misleading to speak of Strindberg as an "obstinate male" or an "impudent titan" as it is to interpret the aberrant situations in his dramas as extravagancies of fancy.

There are certain observations that one can make on the basis of the total picture of his activities, as they are reflected in his letters, his marital conflicts, and his relationship to his friends. Strindberg was egocentric, but his consistent self-absorption included at the same time a discipline. All his activities were controlled by one single relationship: that of Strindberg to himself. This control guaranteed a coherence and a severity to his conceptions. The most obvious difference between him and the expressionists is the absence of anarchistic elements in Strindberg. It is above all in the theater, among directors, actors, and stage designers, that this fact has been observed.

It will be useful to remember that the early plays of Strindberg, those from the early eighties, are characterized not by fancy but by consistency of psychological realism. One example is *Miss Julie*, the most typical play in this style and one that turned out to have just those rich possibilities for role variation that a good drama should have. In Paris, in 1887, it was played with gritty earthiness. In Swedish productions it has occasionally been done with a raging cyclonic fury or, in other cases, in the still, luminescent atmosphere of a Swedish midsummer night (1st and 2nd plates).

As an example of some of the possibilities for variation, one Japanese Miss Julie performed some sort of local hand-clapping ritual the morning after the sinful act, while Jean stropped the razor that was to be the suicidal instrument; and the piece of Western literature that Kristin, dressed for church, had under her arm was not the Bible but rather a copy of *Thus Spake Zarathustra* (3rd plate).

In Brazil one could see a passionate Latin Miss Julie (4th plate), and in India a sultry and realistic seduction (5th plate). Argentine film makers conjured up a kitchen setting clearly fit for any nobleman, stuck away in the "frigid Scandinavian valleys" (6th plate).

As far as Sweden is concerned, *Miss Julie* was the entrance cue for psychological realism on stage. Strindberg has directly analyzed the concept in a preface to the play in which he points out the difference between the internal and external causes of the behavior of his figures.[5]

In the same preface, Strindberg makes what for his time was a sensational statement about the function of the set design. The stage environment should be such that the audience believes in it, he says, but first and foremost it should be so convincing that the actors who move about between its walls and among its props should be able to believe in it, experience it as real and correct. The burden of realism is assigned to the consciousness of the interpreter instead of being placed on the physically enclosed space. Before the audience can be expected to have a deeper sensation of reality, the actors must be capable of making it

Inga Tidblad and Ulf Palme as Julie and Jean in Olof Molander's famous production of *Miss Julie* at the Royal Dramatic Theater in Stockholm during the Strindbergsjubileet (1949). (Courtesy Institute for Drama Research, Lund)

Inger Liljefors and Carl Åke Eriksson as two modern youths in *Miss Julie* (Malmö, 1967). (Courtesy Institute for Drama Research, Lund)

Kaneko Lwasaki as Miss Julie, Tatsuya Nakadai as Jean (Tokyo, 1958). (Gunnar
Ollén, *Strindbergs dramatik*)

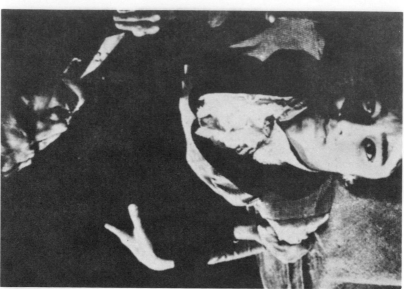

Miss Julie in European costume (Bombay, 1961). Staged by E. Alkazi. (Ingvar Holm, *Drama på scen*)

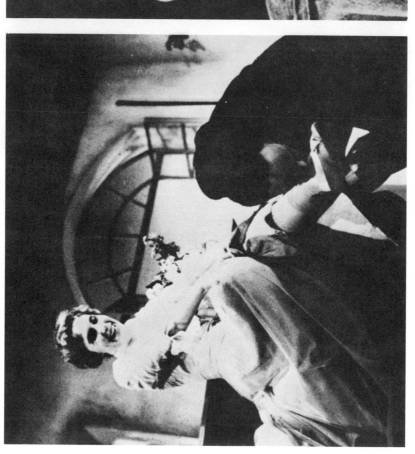

Ana Edler and Antonio Patino in *Miss Julie* (Salvador, Brazil, 1958). (Gunnar Ollén, *Strindbergs dramatik*)

Argentinean film, *Miss Julie* (1947), with Amelia Bence in the title role. (Gunnar Ollén, *Strindbergs dramatik*)

Same as in previous plate. (Courtesy Institute for Drama Research, Lund)

Ingmar Bergman's Malmö production of *The Ghost Sonata* (1954), with Benkt-Åke Benktsson as Hummel. With his 350-pound frame he moved about the stage in much the same fashion as Gordon Craig's supermarionette. (Courtesy Institute for Drama Research, Lund)

Above, premiere of *To Damascus* (1902), with Harriet Bosse and August Palme. *Below*, with Lars Hanson and Märta Ekström; staging by Olof Molander (1937). Both productions at the Royal Dramatic Theater. (Courtesy Institute for Drama Research, Lund)

plausible that they experience the scenic space as an authentic room, an environment necessary to the play.

This idea shows a Stanislavskian concept ten years before Stanislavsky. The most scrupulous of the realistic directors in the twentieth century adhere to these early ideas in Strindberg's theater. These ideas continue through the next stage of Strindberg's development.

The close of the nineteenth century was a time of realistic depiction, but it was also a period when the old view of man as a beautifully balanced, harmonious, and rational being began to be torpedoed. Authors and philosophers sought out regions alien to human experience, investigations into mental illness revealed a dark side of the mind, and the "subconscious" became a concept.

Around 1890 Strindberg began, with scientific ambition, to study such related problems. Brimming with curiosity and prepared to apply what he had learned, he studied in Paris under the auspices of Professors Charcot, Ribot, and Bernheim. The significance of the situation becomes apparent when I mention that in the very same lecture hall and under the same teachers there was a certain young medical student from Vienna who was also soaking up material for later use. That student was Sigmund Freud. But even before the father of psychoanalysis had systematized his views, Strindberg, going on his own introspections, hunted up the secret symbols of the psyche, the repressed dreads and desires of the subconscious. The French teachers and forerunners of psychoanalysis had given him instruments and a plan for his hunting.

The view of humanity that came to be perhaps the most fertile of ideas for twentieth-century fiction was actually anticipated in Strindberg's dramas dating from the years around 1900. In *A Dream Play* (1901) and other plays of that time, the ongoing flow of reality arranged itself in the syntax of dreams, with impacted and convoluted sequences of events, significant similarities, and the appearance of a new and deeper logic than that of waking life. In these plays lies the explanation for why, even today, Strindberg seems so modern. The very latest theater, the new surrealism and the theater of the absurd, has already been anticipated in these plays.

The plays from the time of psychical revelations are somewhat obscure. The characters of *The Ghost Sonata* are a rather sorry lot. In the haunted house of the play, The Colonel carries a noble name, but his title of colonel is false and his noble name is a mistake, and he is not the father of his presumed daughter. Pull off his wig, pluck out the false teeth, shave off the moustache, and unlace his whalebone corset, and all that remains is a former chamber servant. A similar kind of deception is true of his wife and the girl among her flowers in the "Hyacinth Room."

The play is one long revelation, a theater that from beginning to end is a glimpse into the soul. People are unveiled, the death shroud is pulled over them, and life comes to an end (7th and 8th plates).

"There is a moral standpoint in a camera angle" is Godard's often-quoted phrase. This statement is one of the most important things that have been said about the art of film. There is a moral standpoint in a gesture, a tone of voice, a choice of roles, an accent of lighting, or a color in a décor. To speak of drama without bearing this in mind is an absurdity.

Strindberg's later dramas demanded their own style, their own theater. The old theater, with its rigid arrangement of characters before a painted backdrop, was entirely insufficient for the later Strindberg plays. In a production from 1902, the initial performance of Strindberg's *To Damascus*, the meeting on the beach between The Lady and The Stranger is illustrative (9th plate). All productions of the era looked like this, but in Strindberg's dramas, or rather in this production from the first years of the century, there was a throbbing beneath the surface, different from what is being expressed above. In order to interpret what was going on in the soul, a new condensation and concentration was required, a reanalysis of the essentials. There was once an acting art of expressionistic Strindberg mold in the theater of Sweden, Germany, and other countries. It was known that he was a troublemaker, a blasphemer, and a misogynist, and that his dialogues fairly sizzled with emotional violence. As a result a special "Strindberg style" was formed: as soon as the actor got a Strindberg part he pulled down the corners of his mouth, dropped his voice into the bass range, rolled his eyes, gnashed his teeth, and in general carried on like a sex murderer from an old opera or melodrama. The women remade themselves into venomous vampires, beautiful gleaming beasts of prey with long claws and forked tongues.

Strindberg's dramas, however, required something more than just this approach. *To Damascus*, for instance, was written long before high-voltage lamps and cloud projectors had begun to be a part of theater equipment and long before modern textual interpretation and a new expressive acting style had become an ideal. But Strindberg's dramas demanded a new style and stimulated the formation and acceptance of this new style. A picture from the Royal Dramatic Theater in Stockholm, from 1937 (10th plate), shows precisely the same situation seen before, except that here the drama has achieved a new and adequate space to operate in. The figures are no longer propped up in an additive relationship, woman plus man, but are instead forced into a structure of subordinate and superordinate, of dominance and submission. The space is indicated with a few essential details—a beacon light, a half-sunken full-rigger that provides a symbolic Golgotha scene with the three crosses—and for the rest only space, an accentuated space. The characters are no longer two persons engaged in a dialogue—they are signs in a dream or in a guilty mind.

When Olof Molander, the most well known Strindberg director, created his widely admired staging of *A Dream Play*, he proceeded from the assumption that it was a dream, but also from his knowledge of the author's milieu and biographical situation. Allusions to Strindberg were boldly underlined in the three key roles: The Poet, The Officer, and The Lawyer. All these three were played in the type of "Strindberg facial mask" cited earlier. Molander also used as a starting point Strindberg's own understanding of dreams as phenomena. Strindberg has described how in his plays he "sought to reproduce the disconnected but apparently logical form of a dream." A dream is "a medley of memories, experiences, unuttered fancies, absurdities, and improvisations. The characters split, multiply, vanish . . ." For the dreamer "there are no secrets, no incongruities, no scruples, and no law."[6]

The words about dreams are quite striking, but not the declaration that there are no laws and no consistency. The very point of Strindberg's *Dream Play* is consistency in emotion and expression, a coupling of the two, in fact.

Olof Molander also strove to obtain this consistency and, like Strindberg, turned to psychoanalysis to find his way. Molander's correspondence with one of his stage designers in a production of *A Dream Play* is characteristic. Molander relates, in an earlier dialogue between himself and the stage designer, "the thought that perhaps we could arrange it with fewer details, but let it 'reappear' again and again, perpetually. Perhaps we could have the details more or less on stage all the time. What would you think of an arrangement that was partly a revolving stage, partly special wagons, partly hangings, more or less visible? One should in that case ignore all traditional works of illusion and go in for the irrational in the dream world, which is first seen with the fire of the castle."[7]

However, it should be observed that Molander's view here is also fundamentally based upon biographical information. The dream is expressed through masks, accents, and images. The dreamer himself and his situation are carried over to the spectator. The environment around Strindberg and his private conflicts, which had been revealed earlier by literary researchers, made endless appearances on the stage. For the Swedish audience the Molander productions became a conquest of Strindberg. At the same time they tempted danger in a violent way. The audience began to learn too much about the man. He himself as a person began to be too much in the center of interest.

Every country has at some time experienced something equivalent to native classics. In *A Dream Play*, the psychological picture of the poet contained so many strange characteristics that it slowly became caricature. *A Dream Play* gives undeniable key scenes: Poor Strindberg liked red cabbage and couldn't taste it! And all that about crooked candles and untidy curtains! Oh, what a pity about Strindberg!

In this context Molander's Gothenburg staging from 1946 was a little step on the way to discovering *A Dream Play* as a work of an anonymous poet with an appeal to a new era. In the final scene one could see, in that performance, a large wooden cross, but also a background of black ruins. It was a vignette of postwar Europe that had entered on the stage. *A Dream Play* had been removed one step from the poet's situation as a private person, and at the same time the main theme, "What a pity about people," acquired once more a topical application.

The consistency that depends on the intense personal experience of the author is one of the conditions of *A Dream Play*. But this very consistency is also the best help when new directors and new audiences have to use the plays, use them on a new historical occasion to make them instruments in a new world, a new ideological situation.

In the spring of 1955, the German director Oscar Fritz Schuh stage-managed *A Dream Play* at the Theater am Kurfürstendamm in Berlin. It was a step in the history of stage design: it retained simplicity and clarity, and it was an artwork in relation to an environment. The production showed, like so many earlier versions of *A Dream Play*, disappointments and sufferings. "What a pity about people," but not against a background of irritated nerves and religious cramps from a passed-away poet. A likeness of Strindberg (his appearance and face) was not part of Schuh's production; no one in the Berlin audience would have recognized him anyway. And any knowledge about Strindberg's life that could have explained the bizarre things in the play—the cupboard door, the dramatic corridor, disappointments about promotion, and so on—could not be expected from an audience around the Kurfürstendamm.

A Dream Play was dreamed about in Central Europe in the years after the war, a dream play that differed from those in Malmö, Gothenburg, and Stockholm. No one was particularly interested in making certain architectural parts of the setting similar to residential areas in Stockholm. So The Blind Man, The Invalid, and other characters were blown up into terrifying proportions. The dream was adjusted to a new reality. When, at the premiere, the grip of terror on the audience began to loosen, the poet himself presented the formula behind this Berlin production: "I believe I have already experienced it—now I know the true meaning of reality—or dream—or verse."[8]

A Dream Play had been produced and set against the new backdrop of Europe. The colors of the performance were gray; no fragrant Garden of Eden, no towering castle was to be found. Instead a recurrent perspective of eternity was set against the round horizon. In this stylized scenic image, projection screens created dream images in the surrealist scenes. A pattern of iron gratings was often to be seen in the shadows on the screens.

The grating was actually a minor element taken from Strindberg's instructions, yet it came to dominate the overall picture of the production. It called forth associations with jails and escape and liberation. In the final scene the prospect of liberation becomes a cipher, as difficult to interpret as Strindberg himself. During the last monologue, a light fell, as if from a church window, on Indra's daughter. She left the stage through a door, out toward a red dawn far behind the scenic background. There was a humane touch to the departure for the execution at sunrise. She left a prison, but she never entered Strindberg's fragrant castle.

There is much to discuss in the Berlin theater's interpretation of Strindberg, and much to object to. But it was consistent, created by a director who read and listened not only to Strindberg but also to the Europe that was able to follow, recognize, and be astonished by *A Dream Play*. Something was lost in Oscar Fritz Schuh's interpretation, something of the poetry, the weakness, the humble searching. But what was lost was regained in intensity, emotional force, and burning immediacy.

The Berlin staging made *A Dream Play* a tool in a political and social situation. The stage setting was the instrument that directed the audience's attention away from the general things in the play, from the author's situation, to something that was applicable to a certain given aspect of life, after a devastating war, during an increasingly uncertain peace, in a city threatened by isolation, blockades, and barriers.

The relative clarity of the text of the production described above limited the applicability of the drama. Many associations were cut off, while others appeared clear and effective.

Strindberg's plays are plastic, with rich possibilities of variation—the hallmark of all Strindberg's work from *Miss Julie* to *The Highway*. This richness has been interpreted as a fantastic, anarchistic feature, especially in the years of expressionism. But there is always a strong consistency in his plays. In his egocentricity, among other things, lies a guarantee for this consistency. And, finally, the richness and the consistency together make the plays applicable to new historical situations. The theater ought to be not an end in itself but a practicable tool in everyday life. The texts have furnished the new men of the theater with a basis for provocation and challenge. "There is a moral standpoint in a camera angle," as Godard says. The fact that the plays provide a permanent stimulus to find new angles guarantees the continued impact of the Strindberg texts.

NOTES

[1] Rudolf Kayser, *Das Junge Deutsche Drama* (Berlin: Volksbühnen Verlags-und Vertriebsgesellschaft, 1924), p. 85.

[2] Adolf Paul, *Strindbergsminnen och brev* (Stockholm: Åhlén & Åkerlund, 1915).

[3] August Strindberg, *Till Damaskus* (Stockholm: Albert Bonniers Förlag, 1962), part 1, act 1, p. 144.

[4] August Strindberg, *Advent* (Stockholm: Albert Bonniers Förlag, 1962), act 1, p. 33.

[5] August Strindberg, *Fröken Julie* (Stockholm: Albert Bonniers Förlag, 1957).

[6] August Strindberg, Preface to *Ett drömspel*, in his *Samlade skrifter*, ed. John Landquist (Stockholm: Albert Bonniers Förlag, 1916), vol. 36, p. 215.

[7] Olof Molander to Martin Ahlbom, August 27, 1946, cited in Ingvar Holm, *Drama på scen* (Lund: Albert Bonniers Förlag, 1969), p. 252.

[8] More about the performance in Holm, *Drama*, p. 254.

INTELLECTUAL BACKGROUNDS

BOUWSMA: Professor Rehder has suggested that the meeting begin with questions to which yesterday's [May 1, 1972] speakers would then respond.

BAGGESEN: I would like to ask a question of Niels Ingwersen concerning his interpretation of the ending of Schack's *Phantasterne*. I agree with you that the ending, where Conrad is married to a real princess, is appropriate, but not in the way you interpret it. You said that Conrad, in his erotic fantasies, got to know himself, to know certain forces in himself, and he integrated those forces into his mature life as a married man. But you also said that he deprived his sexuality of its sadistic and masochistic complements. I think that, since Freud, we are all prone to think of this as no sexuality at all. What I'm aiming at is the question of whether the ending of *Phantasterne*, appropriate as it is in its historical setting, isn't an expression of the kind of fencing in that you find so much of in Danish literature in the early nineteenth century. I'm thinking of the concept of Biedermeier, which was introduced into the study of Danish literature by Professor Lunding, a teacher of German literature; and I think that, if you take that kind of position, you'll have to restate your conclusion. What happens to Conrad is that he cuts off from himself all the dangerous sides of his own personality, and, once he has done that, it is quite appropriate in the spirit of Biedermeier that he should win the princess, because he has cut off all that is dangerous in his own nature.

INGWERSEN: I think you are suggesting precisely what I intimated yesterday in my remarks on what Alan Friedman called "the closed ending." I would agree with you that I have to continue my interpretation, not only of *Phantasterne*, but also of the two novels by Jacobsen. I have to do so by considering the relationship or tension between, to use Booth's term, "the implied author," the narrator, and his story. In *Phantasterne*, the organization of the book requires me to continue my interpretation. Let me briefly try to suggest what I mean.

This story is told by the older Conrad, who is now married to Blanca and presumably very busy living happily ever after. He tells the whole story from his childhood to the point when he wins her hand. When he focuses on those very dangerous sexual dreams, the dreams in which he imagines himself to be the devil, Moloch, and finally Death, however, he does not tell it himself. He includes excerpts from his diary, the diary he wrote as a young man. One may indeed wonder, "Does the older man, who talks about everything ironically, understand the younger man?" So I do agree with you, and I agree one has to continue in this direction.

GREENWAY: I would like to continue this same line by asking you to elaborate on something that is of great interest to me and that seemed to be buried in your talk, that is, your emphasis on the mythic structure. You spoke about the organization of the novel. It seemed to me that the problem Professor Baggesen raised would be answered in part by the mythic organization, in that the whole novel sounds like an *eventyr* ("adventure") told by somebody from the Biedermeier period. He gets the princess, and then they live happily ever after in their duplex apartment, or whatever it is. Do you see this critical method that you are developing as being an effective tool to explain this? I thought you did quite nicely, using this critical method, this myth-criticism, in *Niels Lyhne* to explain something that has always disturbed me about the novel, namely, the failure of the romantic myth. I would be very much interested in hearing you continue the myth-criticism, either in response to Professor Baggesen's question, or concerning *Niels Lyhne*.

INGWERSEN: What you have to do in all these books, whether they are written before or after 1870, is, of course, discover the underlying myths. We can also call them ideologies. One wonders whether the people who wrote the novels of that time really subscribed to those myths. It seems to me you can see a development here. After 1870, these myths are, shall we say, officially rejected. That's why in Jacobsen's works—at least in *Marie Grubbe* and *Niels Lyhne*—you find them far beneath the surface, to the point where some people maintain they're not even there. What you have here is supposedly pure realism, or naturalism. I really feel that these myths are there, and that they have to be uncovered. You have to take a mythical approach in order to understand and explain the structure. As I indicated yesterday, I don't think you can explain the sudden plot twists in the ending of Jacobsen's two novels unless you take this myth-approach, unless you find the myth beneath the realistic surface. It's a hard task, but it really has to be done.

GREENWAY: You implied, I think, that there was a conflict of myths in the underlying romantic narrative pattern, as in, for instance, Eichendorff's *Taugenichts*. Superimposed upon the underlying romantic pattern of *Niels Lyhne* were the myths of the Modern Breakthrough. Do you see a tension between these two?

INGWERSEN: I do see a tension. I have taught *Niels Lyhne* for some eight years, and I always have a problem with that book. I begin with Kierkegaard, then do Ibsen's *Brand*, then go on to *Niels Lyhne*, and my students become terribly bored. I try to explain the book in terms of the Modern Breakthrough, and my students' response is always that there is more to the book. We finally came to the conclusion that the Modern Breakthrough couldn't explain everything. It is a world of chance we encounter. In terms of mere chance, then, we must understand the endings. But, again, the students' response is that it doesn't explain everything. There is a tension there, and it's probably an unreconciled one. I wonder whether this harms the work's aesthetic quality. It's a very funny thing. The students always respond very positively to *Marie Grubbe*, and even to "Mogens," but with *Niels Lyhne* I always have a pedagogical problem. My problem, perhaps, was that I did not understand that there was a tension between two myths.

GREENWAY: Niels Lyhne fails to dream a good healthy dream. He dreams essentially an ideological dream, one of social myth, secularized, or political. He never achieves any sort of descent into darkness or subsequent reascension.

INGWERSEN: And he dreams this dream in the wrong way. He should dream in terms of society, in terms of the group. When we really analyze his dreams, he dreams in terms of himself. He is still the romantic individual, assuming meaning for himself, not really for society.

MISHLER: But isn't Marie Grubbe doing the same thing?

INGWERSEN: Yes. She is, but, after all, in a different manner. *Marie Grubbe* is a historical novel. We don't have to bother with the Modern Breakthrough. What I mean is this: Niels fails to dream good healthy dreams, be they in terms of society or in terms of himself as an individual, and thus no self-realization on his part is possible. The book *Niels Lyhne* undoubtedly places a high value on Niels's and his generation's cause—atheism can serve as a label for that cause; but self-understanding is, however, more important, for if such an understanding is not achieved, the self-realization deemed necessary by the romanticists and by Jacobsen cannot be reached. Niels may very well be criticized for not grasping his "social cause" correctly, but his real failure lies, as does Marie Grubbe's success, on a personal level.

REHDER: May I ask a question directed to Mr. Ingwersen? What are the exact dates of both *Niels Lyhne* and *Marie Grubbe*?

INGWERSEN: *Marie Grubbe* is the first one. It came out in 1876. And *Niels Lyhne* came out in 1880, about ten years after Brandes had, shall we say, signaled the Modern Breakthrough in Denmark.

REHDER: In connection with the discussion that has developed here, I was struck by a certain resemblance to a much misunderstood, monumental novel, written in Germany, which doesn't seem to have been accorded the proper interpretation. That is Immermann's *Münchhausen*. It has been construed as a late romantic fairy tale, as a satire, even as the fate of an individual who seems to be misplaced. Literary historians and critics have torn the novel apart, taken certain parts out and published them separately. There is, for instance, the famous little story, the interlude of the "Oberhof," which was entirely separate from the main novel. It seems to me that what we have here is precisely a mixture of late Biedermeier realism and romantic fairy tales, along with the introduction of what one would call myth, although it seems we are using the word *myth* to refer to something else, namely, a unifying element—call it culture, or nation, or society. It seems that in style and in direction and in organization, this novel of Immermann, his *Münchhausen*, has certain striking resemblances to the novels of Jacobsen.

INGWERSEN: What is the date?

REHDER: At least twenty years earlier, 1854, if I remember correctly.

INGWERSEN: Brandes commented that Denmark was many years behind. I'm not sure how many.

REHDER: I'm puzzled by one thing. Immermann is somehow bothered by the cultural image of his own country. It was nothing to be proud of, restoration Germany. The conservatism of Metternich was nothing that he was particularly proud of. He developed in this novel something like a wish-image of what, to him, Germany should be. Without being a nationalist or a chauvinist, he seemed to be developing a desirable cultural picture. It's rather interesting that he would name the book after a character as ridiculous as Münchhausen, when the actual hero of the story is Oswald, who seems to represent to him the inward mentality of the desirable cultural image. In the weaving of an outer and an inner frame, of a superior and inferior layer, he seems to have fashioned a vision, in which the individual and the cultural aspects are merged. And it is difficult to see this particular novel in terms of the traditional clichés and in the traditional categories. One cannot say precisely, "It is Biedermeier." One cannot say, "It's romanticism." The critic Gundolf calls Immermann a romantic, but generally we don't include him in the circle of the romanticists. Immermann is a person to whom the clichés do not apply. Similarly, I also feel that Jacobsen exceeds the clichés, transcends them.

INGWERSEN: Within the past five years the critics of *poetik* have changed the picture of Jacobsen completely, and I don't think anyone has really managed to attack these new studies.

TETER: Yesterday, Dr. Arestad, you were referring to Ibsen's relationship to Kierkegaard. I remember Kaufmann's statement in his translation of Nietzsche's *The Will to Power*: when asked how much influence Kierkegaard had had on Ibsen, the latter replied, "I have read little of Kierkegaard, and understood him less." I would like to know your response to that.

ARESTAD: I think that would be a fair assessment, just as a preliminary answer to it. With regard to the possible relationship between Kierkegaard and Ibsen, Ibsen usually refrained from admitting that he had been influenced by anybody, but this is, of course, not true. This question would be in line with, "When Nora leaves in *A Doll's House*, what does she do?" I don't know. Perhaps she goes out to become a bareback rider in a circus, or something like that. Ibsen was always very evasive. Of Kierkegaard's three categories—the aesthetic, the ethical, and the religious—the religious is out because Ibsen said he could have made Brand of a profession other than that of minister. Brian Downs, in his *Ibsen: The Intellectual Background*, and Valborg Erichsen mention that, in their view, Ibsen seems to have used just two minor aspects of each of the categories, the aesthetic and the ethical. It reduces to this as far as those characters are concerned, that in the aesthetic stage, the goal or aim is the person's pleasure, although I don't think that's necessarily true in Ibsen's case. In *Peer Gynt* it's more than that. If an individual in that category makes a decision and then finds that the decision results in too much obligation and responsibility on his part, he does not have to continue in that particular line. He can just draw back —as Peer often does—make another decision, and proceed. In the second category, it seems to me that there is a connection with Brand, in that he is an ethical character, although Ibsen's portrayal of Brand is not the dramatization of the ethical concept of the character of Kierkegaard. Here is an individual who, if he makes a decision, has to assume all the responsibilities. This may not even be a correct analysis of the implications of the aesthetic and the ethical, but I think this is what he got from Kierkegaard. The idea of a one-hundred-percent commitment is found in Kierkegaard. This not only influenced Ibsen, but also had meaning for a great number of writers throughout the nineteenth century in Scandinavia.

TETER: But there is a possibility that there was a slight nuance of that feeling in *Brand*.

ARESTAD: Yes, very definitely.

TETER: How much influence did Nietzsche have on Ibsen?

ARESTAD: That question is, of course, extremely difficult to answer. There is a very good discussion of Nietzsche in Scandinavia by Harald Beyer. It is a two-volume work containing a section on Ibsen. Although he is able to mention a number of correspondences and similarities between the two, it is difficult to know whether or not Ibsen was actually influenced by Nietzsche. If you read Ibsen from the very beginning, you discover that there are many things that he said before Nietzsche ever wrote anything. As I recall, the first thing Nietzsche wrote was *The Birth of Tragedy*, in 1871. In 1873 Ibsen published *Emperor and Galilean*, a play that terminated the first period in his production. Practically every theme that Ibsen dealt with after *Emperor and Galilean* he had already introduced to a large extent as early as *Catiline* in 1850. These themes were intensified throughout the romantic period. Beyer notes that many things that Ibsen said in his early plays are repeated in Nietzsche.

I spoke yesterday of the master builder as *the* Ibsen hero, and I still believe that. Ibsen wrote *The Master Builder* to exemplify his view of what it would be possible for the human being to attain. Here we are witness to an individual and to a magnificent act. I think that Solness is a person of great heroic stature. Ibsen intended for him to be that way, in order to express man as a protest against the leveling process that had taken place during the nineteenth century. Now in *The Genealogy of Morals*, which was written in 1887, and from which I quoted yesterday, Nietzsche speaks of his despair and despondency at the state of mediocrity in contemporary Europe. It corresponds to what Ibsen says, and I suppose there's no doubt but that Ibsen was aware of this. I have no evidence of it, but one assumes that Ibsen knew that this had been written. And then there was the controversy between Brandes and Harald Høffding in Denmark beginning in 1888, during which Brandes helped to revive interest in Nietzsche. Thus, Ibsen must have known about this sort of thing. But, if you go to *Rosmersholm*, which was written in 1886, the year before *The Genealogy of Morals*, and five years before *The Master Builder*—I didn't say anything about *Rosmersholm* yesterday—you find the most frightening statement that Ibsen makes with regard to this question of mediocrity in life. It has been Rosmer's intention as a modern emperor Julian to bring about a synthesis in the country between all the striving forces. Ulrik Brendel, his old tutor, is supposed to deliver a lecture to Mortensgaard's followers—Mortensgaard, the new liberal element in the community, who is opposed to Kroll, who represents the old order. Arriving at Rosmer's house, Brendel says: "Never have I stood in a more august presence. Peter Mortensgaard has divine power; he is omnipotent; he can do anything he wills! . . . For Peter Mortensgaard never wills more than he can do." In other words, just do the things that are easy for you. Don't make any effort. In other words, forget excellence.

I can cite another example to show how early Ibsen had been concerned with this theme, and that is from the fifth act of *The Pretenders*, written in 1864. Bishop Nicholas dies at the end of the third act, and goes down into the nether regions. He then returns in the fifth act as Earl Skule, now King Skule, and is going up to the monastery where he is about to meet his death. The bishop is then speaking about the state of things in Norway. He says: "Går til sin gjerning de norske menn—viljeløst vimrende, vet ei hvorhen,—skrukker seg hjertene, smyger seg sinnene,—veke, som vaggende vidjer for vindene,—kan kun om *en* ting i verden de enes—*den*, at hver storhet skal styrtes og stenes.—"

They go about their tasks, the Norwegian men—weak-willed, wavering, they don't know where they're going
Their hearts shrink, their minds steal away, weak, like waving willows before the wind
They can agree on only *one* thing in the world, namely, that every great person shall be toppled and stoned.

Once again, Ibsen states the idea that excellence cannot be achieved in the country. This would seem to be an expression of the superman ideal—and this is 1863. But many of these things had occurred to Ibsen, and he had given expression to them. He echoes, in a word, quite a number of the things that Nietzsche says. So Nietzsche reinforces, in the end, Ibsen's view of the artist, the genius, and the role that he plays. I find—at least to my own satisfaction—that this is Ibsen's own personal understanding of the artist, and of the artist's evolution. This doesn't mean that a person can't have read an individual like Nietzsche, a kindred spirit who reinforces his own ideas. Writers are rather independent and very wary of admitting that they ever learn anything from anyone else. And they like to quote themselves.

TETER: I remember where someone—this is also in Kaufmann's book—asked Ibsen what he thought of Nietzsche, or if he thought that Nietzsche was a Satan. Ibsen's reply was "No, I don't think so."

ARESTAD: Yes. I think that Ibsen was right in doing that. On the other hand, I thought Nietzsche was very uncomplimentary when they asked him what he thought of Ibsen. He was about as bad as Johannes V. Jensen, who called Ibsen a pansy, a *stemorsblomst*. He looked like that, anyway. Nietzsche called him an old maid, the reason being that Ibsen was a little too soft on the woman question.

REHDER: Are there any further questions?

ARESTAD: I should like to pose this question: when we speak of the intellectual background, and list Kierkegaard and Nietzsche, how far does that take us? Let me just mention either Sigurd Hoel or, perhaps, Nordahl Grieg, in Norwegian literature the forerunner of Brecht, for instance. What do these people contribute to the intellectual background? What about Kielland's novels, or Ibsen's role in the woman's question?

REHDER: Perhaps Professor Weinstock or Professor Rovinsky could answer that better. I also was somewhat concerned, even worried, about limiting the intellectual background to Kierkegaard and Nietzsche. I would like to counter this question of the hero with another question concerning the influence of Carlyle, or that romantic tradition which came down through Carlyle. I ask this question because of a study that appeared in the late thirties, in one of Eric Bentley's first books, *The Century of Hero Worship*, in which he throws a great many similar characters into the same pot, beginning with Carlyle, working through Richard Wagner and Nietzsche, and ending up with D. H. Lawrence. It seems to me that that is not what we are looking for in the intellectual background of the problem of the hero.

TETER: I assumed we would be speaking about Nietzsche's concept of the hero, or rather the creative being.

GREENWAY: It seems to me that the background is quite fitting and that the Scandinavian authors we've been talking about form an appropriate foreground. I notice a recurring pattern in the papers that we've been listening to thus far, namely, the assertion of freedom and the general failure on the part of the literary manifestations to attain this. Kierkegaard and Nietzsche are the authors who assert the possibility of the individual attaining freedom, not the collective man, or the people —it is an assertion of the primacy of the individual will. The literary people whom we have been discussing seem almost to a man to say that this is not really possible. Brand, for instance, who Ibsen said is "me in my best moments," is still terribly guilty at the end. He is true to himself, and, as with so many of Ibsen's heroes, you can't help but sympathize. One can't condemn him completely. Yet he's so horribly wrong. All of Ibsen's other dramatic assertions of self—witness, for example, *Rosmersholm*—end essentially in failure. I find Ibsen's "happy endings" rather second-rate. Take the ending of *Little Eyolf*: Rita and Allmers are standing hand in hand, looking up to the stars. It's a very cliché-ridden ending. Ibsen is at his greatest with the tragic ending.

I think that Kierkegaard and Nietzsche do form a viable intellectual background. Strindberg, in *To Damascus*, for example, allows Den okände, the stranger, the unknown, to assert, in very Nietzschean terms, that he is going to create. He fails. And Professor Ingwersen's paper essentially dealt with such a failure, the failure of heroes.

Does the Scandinavian hero, if there is such a creature, ever succeed? We might well bring in Dostoevsky's *Crime and Punishment*, of 1860. One thinks of Raskolnikov's assertion of freedom in much the same way, and his failure results in a problematic ending to the novel.

TETER: Would you say that Raskolnikov failed?

GREENWAY: To assert his freedom in an intellectual sense, yes, of course. The whole novel is the failure of his Superman theory.

TETER: Many people consider the ending to be very unartistic . . .

GREENWAY: We've been talking about problematic endings for some time.

TETER: But the ending seems to show me that, with all the suffering he had undergone, he did succeed in one sense, by translating this negative freedom into a positive one, even though he was incarcerated in Siberia.

GREENWAY: Yes. It's been brought out by Berdyaev quite well. In terms of Dostoevsky providing perhaps a third element to the intellectual background, he recognized the failure of the assertion of individual freedom through self-will.

ARESTAD: I feel impelled to make a short statement. And that is, if we take as an example Solness, how could he succeed in any way other than he does? You spoke of *Little Eyolf* as having a cliché-ridden ending. But it seems to me Solness aims rather high, doesn't he? Does Solness, or any other human being in his right mind, for that matter, ever think that he can attain the goal he sets out or aspires to achieve? The thing that Ibsen is saying, in his plays, is that the individual cannot compromise with the ideal or the absolute goal. Now Solness's task is a formidable one. He challenges God, as artists do. He tells God: "I want to be the creator in my sphere, just as you are in yours. Leave me alone. I'll go my own way." We've discovered in tragedy, and I suppose everywhere else, that the individual cannot set himself against a universal force with the idea that he can conquer force. If he could, it would end in mockery. Man is too far below this universal force in stature. Even in defeat, however, one can still say that he has aspired to a victory that is as great as any human being can attain. And in that sense it's not a failure.

GREENWAY: You will recall, I did use the words *tragedy* and *tragic*, for which Solness would be a perfect example. In this play, as in others, Ibsen places the protagonist in one of the most dramatic situations a person can find himself in. He puts a sensitive man between two women. Solness had sold out his ideal of building houses for men, and he is now attempting to recapture this initial inspiration, or synthesis, through the building of the tower. In a literal sense he fails. Solness is a tragic hero. I would disagree with you concerning the basically romantic assertion that adherence to one's ideal generally implies success.

ARESTAD: No, it doesn't. It just simply cannot.

GREENWAY: I agree with you there. We're talking about the background, about Kierkegaard and Nietzsche, and this is the way I would measure Ibsen. Ibsen goes against this background and sees that, while the ideal is not possible, there is value in the assertion. Solness has performed an act of value. He asserts himself and dies, but that isn't necessarily a defeat. He attempts to recapture something he had lost in himself.

ARESTAD: Are you sure that he doesn't recapture it? Here is a man who at the beginning of that play is ridden with guilt. He overcomes that and regains the robust conscience. Both Reichardt (in *Tragic Themes in Western Literature*) and Koht maintain that the great tragedy of Solness was that he did not regain his robust conscience. Of course he does. At the end, when he climbs the tower, Solness reasserts his dedication to his art. He has no doubt when he goes up there but that he is going to win. He doesn't falter in going up the stairs, and he doesn't fall down because of dizziness. The scaffolding breaks, that's it.

GREENWAY: Ibsen's ending of the play affirms the value of what Solness does but also says that it must end in death, in the destruction of the individual as a human being. There is a value in asserting the primacy of the ideal and of artistic inspiration, and I don't think that Ibsen questions that. I do think, though, that he goes one step beyond it and says that, while this is valuable, the price one must pay is destruction, rather than a "happy ending," whereby Solness climbs back down and hears music in the air.

ARESTAD: Who in the world would ever want to look at a thing like that?

GREENWAY: I wouldn't. I think it would be very mediocre.

ARESTAD: I think it destroys the tragic concept wherein the hero seeks to attain some unattainable goal. That which impels certain people to achieve is beyond the average.

GREENWAY: I'm just saying that Ibsen had a certain ironic distance from a blind faith that such an act would produce happiness. He believes in the value of what Solness is doing but also says that there is a mortal consequence to it.

ARESTAD: Who is the only ecstatically happy person at the end of the play?

GREENWAY: One of the alter egos, Hilde. Yes, of course, Hilde.

ARESTAD: The other people aren't too happy about the whole thing.

HEINEN: Rather than suggest that Nietzsche influenced Ibsen directly, it might be simpler to say that they were expressing parallel thoughts. The main point, it seems to me, of Nietzsche's Superman is the joyful acceptance of sorrow and death, and a very parallel joy in pain as well as in pleasure. This exists, essentially on a symbolic level, in *The Master Builder*: a joy in creation that encompasses not merely that which is pleasant, but all experience, all consequences, a serenity in the face of tragedy. You suggested that the philosophers had a positive belief in the ability of the individual to achieve freedom. The exposition of this idea in *The Master Builder* points out a fundamental similarity between Nietzsche and Ibsen.

GUSTAFSSON: I must admit that, in my reading of Ibsen, I find it, if not confusing, at least rather difficult to describe the Ibsen hero in Nietzschean terms. For me the Ibsen hero—and I think it comes out so very clearly in Ibsen's last play, *Når vi døde vågner*—is in some important respects a hero of political liberalism, in that his life, with success or failure, is an attempt at individual self-realization. For the interpretation of Nietzsche, I think it is very important never to forget the very first premise of his philosophy, which appears in *Zur Genealogie der Moral*, namely, the moral of the slaves, those people who are weak and who have made a virtue of their weakness. And the Nietzschean hero must be opposed to the moral of the slave. If you look for a Nietzschean hero in the Scandinavian literature of that period, I think you'll find a much better candidate in Doctor Borg of *I havsbandet* (*On the Seaboard*). What he does is to maintain himself against the moral of the slaves. In his view of the world, he represents all the theoretical ideals of the Breakthrough, the scientist, the materialist. Dr. Borg, this Nietzschean hero, also fails. In some ways this discussion of ours has turned into a discussion of the way to end novels, which I find quite interesting. Here you have another type of ending: Dr. Borg, mad, sails out into the winter storm, navigating by the star in Orion, because, helpless, he has become a kind of anti-Christ. Of course he fails, and woman is the main cause of his failure; the slaves in a Nietzschean sense are another. Even in his failure, however, he refuses to accept Christ, which is very significant. So if you look at this novel by Strindberg, which, in some sense, is not very representative of his work—but that is another problem—I think that you'll see the immense difference between such a hero and the protagonist of *Når vi døde vågner*. How very differently they react to their surroundings!

CURRIE: It seems to me that if one is to find out what this hero is, from the viewpoints of Nietzsche and Kierkegaard, the ideas of these two men need to be pinned down pretty closely. In the case of Nietzsche, reference was made to his idea of slave. Now, if I understand him, he made himself quite clear as to what he meant by slave morality. He was talking about compassion and pity, the kind of thing taught by Christianity and Judaism. He states very definitely that Christianity and Judaism were subversive to the Roman Empire and undermined it, undermined the heroic quality of Roman life. And this he disliked intensely. I remember one very interesting line of his: "Be hard. Again I say be hard." Perhaps, in searching for a Scandinavian hero, one should keep in mind Nietzsche's criteria.

TETER: You're talking about the Nietzschean concept of the hero as exemplified by *The Genealogy of Morals*. As far as I can see, Nietzsche doesn't posit any type of hero as such here—he just sets up the strong and the weak. He doesn't consider the strong to be the Superman at all; rather he considers him to be more positive, more healthy valued than the weak. The Christian or the Jew is used resentfully as a very cunning and powerful tool, a sort of negative will to power. Thus it is rather difficult to talk in terms of the Nietzschean hero in relationship to *The Genealogy of Morals*, except when Nietzsche is referring to Zarathustra.

CURRIE: My point is, if he were to construct a hero, wouldn't he tend to construct it in terms of his ideas, his own values?

TETER: Yes, the only reason I brought that up was because I didn't think that talking about the strong man would be profitable.

CURRIE: I think it would; I think he's serious about that.

TETER: Yes, I agree, but his hero—if he would even use the term— while he would possess the strong characteristics, would be controlled by some type of Apollonian suppressor or governor, so as not to tear himself apart with Dionysian vehemence. That, of course, is what the strong person did in the Dionysian sacrifices. Such orgiastic rites quite often got out of hand. And Nietzsche, even though he is intrigued by all these events, would not consider these people to be overmen at all. In fact, they haven't even questioned their own values, so they can't be Supermen.

MONAS: He does greatly admire Dostoevsky, Nietzsche does. He does greatly admire Dostoevsky and Dostoevsky's heroes. Let me introduce some themes here, and perhaps you could respond to them as though they were questions. I want to leave Nietzsche for a minute, and Kierkegaard as well, and introduce a very odd figure here, Robert Frost. I want to quote the last two lines of one of his poems in connection with the situation in Scandinavia, the historical situation of the Scandinavian countries in mid-nineteenth-century Europe, looking back and coming to a certain consciousness of their past, and also looking at their present in relation to civilized, bourgeois nineteenth-century Europe. This very beautiful poem is called "The Oven Bird." It has to do with a bird that sings at midsummer about diminution, about going down. The last two lines are, if my memory serves me right:

The question that he frames in all but words
Is what to make of a diminished thing.

I wonder if this has any resonance for you in the sense of the significance of Scandinavian literature as it appears on the stage, as it becomes European literature in the late nineteenth century. I am reminded of the second theme by this recounting of the marvelous ending of *The Master Builder*. Marvelous as it is—and I think it's a very great play, and a very great ending—it trembles on the edge of absurdity, as I think has already been demonstrated. I can't help thinking of the last remarks that Socrates is heard to make in the final part of the *Symposium*, when everyone else is drunk. He says, seemingly casually, but I think not casually at all, that the man who can write a tragedy can also write a comedy. This introduces me to another question: isn't the proper sequel, the proper self-conscious, conscious, and unconscious sequel to *The Master Builder, Finnegans Wake*?

BULHOF: I would like to agree with what you said about Nietzsche and about the other people who are not Supermen. I think that what Nietzsche meant by Superman was a kind of savior. Zarathustra compared himself with the descending sun, he was not going down in the sense of diminishing or declining; rather, he was going down to save that world. I would like to ask Professor Bouwsma whether there is anything like this in Kierkegaard, with whom I'm not very familiar. I would like to know whether Kierkegaard's heroes also have something of a savior aspect?

BOUWSMA: I'm not sure that I understood all of your question. I take it you were asking whether there was something in Kierkegaard that could be identified with the idea of the hero?

BULHOF: With the savior.

BOUWSMA: The savior in Kierkegaard is not a human being.

BULHOF: No. That's the way I feel about Nietzsche's Übermensch, too.

BOUWSMA: If by that you mean the Nietzschean Superman, then the idea of the Christ as put forth by Kierkegaard is something quite different. For Kierkegaard, Christ is God and doesn't have to try. Do you think that Nietzsche's Superman is a man? Are there such human beings? Or is this his little dream? This is why, if the dramatist tries to represent this, he is bound to fail.

CURRIE: Kierkegaard seems to fit a little better there, doesn't he? I believe that Kierkegaard reacted against this overall, wonderful, logical world of Hegel and emphasized paradox. He was even able to write one book and then write another book in complete opposition to the first.

SHERRY: Nietzsche pointed to several figures as overmen: Napoleon, Goethe, and Cesare Borgia; and he equated them, in *Twilight of the Idols*, with the figure of a genius who is simply a tremendous burst of energy, an accident, you see, a force in the world having no relation to the world into which he comes. He is simply there as a tremendous burst of energy. Note, too, the figures of the statesman, the artist, and the condottiere: the statesman as the founder of the state, the artist as the creator of a work of art, all of them participating in Nietzsche's aesthetic or metaphysic of creation. He said in the book on tragedy that only as aesthetic phenomena are the world and life eternally justified, and even at the end of *Twilight of the Idols* he refers back to the book on tragedy as his first reevaluation of values. The problem is that, if we want to talk about the relationship of Ibsen and Nietzsche and also of Kierkegaard and Nietzsche, we have to push the question back even further into a kind of metaphysic and think of Ibsen as the embodiment of a metaphysic of the artist and see if it has any correlation to the metaphysic of creation found in Kierkegaard and in Nietzsche, particularly Nietzsche. Because there you have the figure of the artist as the one who wills meaning into being through that agonizing act of creation by which he imposes his own will on the world. It seems that, if we want to talk about a hero in Ibsen, we have to try to understand what it meant to Ibsen to create a hero like Solness.

REHDER: Speaking in terms of background, I am wondering whether a question dealing with orientation might be helpful. I have the definite feeling that, when we speak of Nietzsche and Kierkegaard as possible influences upon Scandinavian writers, that's a matter of historical perspective, a thing of the past. I'm struck by the fact that the evaluation of Nietzsche has gone through several stages within the last hundred years. The particular concept that can perhaps be derived most directly, most bluntly, and perhaps most unsophisticatedly from his plain statements—slave-morals, master-morals, will to power, and similar slogans—would be rather clumsy, it seems to me, because it has led to Nietzsche's being blamed for two historical occurrences, namely, World Wars I and II. This, of course, is ridiculous. The surprising thing is that Nietzsche and Kierkegaard have been connected. I personally feel that Nietzsche was not acquainted with Kierkegaard to begin with, but that the two were brought together by the inquiries of existential philosophy, which introduced an entirely new evaluation of both philosophers. The Nietzsche that we find in the writings of Heidegger and Jaspers is an entirely different Nietzsche from the one who was known to be the muscle-flexing proponent of the Superman in the early twentieth century. I think it is the rethinking, the reinterpretation of *Zarathustra* that has, with its natural philosophy of growth, of *werden*, of becoming, of constant change, brought on this stimulating problem of continued creativity. This is a new type of artist Nietzsche envisaged when he concentrated on the metaphysical problem of growth. It seems to me that the matter of influence is somewhat vague. It is not Kierkegaard or Nietzsche who have produced Ibsen and

Strindberg, but Ibsen and Strindberg who have produced themselves. Kierkegaard and Nietzsche have formed the background to a modern philosophy that we now call existential philosophy, but what does the name mean? It is not a particular school. It is merely the attempt by man to orient himself and is therefore an eclectic type of philosophy. It makes use of any kind of values from the past that can contribute to its purpose.

THOMPSON: Professor Bouwsma, I would like to ask you two questions concerning the Superman. The first is: are there any Knights of Faith? And the second is: how do you and I decide whether there are either any Knights of Faith or any Supermen?

BOUWSMA: Are there any Knights of Faith? I don't know. So how do I decide? I don't. I think, at any rate, that Kierkegaard would have replied in this way. This is the secret he speaks of between the believer and God. No man can tell another "I am."

THOMPSON: But doesn't Kierkegaard go so far as to give one characteristic of the Knight of Faith, namely, that we won't be able to recognize him?

BOUWSMA: I guess you're right. If there are no questions just now, I would like to ask Professor Monas to explain his last remark. I know that Joyce was not a Dane, but if Joyce had been a Dane, we should have understood perfectly how he was the sequel to Ibsen.

MONAS: Well, I meant it as a question really, and not one that I would particularly care to answer, but one that I would like to see injected into the discussion. I think that Joyce was Scandinavian enough in his . . .

BOUWSMA: Oh, yes, the Danes went to Ireland, that's right.

MONAS: His earliest literary hero was, indeed, Ibsen. I didn't have that so much in mind as the unusual plot and structure of *Finnegans Wake*, for which I think the early biography of Joyce is only secondary evidence.

BOUWSMA: This wasn't related to the plot of *The Master Builder*?

MONAS: I think it is.

BOUWSMA: I see.

NAESS: There is, of course, a book on *Finnegans Wake* and *The Master Builder* [by Dounia Christiani; see also Bjørn Tysdahl's *Joyce and Ibsen*]. I was just going to add that I also feel exactly like you about this. I do feel that Ibsen is a romantic writer. I have to go back to Mr. Ingwersen again because I am using the word *romantic* in a different sense from you, Niels, from the feeling that there is a lot of irony in the ending of *The Master Builder*. Sverre, you said Solness has regained his robust conscience. I don't know that he ever had one. When he was building that church up there, he was very nervous even then. Doesn't he recognize Hilde as "that little devil" who nearly caused him to fall down? So she does it the second time. I think it is this doubleness that "makes" *The Master Builder*, the fact that there is an absurd element there. It is comedy at the same time. I think a very remarkable thing about Ibsen is that he is one of the great literary caricaturists of the nineteenth century. He sees two things at the same time, tragedy and comedy. That adds a dimension. At the end of the play, you know that he is really shaking as he climbs the steps.

ARESTAD: If you say that, Harald, how then do you account for the impression that his venture on the tower makes on Hilde? At the end there is a little exchange between Hilde and Ragnar, who are standing on the ground, looking up. Then Solness falls down. Perhaps that's amusing, I don't know. In any case, the scaffolding collapses, so that the fall cannot, with certainty, be attributed to vertigo. Ibsen deliberately leaves this open. Hilde stands there, waving her handkerchief, and saying, "My master builder, my master builder." She says to Ragnar, "Can't you hear the music, the music of the spheres?" He's contending with this universal force. At the end of the play we have Hilde, who knows the master builder and who is the only person in the play, if you can call her a person, who knows that Solness is involved in this struggle. Nobody else knew the master builder at all, nor understood him. Not his wife, not the doctor, no one but Hilde. And it took nearly the whole play before she was introduced to the master builder's world, the world of the artist, and he was finally able to tell her what his problem was. And then, as a result of this whole process, he regains his robust conscience, gets rid of his guilt, and climbs the tower. Mrs. Solness comes by and asks Hilde to prevent her husband from going up the tower, because she knows that Hilde can do this better than anyone else. But what is Hilde doing? She's saying, "Get up

there, get up there, and do it." Mrs. Solness doesn't understand that
Hilde is egging him on. He needs support and encouragement. The
significant thing is what Ragnar says when the master builder falls
down, namely: "So he couldn't make it after all." Hilde, in ecstasy, is
communicating with this person who stands up there defying God, demanding his right to be a creator in his own sphere, just as God is in
his. Of course there's irony there. But I don't know that the humor
is so devastating.

NAESS: I think the irony is represented by the two people, Ragnar,
on the one hand, and Hilde. They're both there. It's attempted greatness, and that constitutes tragedy.

ARESTAD: From one point of view you can look upon that whole
spectacle as absurd. I agree that it is romantic, certainly. The goal that
Solness sets for himself—his "will to power"—comes out in the end.
Ibsen's heroes, however—in contrast to Nietzsche's—are not driven
by an impulse to gain power for themselves. The artist does certain
things only because he has to fulfill his creative urges. It only *appears*
that he seeks power to trample other people down. Borkman is the
same way. He is not an individual who wants power for its own sake.
There is no such thing in Ibsen.

MISHLER: It seems to me that Nietzsche is important for Ibsen, and
for this discussion, because he was the exemplary figure who tried to
make meaning when the social and religious basis for meaning had
fallen away. Ibsen once made the remark that his job was not to answer
questions but to pose them. One could go further along this line and
say that Ibsen actually saw his task as one of asking questions in such a
way that they could not be answered, putting sign against sign, element
against element in such a manner that what one winds up with is a kind
of puzzle. If you look at the plays as neither mimesis nor psychology,
but as a process of making meaning, and if you subject them to close
semantic scrutiny, you wind up with a plus-minus at the end of every
major play. This accounts for what I consider to be the static ending of
The Master Builder, static because Ibsen felt this way within himself.
He was being drained by the problem of making meaning when
actually there was no basis for it, and so the play had to be perfectly

self-enclosed and perfectly honest at the same time. In other words, it had to contain its own negation.

GREENWAY: Hilde is his alter ego, a kind of muse. She has been described earlier as a bird of prey. She represents more than inspiration, communion with the gods, for there is a potential within her for negation, for destruction.

MISHLER: So one gets nowhere by asking whether he wins or loses, or whether it is a comedy or a tragedy. It's like one of those boxes that opens up and turns itself off, builds itself up, and undercuts itself in the process.

SHERRY: As Rilke says, it's a question not of triumph but of survival. I would also say that it is not really so much a psychology of creation but a metaphysic, literally, because it's the source of all meaning—it's dasein in the world. This is Heidegger's reading of Nietzsche. I think it's very important that we try to think of the aesthetic, the metaphysical aesthetic, that Nietzsche has created, and of Ibsen's work as an artist in relation to that. I wonder if it's possible to illuminate Ibsen's own sense of himself as an artist in relation to Nietzsche's aesthetic of creation.

MISHLER: I think you can do it in a very concrete way, namely, by reading those plays and taking seriously every statement that every character makes, because you find that they have an extremely logical structure. When a character defines a term, sets up a context in which the term is defined, it is best to take it exactly as given, as defined. The plays, too, give a series of definitions that ultimately become self-canceling. Taking this kind of structure, then, one can ask what significance it has in the creation of meaning. The basis for answering this kind of question, in a word, is close reading. The interpretation of Ibsen has been such that, each time a remark is made, it supposedly illuminates a character's fictive consciousness. I would suggest, however, looking at the whole thing as a kind of field with no real people in it at all, a kind of senseless making of definitions.

DESCHNER: I'm very glad that someone has brought out the question of tragedy and comedy, and the point that they can take place simultaneously, because I've been troubled here by some of the concepts that we are superimposing on Scandinavian literature. What is a hero? What is tragedy? We are quite sure that tragedy is dead today, but as yet we haven't anything to replace it with. It is good that comedy comes in. I have just struggled with a class through *A Doll's House*, and, of course, the women in the class were absolutely dead sure that *here* it was, a marvelous, noble character, Nora, who finally realizes her own potential. Then we read Hermann Weigand's commentary in *The Modern Ibsen*, where he analyzes what a lark Nora is, a real twittering lark who lies all the time, who plays the game and caters to the man. He then points out that Ibsen started with one idea, namely, to write a tragedy, perhaps of modern woman, but mainly of a modern human being. As he was writing, he said, for the first time he saw Nora and could tell what she looked like. Then she took over and became a real human being who was neither tragic nor comic but both things at the same time. I think that's a very good observation and a very helpful one for us in 1972, and I think it shows Ibsen as a very modern author. I'm thinking of Karl S. Guthke's book on the modern tragicomedy, where he says that one finds throughout ancient literature tragedy and comic relief. The very sense of what he called "synthetic tragicomedy" is that comedy and tragedy occur in the same character at the same time, which is the way we see existence today. It's both things at the same time, and this makes the tragical more tragic and the comical even more comic. In this sense, I would think that Ibsen qualifies eminently as a forerunner of modern authors.

ZENTNER: I think that I would agree with Professor Arestad in almost everything he says, except one of the things he would most want me to agree with him on, namely, that the master builder is the best example of Ibsen's hero. We made a few references to the fact that Ibsen wrote plays after *The Master Builder*, and I would like to substitute Rubek as an even more ideal hero. Here again, picking up from a more recent remark, there are both tragedy and comedy at the end. Certain people unite and go up, certain people unite and go down, the former providing the heroic, the latter the comic aspect. I think that Ibsen goes beyond the ending of *The Master Builder*, which has confused some of us as to what situation Hilde is in and what her response is, and in what circumstances the master builder dies, whether it is because of dizziness or because of the scaffolding. The master builder cops out on Aline, on her creativity, on her artistry. Rubek, on the other hand, when he's united with Irene, does both the personal and the social things that we were referring to in another context much earlier. He becomes an artist by rededicating himself to his art. He also pays attention to the social thing that we were discussing under the guise of Breakthrough, because in this case the idea of art was to give birth to the human spirit. In reuniting with Irene he does this on both levels. Ibsen wrote beyond *The Master Builder* and used the same problems in his later dramas. I don't think it's an accident that *When We Dead Awaken* is his last play. The things that obtain in *The Master Builder* are brought to fruition in *When We Dead Awaken*. More of the pluses and minuses are resolved. It is the culmination of the things Ibsen had been working on. He gives more weight to the pluses, there, than he was able to do in earlier plays.

SHERRY: I would like to ask how a play can be both tragedy and comedy at once. It seems to me similar to the old idea of yoking two opposites together and saying that such is the nature of existence. I wonder if there isn't a third element present here, linking together tragedy and comedy, and that is irony. There isn't the kind of ironic position here, where you have neither tragedy nor comedy in the usual senses of the words, but, rather, an attempt to balance the two views, neither of which we can call tragic or comic, but ironic. We've already been talking about myth in terms of *Niels Lyhne*. Was it not Northrop Frye who said that irony turns into myth? There's no reason why the process can't be reversed. That is a question.

MISHLER: Along the line of the ironic, I think that a good example is the play *The Lady from the Sea*, which ends up with the husband affirming that famous chestnut about freedom with responsibility. If you go back and look at the history of the terms throughout the play, you'll find that they've both been turned into ridiculous figures, so that at the end, when he stands up and delivers the chestnut that most viewers take as Ibsen's final statement, they've actually been given a slap in the face. Ibsen has cut away all the ground from under the characters just before the husband stands up to deliver the solution to the thing, and so ends in a perfect fireworks of irony.

DESCHNER: I believe that modern playwrights tussle with that very question, an example of which would be Dürrenmatt, who writes something like *The Physicists: A Comedy*. He says that nobody, first of all, would come to see a play called *The Physicists: A Tragedy*. And second, he says, whereas the Greek plays contain, first, the tragedy and then the satyr play to cheer everyone up at the end, I start with the satyr play and make a big and hilarious comedy. People laugh their heads off until the horrible moment when they are caught up in the "mousetrap of comedy," as he says, and the tragedy all of a sudden leaps at you. He says one can't write a modern tragedy. But the elements of comedy and tragedy still exist in modern life. I do not think a play like *The Physicists* is a satire; I think it is genuinely comic and genuinely tragic.

SHERRY: Perhaps it's what Adrian Leverkuhn in *Doktor Faustus* defines as parody, the form of art with the life taken out of it, the sheer technical performance.

THOMPSON: Following up on your pluses and minuses and looking to Nietzsche, in Ibsen there is evidently a constant cancellation of one work by another work, and of one character by another. Do you expect to find this in Nietzsche as well? Do you find the cancellations specifically overlap in any way?

MISHLER: No, I was simply looking at Nietzsche as someone who dramatized the problems, and then moving very close to Ibsen, and showing how he was doing this textually.

THOMPSON: I was not sure how close an analogy you could make here between cancellation of metaphysics and creation.

MIDDLETON: I think there is something in Nietzsche, though, with this positive-negative polarity, or binary opposition, or ambiguity, or whatever. It's most simply put in the way in which he concludes some of his last letters. When writing to relatives he calls himself *Das Tier*—"the beast"; and when he's writing to Strindberg he calls himself *Der Gekreuzigte*—"the crucified." So, on one hand, he's the great beast, on the other, he's the Christ, and he's both at once in the same person. Also, in his moments of supreme lucidity he was already plummeting into madness.

MISHLER: What counters, what negates Zarathustra?

KRASNOW: The spirit of gravity, or eternal recurrence.

THOMPSON: Does that cancel him? That's not what he thinks.

TETER: I agree with what you said, but you're not saying that Zarathustra is the Superman, are you?

THOMPSON: No, he's not the Superman.

TETER: Zarathustra says he's just a heavy drop from a cloud.

THOMPSON: I think that the Superman is really the issue, but that it can be stated with Zarathustra as being different from Nietzsche, rather than seeing Nietzsche as the Superman. Zarathustra is somewhere between these two. The issue is what gets canceled and how far one can push the canceling in respect to Nietzsche's ideas on creation. That's what I'm really after.

KRASNOW: The cancellation of one Zarathustra immediately gives birth to another.

MIDDLETON: Well, all right, but, hopefully, that ends sometime, or we haven't gone very far.

KRASNOW: Well, this is the purpose of the artist, to create and change in Zarathustra, to continue a life of creativity.

MONAS: To negate is not to cancel. To negate is to charge and to transform with energy. Negation is not cancellation. I don't think that Ibsen's heroes are canceled, and I don't think that this process in Nietzsche's mind involves any cancellation, but, on the contrary, it involves intensification—extreme intensification to madness.

MISHLER: In Ibsen's case too?

MONAS: No, I was speaking of Nietzsche.

MIDDLETON: I think there are three other examples of this sort of thing in modern German fiction, and they're all the ends of various prose fictions, which might be read as developments of the same situation. One is the end of Kafka's *Metamorphosis,* when shortly before he dies Gregor has the thought that perhaps the music was the unknown nourishment for which, all this time, he'd been craving, but which had never been provided. So he reaches his vision of the utmost disembodiment or angelic ethereality just at the moment before his physical extinction as an insect. The second one is the end of *The Trial,* which is, perhaps, not so finished. It's rather difficult to tell, but there is a light that shines from a window far off, and as Joseph K. lies there, spread out on the stone, he sees a figure gesturing, silhouetted against this light, and he wonders if this is someone who might be going to save him. Thus, he has here, on an analogical level, a vision of a potential savior, while he himself is spread-eagled on this rock as a sort of savior figure. The knife is plunged into his breast, and, the boy says, he is killed "like a dog." So again there is a very high degree of polarization between positive and negative valuations that might be put upon the situation. The third one is the end of Hesse's *Glasperlenspiel*, where Josef Knecht leaves Kastalien, apparently to devote all his genius to the world of everyday historical, personal human beings, and he's gone out of the encapsulation of Kastalien and met the boy whose tutor he's going to be. He takes a swim and dies of a heart attack, and the boy, who happens to be there—there has to be a witness like Hilde in *The Master Builder*—absentmindedly puts on Knecht's bathing robe. You can read all kinds of symbolisms into this, and it depends on which frame of reference you're using. If you use Chinese symbolism from the *I Ching*, you find that it works out perfectly well: this is the savior-hero who perishes in combat with the elements, but whose very perishing is an act of supreme transcendence. This act is then noted subconsciously by the boy, who, in putting Knecht's bathing wrap on, is actually imitating an ancient Middle-Eastern bit of symbolism, where the recipient of the robe accepts the authority of the lord or master. But you could also read it in a rather supercilious way as the sad story of a jaded intellectual, who, as soon as he moves out of the university, simply cannot survive the strains of ordinary life. The message might be completely lost. This all happens when someone casually puts on a bathing wrap and walks off. But there are many more possible valuations of this fiction, and I think this is an extraordinary example of this kind of polyvalence or multisignificance that surrounds the hero of ambiguity or the hero of binary oppositions all the way through. It doesn't necessarily begin with Nietzsche. I think it goes way back. But I think savior figures, or even antisavior figures, do have this iridescent context. This is their halo, and it may be a black halo in the twentieth century rather than a radiant one.

GUSTAFSSON: You mean that heroes are defeated, *überwunden*, but that this *Überwinden* is taken in a Hegelian sense.

MIDDLETON: Yes, to the extent that negation is not cancellation.

GUSTAFSSON: I think that's a very important point.

REHDER: Yes, this is the point that you made about negativity.

MIDDLETON: As long as the burst of energy that Charles Sherry is talking about has been articulated sufficiently. If it's just inarticulate energy, then there's neither negation nor the new thing that comes after.

BERGMAN'S MOVEMENT TOWARD NIHILISM

DESCHNER: You mentioned that Bergman is not particularly renowned for themes concerning women that would be accepted today by Women's Liberation. Yet it seems to me that in *The Silence* Bergman is very sensitive to the plight of the woman. It seems that, even if he does not allow his women to transcend the roles, or the traps, that society has created for them or conditioned them to, he certainly employs a great deal of sensitivity in depicting the nature of the problem and its origins. How do you feel about this?

STEENE: Yes, I think you are correct. I think, too, that I know why this film is under particular attack by members of Women's Liberation. It is because of the sexual implications and the portrait of the lesbian in the film. In fact there was an article in a Women's Liberation magazine, quite recently, that discussed this film in particular and also, to a certain extent, *Persona*. The main charge was that here were all the old clichés about lesbians. Many members of Women's Liberation feel that lesbianism is just another form of sexuality, as "normal" as heterosexual life and love. Thus they object to the fact that Ester in the film is dressed up in very masculine clothing. Her hair is pulled back in very intellectual fashion, whereas Anna's body is much more traditionally feminine. She wears décolleté dresses, and she has long flowing hair. Bergman does seem to subscribe then to the traditional images of woman, sensuous woman, and of the lesbian woman as a kind of freak, a male freak. But I would agree with you that Bergman very often uses the clichés, the traditional metaphors, of society. This does not mean that he subscribes to them, and I think you are quite right that in *The Silence* he is sensitive to the roles society has created for women.

DESCHNER: Could I ask you to reiterate something from the beginning of your lecture? Did I understand you to say that Bergman's interest in portraying women as central characters in his plays was partly an expression of his feeling that woman's role is less clearly defined? Did you say that he slips into this persona and seeks to elucidate a human predicament by trying to investigate a particular area that has been less investigated?

STEENE: Yes, I suggested that Bergman uses women in much the same way as Ibsen often does, because women are not traditionally involved in society, certainly not in the professional way that men have always been involved. For this reason they are removed from the external pressures of life, and it is easier under these circumstances for Bergman to get right down to the central human issues. Of course this has also been taken in a negative sense by the critics, who say that Bergman is so antisocial, so asocial, that his whole approach is psychological and metaphysical rather than social and political. And it has been a constant source of irritation to Swedish critics, in particular.

DESCHNER: Did I understand you correctly to say, in your statement concerning the development of Bergman's women up to *The Silence*, that he is not only attacking intellectuals, but also in a way doubting the power of language?

STEENE: Yes, but what I was trying to show was that Bergman's interest in women begins as a psychological interest. Then he gradually begins to use them as metaphysical questers. In the beginning he would use a male figure, such as the Knight or Isak Borg, but in later films there is an interesting shift back to women.

BAGGESEN: I would like you to comment a little further on the political implications of *The Silence*. I think you interpreted that strange country they are in as somehow being part of their predicament. But is it not so that something significant was going on in that country, something from which they were excluded? I am referring to the war that was going on as the significant event from which they were excluded.

STEENE: I find that a little difficult to accept, because I think that Bergman uses the camera in such a way that one becomes very much aware of the world of the war very early in the film. In the first sequence, there is Johan, the young boy, standing and looking out the window, and we actually assume his point of view and we look out at the world of the tanks. But we also get shots of Johan from the outside, so it does seem that Bergman is trying to connect the two. To me, what he is doing is presenting this outside male-oriented world. One finds only men there. There is just one shot from the outside world, where we see two women on their way to church. The rest of the film is all men, and constant references to war and destruction, which leads me to view the whole thing as a collapse of the patriarchal world. And this is something that the two sisters and Johan have to cope with. What happens, I think, is that Anna survives because she holds on to that aggressiveness of language which is perhaps a male or an intellectual characteristic, whereas Ester is destroyed. Johan possibly survives, because the ending is very open, very ambiguous. He sits there reading the note. Anna comes over and asks what it is. He says, "Well, it's some words that Ester gave me." Anna just shrugs her shoulders and says, "Well, that's nice," and she leaves him. The last thing we see in the film is a close-up of Johan, his lips moving as he tries to pronounce these new words. The film does end just as it began, with a close-up of Johan's face. Much of the focus of the film is from the point of view of the child. There are an amazing number of Lilliputian angles in the film, so that to a large extent we do identify or see the normative pattern of the film through the child.

KACIRK: I have a question about Bergman's significance as a film maker. He reaches a large audience, consisting of many non-Scandinavian people who do not dig deeply into the society and subject matter represented in his films. Does Bergman give a valid impression of what it is to be Scandinavian or Northern European? Is he regarded highly among his own?

STEENE: No, not really. I think that Bergman's reputation abroad is quite different from his standing in Sweden. In Sweden he is almost canonized in some ways now, but it has been a long struggle. I do not think that people have really ever accepted his metaphysical probing. It has always been considered slightly obsolete by the Swedes. When one looks at the foreign reaction to Bergman, there are great variations. The British have never liked him, because they feel that he always evokes the image of Nordic brooding, and they do not want that. The French have been fascinated by him as a cinematic craftsman. It is significant that among Bergman's films the French have as their favorites the most visually striking, for example, *The Naked Night* and *Summer with Monica*. In this latter film Bergman uses a hand-held camera; the French were intrigued by this, because it was done in a very early film. They also like the Chamber films, where Bergman begins to approach film making completely from a visual perspective, rather than starting with the verbal dialogue and then adding to it or complementing it with the image. But it is in America that he has really been most successful. Somehow he has posed several problems that have been very relevant to Americans, whereas the Swedes were by and large left cold by his metaphysical angst and his religious questioning. I feel, too, the Americans have been less reluctant to reject what I think you can call the Gothic, the excessive pictorial element in Bergman. There has always been much more resistance to this among the Swedes. I don't know how you felt about *Hour of the Wolf*, that we saw last night. I know that many of my students are quite fond of that film, whereas it is extremely difficult to find any Swede who really likes it.

LINNÉR: I would like to ask you about *Nattvardsgästerna*.

STEENE: *The Communicants* or *Winter Light*.

LINNÉR: As I remember it, during the final scene the service begins and he reads the ritual, then it's all over. The way you interpreted it, it was quite clear that this was empty rhetoric. As I recall it, I felt that the ending was more open. I would like you to comment on that. How sure are you of your interpretation?

STEENE: I am not all that sure. I will give you a beautiful reference that you can build up your own argument with and undercut mine. Bringing in Bergman's own personal view might of course be an intentional fallacy, but he said that he was trying to do three things when he made *Winter Light*. He said that the film is actually composed in three movements. The first and the last ones take place in the church, and the middle one outside, although part of it is also shot in the schoolhouse. In the first movement, which comprises the first church service, Bergman is testing the security god of Tomas, that is, the providential concept of God, God as the loving father, which is part of

Tomas's religious baggage and which is really the reason for his going into the ministry. In the second movement he is smashing the second concept of God, God as a spider, the diabolic God figure. And Tomas frees himself from this, although in a negative way, because he confesses to the fisherman, who then goes out and kills himself. Thus Tomas is at least partially responsible for Persson's suicide. In the last movement, Bergman says, he wants to depict the emergence of a new faith through the beginning of a rapport of Tomas and Märta. And I think it is possible to see that final scene as a very tentative rapprochement between the two in that Märta stays there. She doesn't leave, and he speaks to her more than to anyone else.

LINNÉR: Well, thank you. I think that was extremely interesting, and I must say that the very possibility of an interpretation of this kind makes the film a better film, a richer film.

STEENE: We're back to the open endings.

LINNÉR: Just one more question. Did it ever occur to you that this distrust of language—which I am sure *is* found in Bergman, as you have demonstrated very convincingly—could be in some way related to the curious fact that he is not a really good writer himself? It is hard to say what is wrong with his language, but it is not the right language.

STEENE: Yes. I would advise you to go and see *The Seventh Seal* again, and you will know what is wrong. The language is terribly archaic, stilted, very literary. You were asking about Bergman's reputation in the United States. While this may sound flimsy, I would say that one reason he is more popular here is that the translations are better. The English subtitles take away some of that literary quality to which the Swedes are so opposed. I am always bothered, for instance, by the Knight's speech in *The Seventh Seal*. There is a beautiful article, incidentally, by Harry Schein, in which he debunks Bergman's use of language. The question of language has been a sensitive point with Bergman all along. He has been terribly defensive about this.

Of course, he really wanted to become a playwright. As you know, he wrote plays in the late forties, and he wanted to move into the theater as a dramatist. At the same time he was fascinated by the cinema, but I don't think he was quite aware of his own visual talent. He distrusted it for a long time, and, as I mentioned, until the making of *The Silence* he would proceed from the verbal content and construct his film outward from dialogue.

LINNÉR: May I make just one final point? It is about "the underground man." It is traditional to point to him as one of the prototypical antiheroes. However, there is a tremendous craving for life in that film, and potentially, if not actually, a solution is pointed out. It is not just empty rhetoric, although the man is, of course, a failure. Would you say that you have nothing of this craving for life in Bergman?

STEENE: I would say that in *Brink of Life* you do.

LINNÉR: Oh yes, indeed. But in the later works . . .

STEENE: In the later works it disappears more and more. It is a movement from the antihero, with his occasional craving for life, to the nonhero, the nihilist, as personified by Ester. I think you see a kind of gradual realization of the meaninglessness of life, and the futility of life, in the Bergman characters. They hold on to various things, but the kind of affirmation of life that you sense coming through as a kind of communion in *Brink of Life* disappears more and more. You can even take a visual image in Bergman's films and see how it changes. If you go back to *The Seventh Seal*, the most important and most affirmative scene in that film takes place on the hillside, where the Knight shares a meal with Jof and Mia, which is a kind of secular communion. They share strawberries and milk. In *Wild Strawberries* there is again a luncheon. Bergman brings people together to share a meal. And you realize, if you know the Bergman of the early films, the films of the fifties and still in the early sixties, that we are *now* going to see people who are trying to reach out for each other. In *Through a Glass Darkly* there is an awful breakfast scene where the father is very clumsy. He has absolutely no way of reaching his children. This lack of rapport becomes more and more intensive in later films, and, finally, in *Hour of the Wolf* you end up with a horrible ghost supper with all the nightmarish aspects of Strindberg's ghost supper.

QUESTIONER: In which film does the helicopter collect the sick girl?

STEENE: *Through a Glass Darkly*.

HAUGEN: I don't think you completely answered the question of this gentleman over here who asked whether Bergman reflected what it was like to be a Scandinavian. I might suggest that one reason he is not popular or has not been popular in Scandinavia is that he is so intensely Scandinavian. And Scandinavians do not like to think of themselves as gloomy, morbid people, which, of course, they are. All you have to do is look at the program for this conference and see what authors are being discussed: Kierkegaard, Ibsen, Strindberg, Bergman. All this goes back, in some sense, to that brooder, Nietzsche, who, though not Scandinavian, was first discovered by Georg Brandes, a Scandinavian. I always ran into this problem in the years when I taught Scandinavian literature. Students would say, "Look. Scandinavian authors are so gloomy!" Yet it had never occurred to me that they were gloomy. To me, this is the way life is. I grew up in this country in a Scandinavian tradition, in which I started reading these authors as a child. As a consequence, it seemed natural to me. This is the way things are. You don't expect life to be sort of tra-la-la on the surface, the way most Americans do. As a result one is always getting this reaction. And yet these are the very authors who are most widely read, because they are the most characteristic of the northern countries.

STEENE: Perhaps the reason why Bergman has had so many young followers in this country can be put in relationship to changing philosophical attitudes. It is obvious among the young today that they are more questioning and more serious. They are less willing to believe in the tra-la-la optimism of their ancestors or parents. It is also interesting that, when the Swedes begin to attack Bergman, it is first of all an unwillingness to accept him. Then they reach a point where he becomes so important that they've got to kill him because he is just too influential.

In 1961, Bo Widerberg, the maker of *Elvira Madigan* and *Ådalen 31*, published a kind of manifesto [Vision in the Swedish film], which is really one long assault on Bergman. He attacks Bergman for being too life-denying, for creating this morbid, mythical Swede, who is exported like a Dalecarlian horse. Although a Dalecarlian horse is gay or colorful looking by comparison, it, too, is a kind of cliché, a souvenir, and Bergman has made films that have that kind of superficial, mythical quality. Widerberg then goes on to proclaim a new anti-Bergman program in the cinema. He declares that from now on film makers are going to look out to society. They are going to make documentary, socially oriented, and political films with none of this meta-physical angst. They are through with that. The Swedes are no longer like that.

HAUGEN: But this is what they've been doing to all these men. They killed Kierkegaard, they killed Ibsen, they killed Strindberg. And then, when they're dead, they revive them again.

STEENE: Because then it's safe.

HAUGEN: The "Strindbergolatry" in Sweden is incredible, when you realize that he died lonely and hated in his own country. In 1912 you couldn't mention his name in polite society.

STEENE: Bergman said, not too long ago, that he felt like a stuffed mummy in a museum. I think this was when he began to sense that he was being canonized by film critics and that the Swedes are rather proud of him now. This is apparently safe, because it is also quite clear that Bergman does not have a following, that he does not form a school, that he will not become the completely autocratic film maker in Sweden, that he has been very generous, in fact, in helping young film makers, many of whom started out by attacking him. Thus the very generosity of Bergman has made it possible for the Swedes to accept him. In other words, he senses that he has been canonized, that he has already been placed in a museum to be admired.

DESCHNER: I would like to add one more thing. I don't think that the Scandinavians have a monopoly on gloomy writing today. You can't claim that modern German writing is exactly cheerful, which is not to deny what you said here. But I had not realized that Bergman's language was bad. I don't even know for the moment whether I have heard him dubbed here. I thought that Bergman's attack on language was deeper.

STEENE: Yes, it is. It is.

DESCHNER: My question is, would it be to some extent parallel to Peter Handke's *Kaspar*, where language simply brings a person into life, and, the minute he masters the language, it begins to manipulate him and in a way bring about his destruction?

STEENE: Yes. I think that Ionesco, too, is a good example of this— witness the destructiveness of language in *The Lesson*.

DESCHNER: If I understood you correctly, it was Ester, the intellectual, who despaired of using language, and it was Anna, the non-intellectual, who could flip it around and do something with it.

STEENE: Yes.

CARDINAL: Seeing *Hour of the Wolf* last night, I was quite fascinated with the magnificent film making, but when I tried to put myself in the mind of the student who had never read Strindberg, for example, or Rilke in German literature, the film seemed to me to be *Innenraum*, an inner experience. The average young person, however, doesn't see it that way. He would ask himself, "Why is there this fear?" I recall the woman in the film saying, "I'm beginning to feel, to sense fear here." Any young person seeing that film would ask himself, "Isn't the hero becoming insane?" Or is it the alienation in the metaphysical sense that we all are experiencing in the modern world? In the post-Christian world? For instance, Bergman very specifically gives an example. It's the scene where the little boy runs down the cliff and then looks into the man's shoe. Then the man kills him and throws him over the cliff. I developed my own interpretation of that, but I haven't the vaguest idea of whether or not it links up with what Bergman had in mind. I do not feel that Bergman develops the psychological motivation explicitly enough in this scene.

STEENE: No. I don't think he is even concerned with that in this film. The film is a study in madness, as I see it, a study of the kind of schizophrenia, if you will, that was first presented in *Through a Glass Darkly*. What Bergman is trying to do in the film is to visualize, as completely as possible, the process of disintegration, the movement into madness. I'm not so sure that the film works for me, but I think that what he's trying to do is to accelerate the visual images so that they become more and more macabre, more and more surrealistic, as the man moves further and further into this mad world. Aren't we made aware, quite early in the film, of the fact that these characters, apart from the woman, and the artist, the man, are demons? They are projections of his mind, creations of his mind, and he has to face them and fight them and finally is destroyed by them. The woman repeats twice in the film, "When a man and a woman live together for a long time they become alike." To me the most moving element in the film is the fact that she is drawn into that mad world . . . and, at the end, she is not

even aware of whether she has actually seen him or not. She has seen
the demons, but *we* are not sure at the end whether she has actually
held him in her arms or not. The whole thing might just be a hallucination. But I don't feel that Bergman's approach is that literary. I think
that he is interested in trying to see if he can build up a film that
describes this disintegrating process, this movement into madness, and
in doing it entirely, or as much as possible, on visual terms. I don't
know if I answered your question. You asked for motivation, but I
don't think that that is Bergman's concern. I don't think he offers you
motivation, and I don't even think he intends to.

CARDINAL: Is Bergman interested in metaphysical situations, the
modern spiritual malaise, or is he interested in psychopathic, psychological cases?

STEENE: Well, neither, in a way, if you're talking about *Hour of
the Wolf*. I think that he is interested in the metaphysical malaise in
the films up to the point where I left off, the films up to *The Silence*.
After he made *The Silence*, he said: "I've left all that metaphysical
search. That means nothing to me now. God is dead, and that whole
business is something that I'm going to leave behind." And if you
notice, beginning with *Persona*, which is the next film after that, and
then *Hour of the Wolf*, he shifts all his interest to a theme that has
been a minor one in the earlier films, a very minor one, namely, the
portrait of the artist. This becomes his great concern, the egocentricity,
the parasitical nature of the artist, the artist as a vampire; and this, I
think, is what he explores in the film. The film is very ugly. The man is
really a male chauvinist pig, as far as I'm concerned. He really treats
his woman in a horrible way—he uses her. On the other hand, he is
used by others. The original name of the film was *The Cannibals—
Människoätarna*. Bergman is intrigued more and more by the destructive possibility of, and destructive potential in, people in general and
the artist in particular. This takes the form of a development of the
vampire motif, or the parasite motif, which all comes from *The Ghost
Sonata*.

SUMMING UP

BAGGESEN: I would like to make one comment on the lecture by

Linnér. It seems to me that we lack one step when we talk about the Scandinavian hero. It struck me that, somewhere between the very individualistic hero of Ibsen and the nonexistent hero of recent Swedish fiction, we lack the collective hero. Professor Linnér's contribution somehow made me think of *Fiskerne*, by Hans Kirk, because there you've got another kind of hero, a collective group of persons being a hero. My question to Linnér concerns Sara Lidman's *Gruva*. It was your impression that she felt that kind of thing much more worthwhile. Is that because it is reportage, or is it because she succeeds there in turning to a more collective kind of hero, the anonymous workers of Kiruna?

LINNÉR: I have no access to her mind. My guess is that *Gruva* had a political effect. I think it had. I don't know why she has not written novels for some time. She may return to fiction. It may be a sort of productivity crisis, or it may be that she's so involved in other activities. I have no information on this.

BAGGESEN: But you wouldn't comment upon it yourself from your impression of it?

LINNÉR: I don't feel that the term *collective hero* captures the main point. In my mind the fact that there is a political effect is what matters.

BAGGESEN: I could continue my question. You mentioned a book by Delblanc. I've just been reading *Åsnebrygga*, and there he seems to be lamenting the impossibility of reaching from "I" to "we." Would you comment upon that? I'm still seeking this collective hero.

LINNÉR: Yes, I suppose a great many writers have, shall we say, a romantic dream of being part of a fellowship. Most of them aren't, most of them are extremely individualistic, as we know. And certainly he is. This longing for a group fellowship need not at all lead him into the political direction. There are other ways, too. I guess what matters in the last ten years is precisely the political thing. We may ask Lars Gustafsson whether or not he accepts my hypothesis.

QUESTIONER: What is the collective hero?

LINNÉR: I didn't bring up the term, but I would like to interpret it. It is a man who feels himself to be part of a group and who is regarded by the group as being their man—in a working team, for instance.

BAGGESEN: Well, I think that, if you read Hans Kirk's *Fiskerne*, you really find a collective hero. *Fiskerne* is a novel about a group of fishermen from the western coast of Jutland, who settle down on a small island in Limfjord, moving from a very rough to a rather fertile countryside. And they bring with them from their rough existence on the western island the "Indre Mission," a popular evangelical movement in Danish Christianity. And they perpetuate this mission of Christianity in their new settlement. The novel is about the struggle of a collective seeking to impress its view of life, especially of Christianity, upon a new community. So it is really a novel of quest. What Hans Kirk, who was a Marxist Communist, is exploring in this novel is the way in which a collective works inside a societal frame to press its point of view and make that point of view prevail in a new community. Here you really have a collective hero. There's no one person in this collective who is the hero of the novel; rather, the group is the collective hero, going on to its quest and winning its victory. And that I think is one of the ways of defining a hero.

NAESS: I could mention one example from Norwegian literature which would bear out that point. That would be what in English translation is called *The Floodtide of Fate, Menneske og maktene* by Olav Duun, in which the author groups all the characters into two categories, those that do not survive the catastrophe and those that do, the latter of which he upholds. The criterion is then their ability to survive. The survivors are very different people, and you couldn't point out one of them as really being the hero. But they do represent various aspects of this little community. Another example is, of course, Jens Bjørneboe's play *The Bird Lovers*, in which the entire little Italian town collectively provides the idea of a heroic front against the invaders. This is just to mention two antiindividualistic kinds of works.

GUSTAFSSON: I have three small questions or comments for Professor Linnér. One of the most interesting heroes that you've mentioned, of course, is engineer Andrée in Per Olof Sundman's novel *Ingenjör Andrées luftfärd*. When I heard you describe him, it seemed to me that he comes very near to that genre of hero which is sometimes called "reluctant hero." And, as I think you know, Frans G. Bengtsson published in the 1930's an essay about the real engineer Andrée, which Sundman, strangely enough, never has mentioned. It is in one of the

volumes of Frans G. Bengtsson's collected works. It is quite obvious to
anybody who has read this essay on the real Andrée that it must have
provided the pattern for Per Olof Sundman's novel. Bengtsson analyzes the situation at the start of this traveler's journey and comes to
the conclusion that Andrée does know, more or less *has* to know, when
he starts his journey, that it will end in a catastrophe—because the
material of which the balloon is made does not meet the specifications.
By this time, he has received money from both the Swedish king and
important Swedish sponsors; he has been spoken of for months as the
person who will be the first to fly to the North Pole using modern
means. He simply can't get out of it. This is Frans G. Bengtsson's interpretation of it. And Sundman follows this pattern in all important
respects. I don't know if this is an objection to your description, but it
is very typical of this type of hero that he is made a hero from outside.
As you remember from the novel, there is another person who takes
over the initiative when they have landed on the ice, and this develops
into the sort of hierarchic struggle that is so typical of Sundman's
novels. I only mention this as a little footnote. I think that you said,
in connection with Sundman's heroes, that he has been accused of
ruthless authoritarianism. I gather that you are referring to two essays
that were published in *Bonniers litterära magasin* in the spring of
1970, namely, Tobias Berggren's investigation of the heroes of the
expedition and Jan Stolpe's study of the language of the early Sundman. I feel somewhat reluctant to accept your description of these two
critics. Berggren and Stolpe, I think, are important in one respect:
they introduced the methods of Russian formalism into Swedish literary criticism for the first time. This was decades after the original
formalists. Stolpe, to my reading, is certainly not trying to accuse
Sundman of ruthless authoritarianism; rather, as a result of a structural analysis, or formal analysis, of Sundman's special, very laconic
language, he tries to derive a pattern that he finds to be an appropriate
mirror of the Swedish postwar political structure. What he does is to
describe what he regards as a structural similarity between a linguistic
pattern and a specific political pattern. By this political pattern, he
means a pattern where different pressure groups have a greater influence than Parliament. I think that these two critics are studying the

language much more than the person. And I am aware of Sundman's objection that he is not an authoritarian, but I don't think that these two critics ever meant that. They meant that there is an authoritarian linguistic pattern. Stolpe stresses very heavily what he calls "these Ture Sventon sentences," such as "When it is cold, the snow crystals get smaller; when it is warm, the snow crystals get bigger." Of course, these things can be discussed. And I should like to recommend these two papers by Berggren and Stolpe, because I think they are both controversial and interesting as the first specimens of a formalist method used on a modern Swedish writer. Second, I am not quite certain that I understood what you said about Lukács. Would you please elaborate on that point? Sorry for having spoken so much.

LINNÉR: May I comment first on Sundman. I'm sure I've not done justice to the subtleties either of the novels or of the articles directed against him; when I worked out this paper I did not have the time to reread everything. Maybe certain phrases of mine ought to be revised. But you bring up a point here that I would like to have discussed generally. It has some connection with your paper yesterday on Strindberg, where you said that he introduces something new, a new pattern of composition, and that you would rather discuss his accomplishment in terms of that than in psychological terms.

GUSTAFSSON: Certainly.

LINNÉR: This is a very similar problem. Before you brought this up now I had in mind that in Strindberg the two patterns simply cannot be distinguished. It is fully legitimate to discuss his work—in fact it actually *has* to be discussed—in psychological terms, too. Again, the same thing when it comes to Sundman—I don't think Berggren and Stolpe just demonstrate a linguistic pattern. The political implications are also very strong and directed against the writer. Maybe we can return to Strindberg later, because that is of much more general interest than this Sundman question. As to Lukács—well, good heavens! I quoted a statement of his from his great essay on Tolstoy, which is certainly very representative of his best criticism. I think his view was that the writer depicts a world similar to the one in which he lives—which is not necessarily so—but Lukács assumes that it is. If this world is of the kind where no moral action—and moral action implies social-moral action—is possible, then it won't be possible in literature either. That is what he says, and I think there is no way of getting around that. It's a very simplistic idea, but it belongs to Lukács. I brought this up because I don't think we can draw conclusions of this kind from fiction. There is no such simple mirror relationship. That was why I introduced it.

GUSTAFSSON: As to this question of psychology and formal properties of a text, I think that might be one of the most interesting points to discuss. I certainly agree that psychological study must remain legitimate in all situations. Why should it be forbidden to be interested in human beings? One of my major points yesterday was to state a use of Occam's principle, namely, that, if a literary work like *Inferno* can be understood much better without psychopathological assumptions and theories, then we ought to do exactly that, because Occam's principle is such a tremendously good principle. We have here, among other things, the distinction between psychological study and psychological theories. Psychological study in turn does not necessarily presuppose definite psychological theories. That is one of the distinctions. Another, of course, is the distinction between a psychological study and a study that is more text oriented. I think you are quite right in saying that it is very hard to see where psychology starts and where the formal study ends. But, in spite of such vagueness, it is rather easy to see the distinction between a formalist study like those made by Tinianov, Jakobsen, and Shklovsky, on the one hand, and the typical psychoanalytical interpretation of a novel, on the other hand. Even in hell there are distinctions. May I just add that I feel somewhat reluctant to begin discussing Lukács, because if we start on that, we'll never get out of here.

LINNÉR: You brought it up. May I comment on psychology in Strindberg. First, I think Strindberg's person, that is, the psychological study of him as a man, is not the question at all here. Rather, we're concerned with a text like *Inferno* or similar texts. I'm all for the principle you mentioned to make things as simple as possible. Obviously you're right there, only I think that, if you study the meaning of a work like Strindberg's *Inferno* and if you stop at the linguistic level, it means that you omit many aspects of meaning which are extremely important and that can hardly be described in linguistic terms. You have to use psychological terms. I don't care what theory it is or whether it's just everyday psychology you use, it's psychology all the same. It's just like with Bergman's film last night. I'm not sure that you could really cover the psychological meaning of the film, if you only study it in "linguistic" terms. If it could be done, I would like to have it demonstrated, because that would prove that the same things can be described with two distinctly different frames of reference. To my knowledge that cannot be done. If you don't discuss the psychological meaning of the film, I think you have stopped halfway. And this is how I feel about Strindberg. In your discussion of Strindberg yesterday, you yourself spoke of his having introduced a change in form—something new. I agree that we should concentrate on that, but not exclusively. You also said this implies a change in mind or a change in attitude—those were your words—but that is psychology. And what Strindberg did was to introduce, let us say, the depiction or expression of an extreme state of mind. He changed the focus from so-called normal states of mind to extreme states of mind, and that implied formal innovations, too. Why not describe the psychological implications of this as well?

GUSTAFSSON: I think that your difficulty with my paper on that point has to do with your taking it as a stating of alternatives. It isn't. I don't want to see one method used exclusively like that. It is only the presentation of another suggestion, plus the maintenance that Occam's principle is a very good one. Should this method fail, I'm quite willing to scream for help from other methods. In regard to your last remark, about the linguistic study, or study of forms, I think that very much of what we call psychological significance, even in Bergman's film, is the significance of form, but that would take us too far from the subject.

ALBRECHT: I think the dispute here is that Linnér prefers the psychological interpretation, whereas Gustafsson expresses in his paper the linguistic aspect. I think we stress interpretation because more research has been done in that area. What we ultimately do in psychology is to delve deeply into the human mind, into the deep structure, if you will. That's just what the linguists are doing—witness Chomsky's work from 1965 on. Interpretation of style or even of form, nowadays, would be the transformation a person makes from his deep understanding of language to the surface structure. Whether psychological or historical feeling enters in doesn't make any difference. Thus, the reason we do not get any further with our interpretation, I think, is that we never really explore the linguistic end. We always fall back on Freud and repeat dreams and the like. I think we should go back to the language.

WEINSTOCK: Who would care to comment?

GUSTAFSSON: I think this was a very good contribution.

LINNÉR: Professor Haugen, wouldn't you, as a linguist, care to comment on this?

HAUGEN: I don't know what deep structure is. It doesn't seem to me that there is any very essential contrast between these two views that we have heard. From the linguistic point of view all one can say is that the question Chomsky raised originally in his *Syntactic Structures*, in 1957, and later in *Aspects of the Theory of Syntax*, from 1965, is extremely controversial. For everything that we had traditionally been accustomed to calling the *logical structure* of language, he invented the new term *deep structure*. When we spoke of active and passive sentences—as we always have in grammar—as meaning the same thing, related simply by a change of order of words and so on, we usually said that in a passive sentence the subject was the logical object of the verb. In Chomsky's terminology the logical object is the deep object, the real object. All you are doing is taking various sentences and reducing them to their common denominator of meaning. The result has been that younger scholars in linguistics have taken the further step of saying, "Well, if that's what we're doing, when we speak of transformations from deep structure, then the deep structure is the meaning of the sentence." Chomsky denies this. If the deep structure is the psychology of the utterance, that is, if it is what a person is trying to say, then all language is transformational. It is merely a transformation of what we've got inside our heads into the linear sequence that constitutes language, that is, a formulation. This is as true of a poet as it is of an ordinary speaker of the language. You perform a number of operations, each of which can be specified. This is true as long as you are dealing only with the grammatical basis and are saying that "the man bites the dog" is the deep structure and "the dog was bitten by the man" is a surface structure. But, in fact, they are both surface structures, and the real meaning is somewhere down much deeper, because you are getting at a mythical dog and a mythical man who are related in a certain particular way. I think what you are up against in a work of literature is that the depths are not one deep structure but layers upon layers of structure, going right back to the ultimate primeval thought and feeling of man. Where does psychology begin and linguistics end? Chomsky contends that linguistics is merely a subbranch of psychology, while I could just as well claim that it's a subbranch of sociology, because I am a sociolinguist. Others would say it is a subbranch of physics or of anthropology. Linguistics has always been concerned with the basic ideas people have and the ways in which they express them. There is nothing new in these transformations, and I don't think they solve the problems of literary criticism. They do add certain dimensions and give us certain precisions that are very interesting. But of course you have various kinds of linguists: I have been here to honor Arch Hill, who takes an entirely different view. If anything, he is trying to reconcile the two schools. His contention is that all we have is the message. Let's analyze the message formally, and then we've done our job as linguists. But, of course, the transformationalists are not satisfied with that. They want to start with the mind and to wind up with the message, while setting up rules for how you get from one to the other. I find this very questionable and difficult, and it would take another lifetime for me to learn what it's really all about.

WAHLGREN: Einar Haugen has peeled off the successive layers of the Gyntian onion, and we don't know what we've come to. I would like to say that I'm not much of a descriptivist, but I tried for kicks to analyze some exemplars of that intricate form of poetry known as skaldic verse. I sought to get at the deep structure through transformational grammar. I don't know what I achieved, but I did find, to the limited extent to which I played the game, that it did bring me some comfort in that I thought that I was able to figure out the nominal, the straight meaning, the ordinary prose meaning, of some verses that otherwise had eluded me. If there is anything else to it, it's too deep and has eluded me entirely.

ZELLER: I would just like to do something for those of us who get weighed down with technical questions. That is, the theme of the symposium is the Scandinavian hero, and if we could, for a moment, get off the individual papers and on to this more general topic, I would be most grateful. My major field is Russian and German, and, as I have been sitting here listening to each of you describe these particular individuals, it seems to me that what you have been talking about is a cross between a Slavic hero, a hero of Russian literature, and the German "man of action." I was just wondering if anyone would comment on this.

GREENWAY: It would seem to me that Professor Linnér made a very profound point in his discussion of contemporary Swedish fiction. I must confess that I'm not familiar with most of the works you mentioned, but your descriptions of them were quite good, I thought. As I understood what you said, there is essentially a failure or an inability to synthesize these two demands, the action and the introspection: that is, the political activism demanding essentially a simple, a mythic world versus the technique of the way people learn to write novels, the technique of pure prose style, which implies a certain ambiguity alien to the activist view. It seemed to me that this would be a very profound point to make. Perhaps I'm making too much of this, but, if the goal of revolution is to change the consciousness, it appears to me that, from what you say in general, Swedish writers have been unable to do this in themselves. It would appear to augur ill for the coming golden age, if they cannot do it in their own literary consciousness. As a contrast, witness the thing we saw on television from Nixon's trip to China. Apparently there has been created a cultural consciousness in which this simple world of good and evil has become a viable art form —people charging around with bayonets and such. Apparently you see this as a serious problem for Swedish fiction?

LINNÉR: This is the question of the positive hero that is found in nineteenth-century Russian literature. Do I want positive heroes? I don't know. If a whole culture is so transformed that the creative sources of individual writers become directed this way, then it is conceivable that they may write genuinely about positive heroes. Still, the fact remains that the individual writer is always bound by his personal history, whatever his political convictions, and he can never get beyond that, I am convinced.

GREENWAY: You mentioned several writers who had gone into reportage, and you said that Sara Lidman has not written for a while. Is the problem that writers would just cease writing rather than betray their idealism?

LINNÉR: Of course, you can take another position and say that the writer's job is to ask questions and point out contradictions and doubts. That is not disloyal; on the contrary, it is his valuable contribution. The examples that are very discouraging are, of course, from the Russia of the 1930's, where writers were ordered to write in positive terms. Who would want that? Maybe it is not the writer's task as an artist to be a political leader.

WAHLGREN: Applying deep structure to the young lady's question, one can ask, is there such a thing as a typically Scandinavian hero, as opposed to a European hero? If we answer that one way or another, we may arrive at some common characteristics of the Scandinavian hero that aren't shared by the others. Is that a foolish question, or is it possible to answer?

CARDINAL: I think this is a very interesting point, because I happen to come from Canada, and we are perpetually asking ourselves whether there is such a thing as a Canadian identity in Canadian literature. In this connection, we might go back to Goethe, who said, as early as 1832, that national literature is coming to an end. One of you asked whether Strindberg or Ingmar Bergman is typically Swedish. I don't really see the type that Bergman projects as much in Canadian or German or American literature. My question is whether or not there is a typically Norwegian or Swedish hero. You know, Ibsen struggled all his life over this question, and in Canada we have people like Northrop Frye, who, in his book titled *Modern Century*, says that basically there is no question of a national literature anymore. Or J. B. Priestley, who said you can go from Hong Kong to London to Berlin to Toronto or to New York, get off the plane, and it looks exactly the same everywhere. What really counts, to my mind, is the kind of problem that, for instance, Bergman or, say, Strindberg, or whoever it is, projects on the inner soul of modern man. That has nothing to do with national category. But now you may tell me I'm wrong. Please do so. Prove that to me.

STEENE: I suppose that the reason—if we stick with him for the moment—Bergman has had such an international breakthrough is not that a number of people outside Sweden are terribly fascinated by the Swedish psyche, but that they recognize something of themselves in his characters. Although he can only work in a Swedish milieu—and he himself insists on this very strongly—and can only deal with what he feels to be very personal, Swedish problems, I still think that somehow most of his films transcend that national basis. The foreign audience's reaction to these films proves that they transcend any kind of national identity from which they originally spring. You have to recognize, however, the fact that there is an awful lot of national intellectual baggage that Bergman simply absorbs. There is the main exposure to Strindberg from the age of thirteen, when he began to read him. He never really got over that. There is his almost resentful recognition of Lagerkvist, something that Vilgot Sjöman pointed out to him during the filming of *Winter Light*. Bergman only rather reluctantly acknowledged this, but now he concedes that the metaphysical world of Lagerkvist is also a part of that general national intellectual background that he absorbed. When Bergman grew up, however, the world that he came in contact with as a student was not only the world of Strindberg and Lagerkvist, a world that had special immediacy to him because he experienced the world of Strindberg, especially, in the theater through the productions of Olof Molander's *Dream Play* and *The Ghost Sonata*; part of his intellectual background is also related to the general intellectual climate of Sweden in the 1940's, that is, to the interest in Kafka and T. S. Eliot. Some of the imagery of *The Waste Land* comes through also in Swedish poetry of the 1940's. It's impossible to distinguish between what is national in his characters and what is international.

MISHLER: I wonder if I might make a comment on what makes Bergman interesting and on the sort of questions he's pursuing. The gentleman who just spoke asked this morning whether Bergman was dealing with psychopathological phenomena, or what precisely he was after. In this respect I differ with the view Miss Steene has presented. I find that Bergman is still very much a religious film maker, going on what he himself has said in his book *Bergman om Bergman*, namely, that he's worked through the traditional Christian problems and that he still very much believes in the existence of evil. He has somehow managed to get rid of God, but evil as a positive principle is still very much present in his world. The problem he is working with in his later films is not so much a psychological one, but rather it is the peculiar and very vigorous nature of evil that seems to be loose in the world today. He was doing this in a very baroque sort of way in *Hour of the Wolf*, and in a more restrained fashion in *The Passion of Anna*, where every twenty minutes of the film you have a completely random and senseless act of violence—for example, I am thinking of the hanging of the dog or of the kicking of the old man to death. Bergman is very careful to insist on the fact that there is no explanation for that. There is no sociopsychological explanation for any of these actions; they simply happen. At the same time they are occurring outside, the couple is inside watching scenes from the war in Vietnam, and Bergman seems to be implying that the kind of senseless brutality that is taking place on the screen and outside is very much the same sort of thing and is really unaccountable. It has a positive presence. I think we can understand last night's film in that way. The woman becomes very terrified of that presence of evil. Suddenly it is no longer a privation: it is a very active, religious presence.

NAESS: I just wanted to say a few things about the question of nationalism. We were not really asked to talk about the specifically Scandinavian hero—it might have been possible to do so, but it might have been a little less interesting. Representing a small language, as we do, puts us in a very different position from, let's say, Russians and Germans. We all had to read *Alice in Wonderland*; it was very English. Now, if it had been written in Danish, it would not have been known to the rest of the world. People would not have been interested in that sort of thing. You might say that the English foisted *Alice in Wonderland* upon people like the Scandinavians. One of the greatest Danish books of that kind, Poul Møller's *En dansk Students Eventyr*, is not even translated into English, as far as I know. It is a book that all Danes know. And let's take the most famous of nineteenth-century Finnish works, Kivi's *Seven Brothers*; it was not translated into Danish until 1946, and then the Danes said: "Here you are! This is what we've been waiting for for years. That book is no good, but the Finns have been talking about it for years." And, similarly, we could mention Laxness. His *Independent People* didn't sell very well. You could pick it up for twenty-five cents here for years, until it was sold out. It is a very remarkable book. So, you see, the essentially Scandinavian heroes who are considered great in their home countries might not be equally interesting to the rest of the world. I don't think we were asked to talk about the Scandinavian hero. It's rather the international hero who goes out into the world. Along those lines Peer Gynt is the central Norwegian hero. Of course, Peer Gynt is very popular in Japan, and the Japanese say, "We like him so well, because he is so Japanese." And that really answers some of our questions of nationality.

GUSTAFSSON: I must admit that I feel very confused when somebody starts to speak about such a thing as the Scandinavian hero or the Swedish hero. I simply don't understand what it should mean. Take Charles XII, of Sweden, not the historical one, but the literary figure, as he appears in Heidenstam's *Karolinerna* [The Carolines], and compare this hero to Dr. Borg in August Strindberg's *I havsbandet*. About the only thing they have in common is that they are described in the same language, in the most elementary, rude, and ordinary sense of the word, language—the Swedish language. It would be on the intellectual level of Langbehn's *Rembrandt als Erzieher* to try to prove that one of these heroes does not belong to Swedish literature. Of course, they both do in any possible sense, but they've nothing in common. There is no such thing as a Swedish hero. There will never be, and there has never been. There are different heroes in different historical situations in different literary styles. I feel very unhappy about this concept.

ALBRECHT: But you could still talk about a hero in Swedish literature.

GUSTAFSSON: Of course you can; that is a technical concept.

ALBRECHT: I would like to return to the question of the social engagement.

WAHLGREN: The audience may be quite separated in time and space from any probability calculation on the part of the author that has a bearing on this social-action business. For example, I would like to ask Harald Naess if he has any idea when the Japanese discovered that Peer Gynt was indeed a Japanese?

NAESS: I don't know when they discovered it, but the statement is from the 1940's, as I recall.

WAHLGREN: I don't know if this is a general wave of enthusiasm for Henrik Ibsen, but I discovered a dozen years ago that the Japanese were very much interested in Nora. They had discovered *A Doll's House* and the divorce question. Now you can see why, due to the transformation of the woman's role in Japan. Now I'm sure that Ibsen never thought about that.

KACIRK: I would like to make a few comments. I usually like to express ideas through visual means rather than by carrying on with verbal methods, but the whole idea of the Nordic culture has fascinated me for a number of years. I feel—at the risk of oversimplifying things—that we are dealing with a group of very hearty people that ventured into a climate that was severe and very exacting and, for some reason, remained there. If you study primitive societies other than in the Scandinavian areas—I'm thinking in terms of the Pacific islands and other remote areas—you find that the people, if they hold together as a society, usually devise a religion or a series of beliefs that tend to explain their role in nature, the manner in which they should interact with their environment. As long as this explanation remains valid, as long as it is viable and works, they hold together as a society. Now the Scandinavians, or the Norsemen, were confronted with a nature that was very exacting, very hard, very difficult. It forced these hardy people to sit and acknowledge that in spite of their strength and might they were still impotent, impotent to act or to change or to exert themselves. I think that for this reason, at a very early time, they attempted to develop heroes in lieu of simple explanations. The individual people then attempted to identify with these heroes. Now, in more recent times, these heroes have proved to be inadequate, and the Norsemen have instead resorted to technology to enable them to somehow bolster their egos or muster their feelings of self-esteem. It is at this point that they are becoming men of action as in other more advanced technological nations, to which Lars alluded in his remark on the small dark generator developing light throughout the land. The present-day writer is confronted with the phenomenon of people turned on, being active, attempting to alter nature, but I think that this is simply a reaction to a failure, namely, the inability to generate a hero, a national hero, who would continue to satisfy them. Does this have a bearing on what we are talking about?

GREENWAY: Yes, I think it does. I am also reluctant to put forth some sort of archetypal hero for all the Scandinavian literatures. We've seen the impossibility of this in the course of the discussion. I think, though, Jim, you have a point. Perhaps we have been talking about a certain attitude, namely, the presence of evil—the presence not only of good, but also of inexplicable evil. Now this may be one characteristic. I was thinking in particular of Johannes V. Jensen's novel *Braeen*, in which he goes into what you were talking about. The response to the climate, the response to a malevolent nature, develops in modernism into the inability to respond to a crisis or to an evil that is sensed and apprehended as very real—this is getting into Professor Linnér's point of view—but in order to respond to the crisis, you have to understand it in some way.

KACIRK: I would like to make one more comment. This morning I was intrigued with Birgitta's statement in reference to the Nordic brooding characteristic.

STEENE: It's not mine, it's British.

KACIRK: In any case, to me it is a good thing. I look upon that as a much more valid role, wherein man confronts his world and by brooding, on the one hand, admits to being inadequate and is reluctant to admit to that, but, on the other hand, he searches, continues to search, to look, and to wonder. I feel that people—in this country and other countries—who view technological advancement as the apparent answer to this problem, are now looking back to the Bergman-type character and wishing that that was the solution chosen, rather than to ravage a continent in a couple hundred years in an attempt to reassure themselves. I think that this Nordic brooding should be reemphasized, that this is a good thing, that the world is looking for this. People today, young people, are attempting to turn back or to turn away from the direction that is being taken in technological nations.

WEINSTOCK: Let me just make a brief comment. The original theme of the symposium was, of course, not the Scandinavian hero, but rather the hero in Scandinavian literature. I don't know how we got turned around exactly.

ROVINSKY: I would like to pose a question to either Sven Linnér or Birgitta Steene or any other of the brooding Scandinavians on the panel. Let us note, first, that we've learned today that one of the central problems in Bergman's metaphysical approach is the problem of evil. Second, we've learned that he doesn't write very well. We've learned, third, that he's been canonized in his own time in Scandinavia, particularly in Sweden. I am thinking now of the "Prince of Grubbel," Pär Lagerkvist, whose central problem—or one of whose central problems —is evil and who "discovered" this theme many years before Bergman did. Lagerkvist is regarded by many modern Scandinavians as unsophisticated, possibly because of the superficial simplicity of his language, which *is* merely superficial. Could you tell me why many modern Scandinavians look down on Lagerkvist as being simple, while, at the same time, they are prepared to apotheosize Bergman, who deals with the same problems and, in my point of view, not even as effectively.

STEENE: I don't think that when you talk about the canonization of Bergman, it means an acceptance of his ideas or even an appreciation of themes in his films. It is very simply a matter of national pride. You have a figure here who has a tremendous international reputation, so I think it is really for a rather superficial reason he has become canonized. I don't want to suggest that all his metaphysical brooding strikes home, that the Swedes think it is very subtle or sophisticated, or that they agree with it. I think that they consider him from a philosophical, even psychological, point of view to be quite obsolete. What is operating here is simple national pride. Now Lagerkvist, although he won the Nobel prize and has been translated and so on, does not have that international stature. I don't know if it's even true that Lagerkvist is considered unsophisticated—Sven can probably answer this much better. He's not a *kändis*—a celebrity—like Bergman—he's a recluse. He doesn't have the fascinating personality that Bergman has; that may have something to do with it, too.

ROVINSKY: I don't know that his personality isn't all the *more* fascinating, because nobody knows much about it.

STEENE: Yes, but to the average Swede, there is almost a tabloid presentation of Bergman.

ROVINSKY: I think that Lagerkvist is much more widely read than Bergman. I know he is. He is much more widely translated than Bergman.

STEENE: It's not a question of reading; it's a question of knowing him, and I think that many more people have seen the films of Bergman than have read the novels of Lagerkvist.

ROVINSKY: Yes, the media have changed things to the point that instant recognition is easier with Bergman, but I think the true reason people seem to prefer Bergman to Lagerkvist is that Bergman has a more convoluted approach to life. He isn't as direct as Lagerkvist. People don't want to be guilty of appreciating something simple. So they go to Bergman movies, become confounded and thrice confounded, and appreciate it. Then they come out and ask each other, "What happened?" The more confused the movie is, the more the fires are fed. Whereas, with Lagerkvist, you read a simple line and you can get to the bottom of it very rapidly, which is, it seems to me, the object of all art. The approach should be from the pen or the vision directly to the mind, and I don't feel that Bergman does this. He deliberately leads people around, to the same point, to the same end. It is a matter of haughtiness that makes people appreciate Bergman and look down on Lagerkvist.

STEENE: You mean Bergman has a snob appeal?

ROVINSKY: Perhaps I'm just not a snob.

LINNÉR: It's my guess many young people in Sweden who are interested in literature still don't care for Lagerkvist. He's not relevant. Of course, an empirical study could be made. I think many people would say, "Well, he's a big name, but I don't care." Am I right?

ROVINSKY: Yes. We are saying he's not relevant, yet Brandell has said (and I agree) that Lagerkvist's "personligaste, innersta fråga gäller det onda som makt i tiden och i evigheten," that is, that his main problem is evil. Bergman has the same central idea, and now we're saying that Bergman is relevant and Lagerkvist isn't. Lagerkvist dealt with this problem more than sixty years ago.

STEENE: I really think that the Swedes would say they're both irrelevant.

LINNÉR: I think the key point here is eternity, evil as an eternal force. The kind of people I have in mind are not interested in eternity. That's my guess.

HAUGEN: I think it is very interesting that the organizers of this symposium have hit upon the word *hero* as a unifying theme. It is obvious that you can't have a discussion about a term that is not ambiguous. This term is not only ambiguous, but it is whatever the word is for twice ambiguous. We all know there is no such thing as a Scandinavian hero—we're not even sure there's a Greek hero. There are two kinds of hero: the main figure, the protagonist, in a piece of literature, which is what Harald Naess was talking about in Hamsun, and then the heroic hero, which is what Sven Linnér was talking about. I was quite surprised when he started his paper by saying he was going to talk about the heroic character.

LINNÉR: May I interrupt? What I mean is that the heroic character is also the main character of the book.

HAUGEN: Yes, but you have limited it twice. You've taken only the most central characters who could be described as heroic, thereby ducking out after two or three authors, because there is nothing more to talk about. All of a sudden you ran out of heroes in your narrow sense.

LINNÉR: I would not agree to that.

HAUGEN: That is what I got out of it. I'm sorry! Maybe I missed something at that point. I would say "Thank goodness!" that there are no heroes in Scandinavian literature, for the heroes that are there are rather unfortunate. On the one hand, you have Isak Sellanraa, who is sort of a fascist hero, if I may be nasty in the way I put it. He reflects Hamsun's notion that the hero is some kind of primitive vegetable, to whom we should all return. We should all eat right off the earth. All this business about eating natural foods is all Hamsun. He called it *dåsemat*—canned goods—and *dåsemat* was the worst thing he knew. That was back in 1912, in some of his novels of that period. On the other hand, you have the Communist hero, Bjartur in *Själfstaett fólk*, who is also extremely primitive, but who is ground down by capitalism and is called, ironically, the independent man. He is really a victim of modern society. The character of the modern, collective Bergman hero falls apart into a general European hero.

BAGGESEN: Professor Haugen has made a very important point by noting that a lot of the characters we have been discussing are really not heroes, but victims. That is perhaps a term that Linnér could use in describing the problem. We are somehow, all of us, taken up too much with the victimizing role of society and with human beings as victims of their society, of their surroundings, not with conquering heroes. The heroic hero of ancient times was sacrificed, whereas the modern character that we have been discussing is simply victimized. He is simply ground down by external forces. It is not sacrifice for anything, there is nothing holy about it—he's simply run over by a stray automobile.

HAUGEN: Oswald in *Ghosts* was the prototype of that, a hero who is sacrificed for no obvious reason. He dies simply because of what his father did.

LINNÉR: May I remind you of Ekelöf's *Prince of Emgión*. This is obviously not a portrait, although you might regard it as a kind of lyrical portrait. He is not merely a victim; he has his own identity and strength. To me that is the decisive thing. I'm not just talking about a victimized protagonist, very definitely not.

BAGGESEN: It might simply be the case that you can no longer find a hero in the novel anymore. We have an example of this phenomenon in Denmark today, where a heroic young man with lots of hair, named Ebbe Reich, has been searching throughout the entire history of Europe for a hero. He thinks we need heroes, and he has drawn upon figures like Malatesta and N. F. S. Grundtvig to this end. It appears, however, that the genre doesn't allow for that kind of thing any more.

NOTES ON THE CONTRIBUTORS

Sverre Arestad, now retired professor of Scandinavian languages, and former chairman of the Department of Scandinavian Language and Literature at the University of Washington, earned his doctorate in English and Scandinavian at that institution in 1938. He has also studied at the Universities of Oslo, Copenhagen, and Stockholm. Professor Arestad has been both vice-president and president of the Society for the Advancement of Scandinavian Study, as well as editor of *Scandinavian Studies*. His interests have ranged from Ibsen and Danish, Swedish, and Norwegian drama, to the modern Scandinavian novel, to broader comparative studies, on which he has produced countless critical articles and reviews.

Niels Ingwersen, associate professor of Scandinavian studies at the University of Wisconsin at Madison since 1965, earned his Candidatus Magisterii degree at the University of Copenhagen in 1963 after study in Stockholm, Oslo, and Chicago. He has taught both in Scandinavia and the United States and has received faculty and student awards for teaching excellence at the University of Wisconsin. In addition to having served as Lithgow Osborne Lecturer for the American-Scandinavian Foundation (1972), he has also held the office of president of the Society for the Advancement of Scandinavian Study, for whose journal he is now an associate editor. Professor Ingwersen has published numerous scholarly articles and reviews in the area of Scandinavian literature and is presently completing work on a book dealing with Martin A. Hansen.

Ingvar Holm, professor of drama and theater history and leader of the Drama Institute at Sweden's University of Lund, earned his doctorate there in 1957. He has been theater critic for *Dagens nyheter*, teacher of theater history at the Malmö student theater, and literary advisor for the Royal Swedish Theater. He has written extensively on all genres in the area of Scandinavian and world literature. Included in this sizable bibliography are *Ola Hansson, en studie i åttiotals romantik*; *Harry Martinson: Myter, målningar, motiv*; *Drama på scen: Dramats former och funktion*; and *La Littérature suédoise*.

Harald Naess is professor of Scandinavian languages at the University of Wisconsin at Madison. He is also managing editor of *Scandinavian Studies*. Professor Naess received his Candidatus Philologiae degree at the University of Oslo in 1952 and subsequently taught at the University of Durham (England) and the University of Wisconsin, first as visiting lecturer, then as associate professor and, in 1967, Torger Thompson Professor of Scandinavian Languages. From 1959 to 1961, he was a Fulbright scholar. In addition to a great number of scholarly articles and reviews on Scandinavian literature, Professor Naess has also written *Knut Hamsun og Amerika* and *Knut Hamsuns brevveksling med postmester Frydenlund*.

Lars Gustafsson, a native of Västerås, Sweden, is one of Europe's leading authors and cultural personalities. He received his Filosofie Licentiat degree from the University of Uppsala in 1961 and has served as literary critic for *Expressen* (since 1961) and *Bonniers litterära magasin* (*BLM*); he was managing editor of *BLM* from 1962 until 1972. He has taught on the college level in the United States and held the position of Thord-Gray Visiting Professor (American-Scandinavian Foundation) at the University of Texas at Austin in 1974. Among Mr. Gustafsson's copious works may be mentioned *Vägvila*; *Ballongfararna*; *En förmiddag i Sverige*; *Den egentliga berättelsen om herr Arenander*; *Kärleksförklaring till en sefardisk dam*; *Herr Gustafsson själv*; and *Yllet*.

Birgitta Steene, born in Uddevalla, Sweden, is professor of Scandinavian languages and chairperson of the Department of Scandinavian Language and Literature at the University of Washington, where she received her doctorate in comparative literature in 1962. She began her teaching career as an instructor in English at Louisiana State University in 1959 and has since taught at the University of Alberta, University of Pennsylvania, and Temple University. Professor Steene has been both a Sweden-America Foundation Scholar and American Association of University Women Scholar. Among her many scholarly writings in the area of Scandinavian and comparative literature are *Ingmar Bergman*; *August Strindberg*; and *Focus on "The Seventh Seal."*

Sven Linnér, recently chosen professor of Scandinavian languages at Finland's Åbo University, which post he assumed in September, 1974, has been a docent in literary history at the University of Uppsala. He has taught at Bergen and Kiruna, in Scandinavia, as well as in the United States at the Universities of Wisconsin and Illinois and Harvard University. He is the author of *Livsförsoning och idyll: en studie i rikssvensk litteratur 1915– 1925*; *Pär Lagerkvists livstro*; *Litteraturhistoriska argument: studier i en vetenskaps metodpraxis*; and numerous other scholarly articles and reviews.

James Kacirk, prominent professional artist, earned a master's degree in fine arts from the University of California at San Diego. After a stint in the United States Navy as a member of an underwater demolition team in World War II, during which period he was able to visit Scandinavia for the first time, Mr. Kacirk was an electrical engineer for several years. Since then he has devoted himself entirely to art and has won recognition both in the United States and abroad, particularly in Mexico City, where he has exhibited widely. Mr. Kacirk is currently continuing his work on Scandinavian motifs in preparation for the 1976 annual meeting of the Society for the Advancement of Scandinavian Study, to be held at Austin, Texas, where he plans to exhibit.

INDEX